Howard T. Crocker.
1868 Gaylord St,
Denver,
Colo.

SHADOWS OF THE STAGE

SHADOWS OF THE STAGE

BY

WILLIAM WINTER

" *The best in this kind are but shadows* "
SHAKESPEARE

NEW YORK
MACMILLAN AND COMPANY
AND LONDON
1893

Norwood Press:
J. S. Cushing & Co. — Berwick & Smith.
Boston, Mass., U.S.A.

TO

Henry Irving

IN MEMORY AND IN HONOUR
OF ALL THAT HE HAS DONE
TO DIGNIFY AND ADORN THE STAGE
AND TO ENNOBLE SOCIETY
THIS BOOK IS GRATEFULLY INSCRIBED

" Cui laurus æternos honores
Delmatico peperit triumpho "

PREFACE.

—◆—

*THE papers contained in this volume,
chosen out of hundreds that the author has
written on dramatic subjects, are assembled
with the hope that they may be accepted,
in their present form, as a part of the
permanent record of our theatrical times.
For at least thirty years it has been a
considerable part of the constant occupation of the author to observe and to record
the life of the contemporary stage. Since
1860 he has written intermittently in various
periodicals, and since the summer of 1865
he has written continuously in the New
York Tribune, upon actors and their art;
and in that way he has accumulated a
great mass of historical commentary upon
the drama. In preparing this book he has
been permitted to draw from his contribu-
tions to the Tribune, and also from his
writings in Harper's Magazine and Weekly,
in the London Theatre, and in Augustin*

7

Daly's Portfolio of Players. The choice of these papers has been determined partly by consideration of space and partly with the design of supplementing the author's earlier dramatic books, namely: *Edwin Booth in Twelve Dramatic Characters; The Jeffersons; Henry Irving; The Stage Life of Mary Anderson; Brief Chronicles,* containing eighty-six dramatic biographies; *In Memory of McCullough; The Life of John Gilbert; The Life and Works of John Brougham; The Press and the Stage; The Actor and Other Speeches;* and *A Daughter of Comedy,* being the life of *Ada Rehan.* The impulse of all those writings, and of the present volume, is commemorative. Let us save what we can.

> " *Sed omnes una manet nox,*
>   *Et calcanda semel via leti.*"

W. W.

APRIL 18, 1892.

CONTENTS.

" — *It so fell out that certain players*
We o'er-raught on the way: of these we told him;
And there did seem in him a kind of joy
To hear of it."

HAMLET.

" *Of all the cants which are canted in this canting world — though the cant of hypocrites may be the worst — the cant of criticism is the most tormenting. I would go fifty miles on foot, for I have not a horse worth riding on, to kiss the hand of that man who will give up the reins of his imagination into his author's hands, — be pleased he knows not why and cares not wherefore.*"

TRISTRAM SHANDY.

SHADOWS OF THE STAGE.

————◆————

I.

THE GOOD OLD TIMES.

IT is recorded of John Lowin, an actor contemporary with Shakespeare and associated with several of Shakespeare's greater characters (his range was so wide, indeed, that it included Falstaff, Henry the Eighth, and Hamlet), that, having survived the halcyon days of "Eliza and our James" and lingered into the drab and russet period of the Puritans, when all the theatres in the British islands were suppressed, he became poor and presently kept a tavern, at Brentford, called The Three Pigeons. Lowin was born in 1576 and he died in 1654 — his grave being in London, in the churchyard of St. Martin-in-the-Fields — so that, obviously, he was one of the veterans of the stage. He was in his seventy-eighth year when he passed away — wherefore in his last days he must

have been "a mine of memories." He could
talk of the stirring times of Leicester, Drake,
Essex, and Raleigh. He could remember,
as an event of his boyhood, the execution
of Queen Mary Stuart, and possibly he
could describe, as an eye-witness, the splendid funeral procession of Sir Philip Sidney.
He could recall the death of Queen Elizabeth ; the advent of Scottish James ; the
ruffling, brilliant, dissolute, audacious Duke
of Buckingham ; the impeachment and disgrace of Francis Bacon ; the production of
the great plays of Shakespeare and Ben
Jonson ; the meetings of the wits and poets
at the Apollo and the Mermaid. He might
have personally known Robert Herrick —
that loveliest of the wild song-birds of that
golden age. He might have been present
at the burial of Edmund Spenser, in Westminster Abbey — when the poet brothers
of the author of *The Faerie Queene* cast
into his grave their manuscript elegies and
the pens with which those laments had been
written. He had acted Hamlet, — perhaps
in the author's presence. He had seen the
burning of the old Globe Theatre. He had
been, in the early days of Charles the First,
the chief and distinguished Falstaff of the
time. He had lived under the rule of three

successive princes; had deplored the sanguinary fate of the martyr-king (for the
actors were almost always royalists); had
seen the rise of the Parliament and the
downfall of the theatre; and now, under
the Protectorate of Oliver Cromwell, he had
become the keeper of an humble wayside
inn. It is easy to fancy the old actor sitting in his chair of state, the monarch of
his tap-room, with a flagon of beer, and a
church-warden pipe of tobacco, and holding
forth, to a select circle of cronies, upon the
vanished glories of the Elizabethan stage —
upon the days when there were persons in
existence really worthy to be called actors.
He could talk of Richard Burbage, the first
Romeo; of Armin, famous in Shakespeare's
clowns and fools; of Heminge and Condell,
who edited the First Folio of Shakespeare,
which possibly he himself purchased, fresh
from the press; of Joseph Taylor, whom it
is said Shakespeare personally instructed
how to play Hamlet, and the recollection of
whose performance enabled Sir William
Davenant to impart to Betterton the example and tradition established by the author
— a model that has lasted to the present
day; of Kempe, the original Dogberry, and
of the exuberant, merry Richard Tarleton,

after whom that comic genius had fashioned
his artistic method; of Alleyne, who kept
the bear-garden, and who founded the Col-
lege and Home at Dulwich — where they
still flourish; of Gabriel Spencer, and his
duel with Ben Jonson, wherein he lost his
life at the hands of that burly antagonist;
of Marlowe "of the mighty line," and his
awful and lamentable death — stabbed at
Deptford by a drunken drawer in a tavern
brawl. Very rich and fine, there can be no
doubt, were that veteran actor's remem-
brances of "the good old times," and most
explicit and downright, it may surely be
believed, was his opinion, freely commu-
nicated to the gossips of The Three Pigeons, that — in the felicitous satirical phrase
of Joseph Jefferson — all the good actors
are dead.

It was ever thus. Each successive epoch
of theatrical history presents the same
picturesque image of storied regret — memory incarnated in the veteran, ruefully
vaunting the vanished glories of the past.
There has always been a time when the
stage was finer than it is now. Cibber and
Macklin, surviving in the best days of
Garrick, Peg Woffington, and Kitty Clive,
were always praising the better days of

Wilks, Betterton, and Elizabeth Barry.
Aged play-goers of the period of Edmund
Kean and John Philip Kemble were firmly
persuaded that the drama had been buried,
never to rise again, with the dust of Garrick and Henderson, beneath the pavement
of Westminster Abbey. Less than fifty
years ago an American historian of the
stage (James Rees, 1845) described it as a
wreck, overwhelmed with "gloom and eternal night," above which the genius of the
drama was mournfully presiding, in the
likeness of an owl. The New York veteran
of to-day, although his sad gaze may not
penetrate backward quite to the effulgent
splendours of the old Park, will sigh for
Burton's and the Olympic, and the luminous
period of Mrs. Richardson, Mary Taylor,
and Tom Hamblin. The Philadelphia veteran gazes back to the golden era of the old
Chestnut Street theatre, the epoch of tie-
wigs and shoe-buckles, the illustrious times
of Wood and Warren, when Fennell, Cooke,
Cooper, Wallack, and J. B. Booth were
shining names in tragedy, and Jefferson
and William Twaits were great comedians,
and the beautiful Anne Brunton was the
queen of the stage. The Boston veteran
speaks proudly of the old Federal and the

old Tremont, of Mary Duff, Julia Pelby,
Charles Eaton, and Clara Fisher, and is even
beginning to gild with reminiscent splen-
dour the first days of the Boston Theatre,
when Thomas Barry was manager and Julia
Bennett Barrow and Mrs. John Wood con-
tended for the public favour. In a word,
the age that has seen Rachel, Seebach,
Ristori, Charlotte Cushman, and Adelaide
Neilson, the age that sees Ellen Terry, Mary
Anderson, Edwin Booth, Joseph Jefferson,
Henry Irving, Salvini, Coquelin, Lawrence
Barrett, John Gilbert, John S. Clarke, Ada
Rehan, James Lewis, Clara Morris, and
Richard Mansfield, is a comparatively sterile
period — "Too long shut in strait and few,
thinly dieted on dew" — which ought to
have felt the spell of Cooper and Mary Duff,
and known what acting was when Cooke's
long forefinger pointed the way, and Dunlap bore the banner, and pretty Mrs. Marshall bewitched the father of his country,
and Dowton raised the laugh, and lovely
Mrs. Barrett melted the heart, and the roses
were "bright by the calm Bendemeer."
The present writer, who began theatre-
going in earnest over thirty years ago, finds
himself full often musing over a dramatic
time that still seems brighter than this —

when he could exult in the fairy splendour
and comic humour of *Aladdin* and weep
over the sorrows of *The Drunkard,* when
he was thrilled and frightened by J. B.
Booth in *The Apostate,* and could find an
ecstasy of pleasure in the loves of Alonzo
and Cora and the sublime self-sacrifice of
Rolla.   Thoughts of such actors as Henry
Wallack, George Jordan, John Brougham,
John E. Owens, Mary Carr, Mrs. Barrow,
and Charlotte Thompson, together in the
same theatre, are thoughts of brilliant people and of more than commonly happy displays of talent and beauty.   The figures
that used to be seen on Wallack's stage, at
the house he established upon the wreck of
John Brougham's Lyceum, often rise in
memory, crowned with a peculiar light.
Lester Wallack, in his peerless elegance ;
Laura Keene, in her spiritual beauty ; the
quaint, eccentric Walcot ; the richly humorous Blake, so noble in his dignity, so
firm and fine and easy in his method, so
copious in his natural humour ; Mary Gannon, sweet, playful, bewitching, irresistible ;
Mrs. Vernon, as full of character as the
tulip is of colour or the hyacinth of grace,
and as delicate and refined as an exquisite
bit of old china — those actors made a

group, the like of which it would be hard to find now. Shall we ever see again such an Othello as Edwin Forrest, or such a Lord Duberly and Cap'n Cuttle as Burton, or such a Dazzle as John Brougham, or such an Affable Hawk as Charles Mathews? Certainly there was a superiority of manner, a tinge of intellectual character, a tone of grace and romance about the old actors, such as is not common in the present; and, making all needful allowance for the illusive glamour that memory casts over the distant and the dim, it yet remains true that the veterans of our day have a certain measure of right upon their side of the question.

In the earlier periods of our theatrical history the strength of the stage was concentrated in a few theatres. The old Park, for example, was called simply The Theatre, and when the New York playgoer spoke of going to the play he meant that he was going there. One theatre, or perhaps two, might flourish, in a considerable town, during a part of the year, but the field was limited, and therefore the actors were brought together in two or three groups. The star system, at least till the time of Cooper, seems to have been innocuous. Garrick's prodigious success in London, more than a hundred years ago, had enabled him to engross the control of the stage in that centre, where he was but little opposed, and practically to exile many players of the first ability, whose lustre he dimmed or whose services he did not require ; and those players dispersed themselves to distant places — to York, Dublin, Edinburgh, etc. — or crossed the sea to America. With that beginning the way was opened for the growth of superb stock-companies, in the early days of the American theatre. The English, next to the Italians, were the first among modern peoples to create a dramatic literature and to establish the acted drama, and they have always led in this field — antedating, historically, and surpassing in essential things the French stage which nowadays it is fashionable to extol. English influence, at all times stern and exacting, stamped the character of our early theatre. The tone of society, alike in the mother country, in the colonies, and in the first years of our Republic, was, as to these matters, formal and severe. Success upon the stage was exceedingly difficult to obtain, and it could not be obtained without substantial merit. The youths who

sought it were often persons of liberal education.   In Philadelphia, New York, and
Boston the stock-companies were composed
of select and thoroughly trained actors,
many of whom were well-grounded classical
scholars.   Furthermore, the epoch was one
of far greater leisure and repose than are
possible now — when the civilised world is
at the summit of sixty years of scientific
development such as it had not experienced
in all its recorded centuries of previous
progress.   Naturally enough the dramatic art
of our ancestors was marked by scholar-like
and thorough elaboration, mellow richness
of colour, absolute simplicity of character,
and great solidity of merit.   Such actors as
Wignell, Hodgkinson, Jefferson, Francis,
and Blissett offered no work that was not
perfect of its kind.   The tradition had been
established and accepted, and it was transmitted and preserved.   Everything was concentrated, and the public grew to be entirely
familiar with it.   Men, accordingly, who
obtained their ideas of acting at a time
when they were under influences surviving
from those ancient days are confused, bewildered, and distressed by much that is
offered in the theatres now.   I have listened
to the talk of an aged American acquain-

tance (Thurlow Weed), who had seen and known Edmund Kean, and who said that all modern tragedians were insignificant in comparison with him. I have listened to the talk of an aged English acquaintance (Fladgate), who had seen and known John Philip Kemble, and who said that his equal has never since been revealed. The present day knows what the old school was,[1] when it sees William Warren, Joseph Jefferson, Charles Fisher, Mrs. John Drew, John Gilbert, J. H. Stoddart, Mrs. G. H. Gilbert, William Davidge, and Lester Wallack — the results and the remains of it. The old touch survives in them and is under their control, and no one, seeing their ripe and finished art, can feel surprise that the veteran moralist should be wedded to his idols of the past, and should often be heard sadly to declare that all the good actors — except these — are dead. He forgets that scores of theatres now exist where once there were but two or three ; that the population of the United States has been increased by about fifty millions within ninety years ; that the field has been enormously broad-

[1] This paper was written in 1888, and now, in 1892, Mr. Jefferson, Mr. Stoddart, Mrs. Drew, and Mrs. Gilbert are the only survivors of that noble group.

ened ; that the character of the audience
has become one of illimitable diversity ;
that the prodigious growth of the star-sys-
tem, together with all sorts of experimental
catch-penny theatrical management, is one
of the inevitable necessities of the changed
condition of civilisation ; that the feverish
tone of this great struggling and seething
mass of humanity is necessarily reflected
in the state of the theatre ; and that the
forces of the stage have become very widely
diffused.   Such a moralist would necessarily be shocked by the changes that have
come upon our theatre within even the last
twenty-five years — by the advent of " the
sensation drama," invented and named by
Dion Boucicault ; by the resuscitation of
the spectacle play, with its lavish tinsel
and calcium glare and its multitudinous
nymphs ; by the opera bouffe, with its
frequent licentious ribaldry ; by the music-
hall comedian, with his vulgar realism ;
and by the idiotic burlesque, with its futile
babble and its big-limbed, half-naked girls.
Nevertheless there are just as good actors
now living as have ever lived, and there
is just as fine a sense of dramatic art in the
community as ever existed in any of " the
palmy days " ; only, what was formerly
concentrated is now scattered.

The stage is keeping step with the progress of human thought in every direction, and it will continue to advance. Evil influences impressed upon it there certainly are, in liberal abundance — not the least of these being that of the speculative shop-keeper, whose nature it is to seize any means of turning a penny, and who deals in dramatic art precisely as he would deal in groceries: but when we speak of "our stage" we do not mean an aggregation of shows or of the schemes of showmen. The stage is an institution that has grown out of a necessity in human nature. It was as inevitable that man should evolve the theatre as it was that he should evolve the church, the judiciary tribunal, the parliament, or any other essential component of the State. Almost all human beings possess the dramatic perception; a few possess the dramatic faculty. These few are born for the stage, and each and every generation contributes its number to the service of this art. The problem is one of selection and embarkation. Of the true actor it may be said, as Ben Jonson says of the true poet, that he is made as well as born. The finest natural faculties have never yet been known to avail without training and culture. But this is a

problem which, in a great measure, takes
care of itself and in time works out and
submits its own solution. The anomaly,
every day presented, of the young person
who, knowing nothing, feeling nothing,
and having nothing to communicate except
the desire of communication, nevertheless
rushes upon the stage, is felt to be absurd.
Where the faculty as well as the instinct
exists, however, impulse soon recognises
the curb of common sense, and the aspirant
finds his level. In this way the dramatic
profession is recruited. In this way the
several types of dramatic artist — each type
being distinct and each being expressive of
a sequence from mental and spiritual ancestry — are maintained. It is not too much
to say that a natural law operates silently
and surely behind each seemingly capricious
chance, in this field of the conduct of life.
A thoroughly adequate dramatic stock-
company may almost be said to be a thing
of natural accretion. It is made up, like
every other group, of the old, the middle-
aged, and the young; but, unlike every
other group, it must contain the capacity to
present, in a concrete image, each elemental
type of human nature, and to reproduce,
with the delicate exaggeration essential to

dramatic art, every species of person ; in order that all human life — whether of the street, the dwelling, the court, the camp, man in his common joys and sorrows, his vices, crimes, miseries, his loftiest aspirations and most ideal state — may be so copied that the picture will express all its beauty and sweetness, all its happiness and mirth, all its dignity, and all its moral admonition and significance, for the benefit of the world. Such a dramatic stock-company, for example (and this is but one of the commendable products of the modern stage), has grown up and crystallised into a form of refined power and symmetry, for the purpose to which it is devoted, under the management of Augustin Daly. That purpose is the acting of comedy. Mr. Daly began management in 1869, and he has remained in it, almost continually, from that time to this. Many players, first and last, have served under his direction. His company has known vicissitudes. But the organisation has not lost its comprehensive form, its competent force, and its attractive quality of essential grace. No thoughtful observer of its career can have failed to perceive how prompt the manager has been to profit by every lesson of experience ; what

keen perception he has shown as to the
essential constituents of a theatrical troop ;
with what fine judgment he has used the
forces at his disposal ; with what intrepid
resolution and expeditious energy he has
animated their spirit and guided their art ;
and how naturally those players have glided
into their several stations and assimilated
in one artistic family. How well balanced,
how finely equipped, how distinctively able
that company is, and what resources of
poetry, thought, taste, character, humour,
and general capacity it contains, may not,
perhaps, be fully appreciated in the passing
hour. "*Non, si male nunc, et olim sic erit.*"
Fifty years from now, when perchance some
veteran, still bright and cheery "in the
chimney-nook of age," shall sit in his arm-
chair and prose about the past, with what
complacent exultation will he speak of the
beautiful Ada Rehan, so bewitching as
Peggy in *The Country Girl*, so radiant,
vehement, and stormily passionate as Kath-
erine ; of manly John Drew, with his nonchalant ease, incisive tone, and crisp and
graceful method ; of noble Charles Fisher,
and sprightly and sparkling James Lewis,
and genial, piquant, quaint Mrs. Gilbert !
I mark the gentle triumph in that aged

reminiscent voice, and can respect an old
man's kindly and natural sympathy with
the glories and delights of his vanished
youth. But I think it is not necessary to
wait till you are old before you begin to
praise anything, and then to praise only the
dead. Let us recognise what is good in our
own time, and honour and admire it with
grateful hearts.

NOTE. — At the Garrick club, London, June
26, 1885, it was my fortune to meet Mr. Fladgate, "father of the Garrick," who was then
aged 86. The veteran displayed astonishing
resources of memory and talked most in-
structively about the actors of the Kemble
period. He declared John Philip Kemble to
have been the greatest of actors, and said
that his best impersonations were Penrud-
dock, Zanga, and Coriolanus. Mrs. Siddons,
he said, was incomparable, and the elder
Mathews a great genius, — the precursor of
Dickens. For Edmund Kean he had no enthusiasm. Kean, he said, was at his best in
Sir Edward Mortimer, and after that in Shylock. Miss O'Neill he remembered as the
perfect Juliet : a beautiful, blue-eyed woman,
who could easily weep, and who retained her
beauty to the last, dying at 85, as Lady
Wrixon Becher.

II.

HENRY IRVING AND ELLEN TERRY IN FAUST.

IT is not surprising that the votaries of Goethe's colossal poem — a work which, although somewhat deformed and degraded with the pettiness of provincialism, is yet a grand and immortal creation of genius — should find themselves dissatisfied with theatrical expositions of it. Although dramatic in form the poem is not continuously, directly, and compactly dramatic in movement. It cannot be converted into a play without being radically changed in structure and in the form of its diction. More disastrous still, in the eyes of those votaries, it cannot be and it never has been converted into a play without a considerable sacrifice of its contents, its comprehensive scope, its poetry, and its ethical significance. In the poem it is the Man who predominates ; it is not the Fiend. Mephistopheles, indeed, might, for the purpose of philosophical apprehension, be viewed as an embodied projection of the mind of Faust; for the power of the one is dependent absolutely upon the weakness and surrender of the other. The object of the poem was the portrayal of universal humanity in a typical form at its highest point of development and in its representative spiritual experience. Faust, an aged scholar, the epitome of human faculties and virtues, grand, venerable, beneficent, blameless, is passing miserably into the evening of life. He has done no outward and visible wrong, and yet he is wretched. The utter emptiness of his life — its lack of fulfilment, its lack of sensation — wearies, annoys, disgusts, and torments him. He is divided between an apathy, which heavily weighs him down into the dust, and a passionate, spiritual longing, intense, unsatisfied, insatiable, which almost drives him to frenzy. Once, at sunset, standing on a hillside, and looking down upon a peaceful valley, he utters, in a poetic strain of exquisite tenderness and beauty, the final wish of his forlorn and weary soul. It is no longer now the godlike aspiration and imperious desire of his prime, but it is the sufficient alternative. All he asks now is that he may see the world always as in that sunset vision, in

the perfection of happy rest; that he may
be permitted, soaring on the wings of the
spirit, to follow the sun in its setting ("The
day before me and the night behind"), and
thus to circle forever round and round this
globe, the ecstatic spectator of happiness
and peace. He has had enough and more
than enough of study, of struggle, of un-
fulfilled aspiration. Lonely dignity, arid
renown, satiety, sorrow, knowledge without hope, and age without comfort, — these
are his present portion; and a little way
onward, waiting for him, is death. Too
old to play with passion, too young not to
feel desire, he has endured a long struggle
between the two souls in his breast — one
longing for heaven and the other for the
world; but he is beaten at last, and in the
abject surrender of despair he determines
to die by his own act. A childlike feeling,
responsive in his heart to the divine prompt-
ing of sacred music, saves him from self-
murder; but in a subsequent bitter revulsion
he utters a curse upon everything in the
state of man, and most of all upon that
celestial attribute of patience whereby man
is able to endure and to advance in the
eternal process of evolution from darkness
into light. And now it is, when the soul

of the human being, utterly baffled by the
mystery of creation, crushed by its own
hopeless sorrow, and enraged by the everlasting command to renounce and refrain,
has become one delirium of revolt against
God and destiny, that the spirit of perpetual
denial, incarnated in Mephistopheles, steps
forth to proffer guidance and help.   It is as
if his rejection and defiance had suddenly
become embodied, to aid him in his ruin.
More in recklessness than in trust, with no
fear, almost with scorn and contempt, he
yet agrees to accept this assistance.   If
happiness be really possible, if the true
way, after all, should lie in the life of the
senses, and not in knowledge and reason ;
if, under the ministrations of this fiend,
one hour of life, even one moment of it,
shall ever (which is an idle and futile supposition) be so sweet that his heart shall
desire it to linger, then, indeed, he will surrender himself eternally to this at present
preposterous Mephistopheles, whom his
mood, his magic, and the revulsion of his
moral nature have evoked : —

"Then let the death-bell chime the token!
     Then art thou from thy service free!
The clock may stop, the hand be broken,
     And time be finished unto me."

Such an hour, it is destined, shall arrive, after many long and miserable years, when, aware of the beneficence of living for others and in the imagined prospect of leading, guiding, and guarding a free people upon a free land, Faust shall be willing to say to the moment: "Stay, thou art so fair"; and Mephistopheles shall harshly cry out: "The clock stands still"; and the graybeard shall sink in the dust; and the holy angels shall fly away with his soul, leaving the Fiend baffled and morose, to gibe at himself over the failure of all his infernal arts. But, meanwhile, it remains true of the man that no pleasure satisfies him and no happiness contents, and "death is desired, and life a thing unblest."

The man who puts out his eyes must become blind. The sin of Faust is a spiritual sin, and the meaning of all his subsequent terrible experience is that spiritual sin must be — and will be — expiated. No human soul can ever be lost. In every human soul the contest between good and evil must continue until the good has conquered and the evil is defeated and eradicated. Then, when the man's spirit is adjusted to its environment in the spiritual world, it will be at peace — and not till then. And if this conflict is not waged and completed now and here, it must be and it will be fought out and finished hereafter and somewhere else. It is the greatest of all delusions to suppose that you can escape from yourself. Judgment and retribution proceed within the soul and not from sources outside of it. That is the philosophic drift of the poet's thought expressed and implied in his poem. It was Man, in his mortal ordeal — the motive, cause, and necessity of which remain a mystery — whom he desired and aimed to portray ; it was not merely the triumph of a mocking devil, temporarily victorious through ministration to animal lust and intellectual revolt, over the weakness of the carnal creature and the embittered bewilderment of the baffled mind. Mr. Irving may well say, as he is reported to have said, that he will consider himself to have accomplished a good work if his production of Faust should have the effect of invigorating popular interest in Goethe's immortal poem and bringing closer home to the mind of his public a true sense of its sublime and far-reaching signification.

The full metaphysical drift of thought and meaning in Goethe's poem, however,

can be but faintly indicated in a play. It
is more distinctly indicated in Mr. Wills's
play, which is used by Mr. Irving, than in
any other play upon this subject that has
been presented. This result, an approxi-
mate fidelity to the original, is due in part
to the preservation of the witch scenes, in
part to Mr. Irving's subtle and significant
impersonation of Mephistopheles, and in
part to a weird investiture of spiritual mystery with which he has artfully environed
the whole production. The substance of
the piece is the love story of Faust and
Margaret, yet beyond this is a background
of infinity, and over and around this is a
poetic atmosphere charged with suggestiveness of supernatural agency in the fate of
man. If the gaze of the observer be concentrated upon the mere structure of the
piece, the love story is what he will find ;
and that is all he will find. Faust makes
his compact with the Fiend. He is rejuve-
nated and he begins a new life. In "the
Witch's Kitchen" his passions are intensified, and then they are ignited, so that he
may be made the slave of desire and afterward if possible imbruted by sensuality.
He is artfully brought into contact with
Margaret, whom he instantly loves, who

presently loves him, whom he wins, and
upon whom, since she becomes a mother
out of wedlock, his inordinate and reckless
love imposes the burden of pious contrition
and worldly shame. Then, through the
puissant wickedness and treachery of Mephistopheles, he is made to predominate
over her vengeful brother, Valentine, whom
he kills in a street fray. Thus his desire
to experience in his own person the most
exquisite bliss that humanity can enjoy and
equally the most exquisite torture that it
can suffer, becomes fulfilled. He is now
the agonised victim of love and of remorse.
Orestes pursued by the Furies was long ago
selected as the typical image of supreme
anguish and immitigable suffering; but
Orestes is less a lamentable figure than
Faust — fortified though he is, and because
he is, with the awful but malign, treacherous, and now impotent sovereignty of hell.
To deaden his sensibility, destroy his conscience, and harden him in evil the Fiend
leads him into a mad revel of boundless
profligacy and bestial riot — denoted by the
beautiful and terrible scene upon the
Brocken — and poor Margaret is abandoned
to her shame, her wandering, her despair,
her frenzy, her crime, and her punishment.

This desertion, though, is procured by a
stratagem of the Fiend and does not proceed from the design of her lover. The
expedient of Mephistopheles, to lull his prey
by dissipations, is a failure. Faust finds
them "tasteless," and he must return to
Margaret. He finds her in prison, crazed
and dying, and he strives in vain to set her
free. There is a climax, whereat, while
her soul is borne upward by angels he —
whose destiny must yet be fulfilled — is
summoned by the terrible voice of Satan.
This is the substance of what is shown;
but if the gaze of the observer pierces beyond this, if he is able to comprehend that
terrific but woeful image of the fallen angel,
if he perceives what is by no means ob-
scurely intimated, that Margaret, redeemed
and beatified, cannot be happy unless her
lover also is saved, and that the soul of
Faust can only be lost through the impossible contingency of being converted into
the likeness of the Fiend, he will understand that a spectacle has been set before
him more august, momentous, and sublime
than any episode of tragical human love
could ever be.

Henry Irving, in his embodiment of Mephistopheles, fulfilled the conception of the

poet in one essential respect and transcended it in another. His performance, superb in ideal and perfect in execution, was a great work — and precisely here was the greatness of it. Mephistopheles as delineated by Goethe is magnificently intellectual and sardonic, but nowhere does he convey even a faint suggestion of the godhead of glory from which he has lapsed. His own frank and clear avowal of himself leaves no room for doubt as to the limitation intended to be established for him by the poet. I am, he declares, the spirit that perpetually denies. I am a part of that part which once was all — a part of that darkness out of which came the light. I repudiate all things — because everything that has been made is unworthy to exist and ought to be destroyed, and therefore it is better that nothing should ever have been made. God dwells in splendour, alone and eternal, but his spirits he thrusts into darkness, and man, a poor creature fashioned to poke his nose into filth, he sportively dowers with day and night. My province is evil ; my existence is mockery ; my pleasure and my purpose are destruction. In a word, this Fiend, towering to the loftiest summit of cold intellect, is the embodiment

of cruelty, malice, and scorn, pervaded and
interfused with grim humour. That ideal
Mr. Irving made actual. The omniscient
craft and deadly maglignity of his impersonation, swathed in a most specious humour at some moments (as, for example, in
Margaret's bedroom, in the garden scene
with Martha, and in the duel scene with
Valentine) made the blood creep and curdle
with horror, even while they impressed the
sense of intellectual power and stirred the
springs of laughter. But if you rightly saw
his face, in the fantastic, symbolical scene
of the Witch's Kitchen ; in that lurid moment of sunset over the quaint gables and
haunted spires of Nuremburg, when the
sinister presence of the arch-fiend deepened
the red glare of the setting sun and seemed
to bathe this world in the ominous splendour of hell ; and, above all, if you perceived the soul that shone through his eyes
in that supremely awful moment of his pre-
dominance over the hellish revel upon the
Brocken, when all the hideous malignities
of nature and all those baleful ''spirits
which tend on mortal consequence'' are
loosed into the aerial abyss, and only this
imperial horror can curb and subdue them,
you knew that this Mephistopheles was a

sufferer not less than a mocker; that his
colossal malignity was the delirium of an
angelic spirit thwarted, baffled, shattered,
yet defiant ; never to be vanquished;
never through all eternity to be at peace
with itself. The infinite sadness of that
face, the pathos, beyond words, of that
isolated and lonely figure — those are the
qualities that irradiated all its diversified
attributes of mind, humour, duplicity, sarcasm, force, horror, and infernal beauty,
and invested it with the authentic quality
of greatness. There is no warrant for this
treatment of the part to be derived from
Goethe's poem. There is every warrant
for it in the apprehension of this tremendous subject by the imagination of a great
actor. You cannot mount above the earth,
you cannot transcend the ordinary line of
the commonplace, as a mere sardonic image
of self-satisfied, chuckling obliquity. Mr.
Irving embodied Mephistopheles not as a
man but as a spirit, with all that the word
implies, and in doing that he not only
heeded the fine instinct of the true actor
but the splendid teaching of the highest
poetry — the ray of supernal light that
flashes from the old Hebrew Bible ; the
blaze that streams from the *Paradise Lost;*

the awful glory through which, in the
pages of Byron, the typical figure of
agonised but unconquerable revolt towers
over a realm of ruin : —

    " On his brow
The thunder-scars are graven; from his eye
Glares forth the immortality of hell."

Ellen Terry, in her assumption of Margaret, once more displayed that profound,
comprehensive, and particular knowledge
of human love — that knowledge of it
through the soul and not simply the mind
— which is the source of her exceptional
and irresistible power. This Margaret was
a woman who essentially loves, who exists
only for love, who has the courage of her
love, who gives all for love — not knowing
that it is a sacrifice — and whose love, at
last, triumphant over death, is not only her
own salvation but that also of her lover.
The point of strict conformity to the conception of the poet, in physique and in
spiritual state, may be waived. Goethe's
Margaret is a handsome, hardy girl, of humble rank, who sometimes uses bad gram-
mar and who reveals no essential mind.
She is just a delicious woman, and there is
nothing about her either metaphysical or

mysterious. The wise Fiend, who knows that with such a man as Faust the love of such a woman must outweigh all the world, wisely tempts him with her, and infernally lures him to the accomplishment of her ruin. But it will be observed that, aside from the infraction of the law of man, the loves of Faust and Margaret are not only innocent but sacred. This sanctity Mephistopheles can neither pollute nor control, and through this he loses his victims. Ellen Terry's Margaret was a delicious woman, and not metaphysical nor mysterious; but it was Margaret imbued with the temperament of Ellen Terry, — who, if ever an exceptional creature lived, is exceptional in every particular. In her embodiment she transfigured the character: she maintained it in an ideal world, and she was the living epitome of all that is fascinating in essential womanhood — glorified by genius. It did not seem like acting but like the revelation of a hallowed personal experience upon which no chill worldly gaze should venture to intrude.

In that suggestive book in which Lady Pollock records her recollections of Macready it is said that once, after his retirement, on reading a London newspaper

account of the production of a Shakespearean play, he remarked that "evidently
the accessories swallow up the poetry and
the action": and he proceeded, in a reminiscent and regretful mood, to speak as
follows: "In my endeavour to give to
Shakespeare all his attributes, to enrich his
poetry with scenes worthy of its interpretation, to give to his tragedies their due
magnificence and to his comedies their
entire brilliancy, I have set an example
which is accompanied with great peril, for
the public is willing to have the magnificence without the tragedy, and the poet is
swallowed up in display." Mr. Irving is
the legitimate successor to Macready and he
has encountered that same peril. There are
persons — many of them — who think that
it is a sign of weakness to praise cordially
and to utter admiration with a free heart.
They are mistaken, but no doubt they are
sincere. Shakespeare, the wisest of moni-
tors, is never so eloquent and splendid as
when he makes one of his people express
praise of another. Look at those speeches
in *Coriolanus*. Such niggardly persons,
in their detraction of Henry Irving, are
prompt to declare that he is a capital stage
manager but not a great actor. This has

an impartial air and a sapient sound, but it
is gross folly and injustice. Henry Irving
is one of the greatest actors that have ever
lived, and he has shown it over and over
again. His acting is all the more effective
because associated with unmatched ability
to insist and insure that every play shall be
perfectly well set, in every particular, and
that every part in it shall be competently
acted. But his genius and his ability are
no more discredited than those of Macready
were by his attention to technical detail
and his insistence upon total excellence of
result. It should be observed, however,
that he has carried stage garniture to an
extreme limit. His investiture of *Faust*
was so magnificent that possibly it may
have tended in the minds of many spectators, to obscure and overwhelm the fine intellectual force, the beautiful delicacy, and
the consummate art with which he embodied Mephistopheles. It ought not to
have produced that effect — because, in
fact, the spectacle presented was, actually
and truly, that of a supernatural being,
predominant by force of inherent strength
and charm over the broad expanse of the
populous and teeming world ; but it might
have produced it : and, for the practical

good of the art of acting, progress in that
direction has gone far enough. The supreme beauty of the production was the
poetic atmosphere of it — the irradiation of
that strange sensation of being haunted
which sometimes will come upon you, even
at noon-day, in lonely places, on vacant hillside, beneath the dark boughs of great
trees, in the presence of the grim and silent
rocks, and by the solitary margin of the
sea. The feeling was that of Goethe's own
weird and suggestive scene of the Open
Field, the black horses, and the raven-
stone ; or that of the shuddering lines of
Coleridge : —

> " As one that on a lonesome road
>   Doth walk in fear and dread,
> And, having once turned round, walks on
>   And turns no more his head,
> Because he knows a frightful fiend
>   Doth close behind him tread."

III.

ADELAIDE NEILSON AS IMOGEN AND JULIET.

SHAKESPEARE'S drama of *Cymbeline* seems not at any time in the history of the stage to have been a favourite with theatrical audiences. In New York it has had but five revivals in more than a hundred years, and those occurred at long intervals and were of brief continuance. The names of Thomas Barry, Mrs. Shaw-Hamblin (Eliza Marian Trewar), and Julia Bennett Barrow are best remembered in association with it on the American stage. It had slept for more than a generation when, in the autumn of 1876, Adelaide Neilson revived it at Philadelphia; but since then it has been reproduced by several of her imitators. She first offered it on the New York stage in May 1877, and it was then seen that her impersonation of Imogen was one of the best of her works. If it be the justification of the stage as an institution of public benefit and social advancement, that it elevates humanity by presenting noble ideals of human nature and making them exemplars and guides, that justification was practically accomplished by that beautiful performance.

The poetry of *Cymbeline* is eloquent and lovely.   The imagination of its appreciative reader, gliding lightly over its more sinister incidents, finds its story romantic, its accessories — both of the court and the wilderness — picturesque, its historic atmosphere novel and exciting, and the spirit of it tender and noble.   Such a reader, likewise, fashions its characters into an ideal form which cannot be despoiled by comparison with a visible standard of reality.   It is not, however, an entirely pleasant play to witness.   The acting version, indeed, is considerably condensed from the original, by the excision of various scenes explanatory of the conduct of the story, and by the omission of the cumbersome vision of Leonatus ; and the gain of brevity thereby made helps to commend the work to a more gracious acceptance than it would be likely to obtain if acted exactly according to Shakespeare.   Its movement also is imbued with additional alacrity by a rearrangement of its divisions.   It is customarily presented in six acts. Yet, notwithstanding the cutting and editing to which it has been subjected, *Cymbeline* remains somewhat inharmonious alike with the needs of the stage and the apprehension of the public.

For this there are several causes. One perhaps is its mixed character, its vague, elusive purpose, and its unreality of effect. From the nature of his story — a tale of stern facts and airy inventions, respecting Britain and Rome, two thousand years ago — the poet seems to have been compelled to make a picture of human life too literal to be viewed wholly as an ideal, and too romantic to be viewed wholly as literal. In the unequivocally great plays of Shakespeare the action moves like the mighty flow of some resistless river. In this one it advances with the diffusive and straggling movement of a summer cloud. The drift and meaning of the piece, accordingly, do not stand boldly out. That astute thinker, Ulrici, for instance, after much brooding upon it, ties his mental legs in a hard knot and says that Shakespeare intended, in this piece, to illustrate that man is not the master of his own destiny. There must be liberal scope for conjecture when a philosopher can make such a landing as that.

The persons in *Cymbeline*, moreover —
aside from the exceptional character of
Imogen — do not come home to a spectator's
realisation, whether of sympathy or repug-
nance. It is like the flower that thrives
best under glass but shivers and wilts in
the open air. Its poetry seems marred by
the rude touch of the actual. Its delicious
mountain scenes lose their woodland fragrance. Its motive, bluntly disclosed in the
wager scene, seems coarse, unnatural, and
offensive. Its plot, really simple, moves
heavily and perplexes attention. It is a
piece that lacks pervasive concentration
and enthralling point. It might be defined
as *Othello* with a difference — the difference
being in favour of *Othello*. Jealousy is the
pivot of both : but in *Othello* jealousy is
treated with profound and searching truth,
with terrible intensity of feeling, and with
irresistible momentum of action. A spectator will honour and pity Othello, and hate
and execrate Iago — with some infusion, perhaps of impatience toward the one and of
admiration for the other — but he is likely
to view both Leonatus and Iachimo with
considerable indifference ; he will casually
recognise the infrequent Cymbeline as an
ill-tempered, sonorous old donkey ; he will

give a passing smile of scornful disgust to
Cloten — that vague hybrid of Roderigo and
Oswald ; and of the proceedings of the
Queen and the fortunes of the royal family
— whether as affected by the chemical ex-
periments of Doctor Cornelius or the belli-
cose attitude of Augustus Cæsar, in reach-
ing for his British tribute — he will be practically unconscious. This result comes of
commingling stern fact and pastoral fancy
in such a way that an auditor of the composition is dubious whether to fix his senses
steadfastly on the one or yield up his spirit
to poetic reverie on the other.

Coleridge — whose intuitions as to such
matters were usually as good as recorded
truth — thought that Shakespeare wrote
Cymbeline in his youthful period. He certainly does not manifest in it the cogent
and glittering dramatic force that is felt in
Othello and *Macbeth*. The probability is
that he wrought upon the old legend of
Holinshed in a mood of intellectual caprice,
inclining towards sensuous and fanciful
dalliance with a remote and somewhat
intangible subject. Those persons who explain the immense fecundity of his creative
genius by alleging that he must steadily
have kept in view the needs of the contem-

porary theatre seem to forget that he went much further in his plays than there was any need for him to go, in the satisfaction of such a purpose, and that those plays are, in general, too great for any stage that has existed. Shakespeare, it is certain, could not have been an exception to the law that every author must be conscious of a feeling, apart from intellectual purpose, that carries him onward in his art. The feeling that shines through *Cymbeline* is a loving delight in the character of Imogen.

The nature of that feeling and the quality of that character, had they been obscure, would have been made clear by Adelaide Neilson's embodiment. The personality that she presented was typical and unusual. It embodied virtue, neither hardened by austerity nor vapid with excess of goodness, and it embodied seductive womanhood, without one touch of wantonness or guile. It presented a woman innately good and radiantly lovely, who amid severest trials spontaneously and unconsciously acted with the ingenuous grace of childhood, the grandest generosity, the most constant spirit. The essence of Imogen's nature is fidelity. Faithful to love, even till death, she is yet more faithful to honour. Her scorn of false-

hood is overwhelming; but she resents no
injury, harbours no resentment, feels no
spite, murmurs at no misfortune. From
every blow of evil she recovers with a gentle patience that is infinitely pathetic. Passionate and acutely sensitive, she yet seems
never to think of antagonising her affliction
or to falter in her unconscious fortitude.
She has no reproach — but only a grieved
submission — for the husband who has
wronged her by his suspicions and has
doomed her to death. She thinks only of
him, not of herself, when she beholds him,
as she supposes, dead at her side; but even
then she will submit and endure — she will
but "weep and sigh" and say twice o'er
"a century of prayers." She is only sorry
for the woman who was her deadly enemy
and who hated her for her goodness — so
often the incitement of mortal hatred.
She loses without a pang the heirship to a
kingdom. An ideal thus poised in goodness and radiant in beauty might well have
sustained — as undoubtedly it did sustain
— the inspiration of Shakespeare.

Adelaide Neilson, with her uncommon
graces of person, found it easy to make the
chamber scene and the cave scenes pictorial
and charming. Her ingenuous trepidation

and her pretty wiles, as Fidele, in the cave,
were finely harmonious with the character
and arose from it like odour from a flower.
The innocence, the glee, the feminine desire
to please, the pensive grace, the fear, the
weakness, and the artless simplicity made
up a state of gracious fascination. It was,
however, in the revolt against Iachimo's
perfidy, in the fall before Pisanio's fatal
disclosure, and in the frenzy over the supposed death of Leonatus that the actress
put forth electrical power and showed how
strong emotion, acting through the imagination, can transfigure the being and give
to love or sorrow a monumental semblance
and an everlasting voice. The power was
harmonious with the individuality and did
not mar its grace. There was a perfect
preservation of sustained identity, and this
was expressed with such a sweet elocution
and such an airy freedom of movement and
naturalness of gesture that the observer
almost forgot to notice the method of the
mechanism and quite forgot that he was
looking upon a fiction and a shadow. That
her personation of Imogen, though more
exalted in its nature than any of her works,
excepting Isabella, would rival in public
acceptance her Juliet, Viola, or Rosalind,

was not to be expected : it was too much a passive condition — delicate and elusive — and too little an active effort. She woke into life the sleeping spirit of a rather repellant drama, and was "alone the Arabian bird."

Shakespeare's Juliet, the beautiful, ill-fated heroine of his consummate poem of love and sorrow, was the most effective, if not the highest of Adelaide Neilson's tragic assumptions. It carried to every eye and to every heart the convincing and thrilling sense equally of her beauty and her power. The exuberant womanhood, the celestial affection, the steadfast nobility, and the lovely, childlike innocence of Imogen — shown through the constrained medium of a diffusive romance — were not to all minds appreciable on the instant. The gentle sadness of Viola, playing around her gleeful animation and absorbing it as the cup of the white lily swallows the sunshine, might well be, for the more blunt senses of the average auditor, dim, fitful, evanescent, and ineffective. Ideal heroism and dream-like fragrance — the colours of Murillo or the poems of Heine — are truly known but to exceptional natures or in exceptional moods. The reckless, passionate idolatry

of Juliet, on the contrary, — with its attendant sacrifice, its climax of disaster, and its
sequel of anguish and death, — stands forth
as clearly as the white line of the lightning
on a black midnight sky, and no observer
can possibly miss its meaning. All that
Juliet is, all that she acts and all that she
suffers, is elemental. It springs directly
from the heart and it moves straight onward
like a shaft of light. Othello, the perfection of simplicity, is not simpler than
Juliet. In him are embodied passion and
jealousy, swayed by an awful instinct of
rude justice. In her is embodied unmixed
and immitigable passion, without law, limit,
reason, patience, or restraint. She is love
personified and therefore a fatality to herself. Presented in that way — and in that
way she was presented by Adelaide Neilson
— her nature and her experience come
home to the feelings as well as the imagination, and all that we know, as well as all
that we dream, of beauty and of anguish
are centred in one image. In this we may
see all the terrors of the moving hand of
fate. In this we may almost hear a warn-
ing voice out of heaven, saying that nowhere except in duty shall the human heart
find refuge and peace — or, if not peace,
submission.

The question whether Shakespeare's
Juliet be correctly interpreted is not one
of public importance. It might be ever so
correctly interpreted without producing the
right effect. There have been many Juliets.
There has, in our time, been no Juliet so
completely fascinating and irresistible as
that of Adelaide Neilson. Through the
medium of that Shakespearean character
the actress poured forth that strange, thrilling, indescribable power which more than
anything else in the world vindicates by its
existence the spiritual grandeur and destiny
of the human soul. Neither the accuracy
of her ideals nor the fineness of her execution would have accomplished the result
that attended her labours and crowned her
fame. There was an influence back of
these — a spark of the divine fire — a consecration of the individual life — as eloquent
to inform as it was potent to move. Adelaide Neilson was one of those strange,
exceptional natures that, often building
better than they know, not only interpret
"the poet's dream" but give to it an added
emphasis and a higher symbolism. Each
element of her personality was rich and
rare. The eyes — now glittering with a
mischievous glee that seemed never to have

seen a cloud or felt a sorrow, now steady,
frank, and sweet, with innocence and trust,
— could, in one moment, flash with the wild
fire of defiance or the glittering light of
imperious command, or, equally in one moment, could soften with mournful thought
and sad remembrance, or darken with the
far-off look of one who hears the waving
wings of angels and talks with the spirits
of the dead. The face, just sufficiently
unsymmetrical to be brimful of character,
whether piquant or pensive ; the carriage
of body, — easy yet quaint in its artless
grace, like that of a pretty child in the unconscious fascination of infancy ; the restless, unceasing play of mood, and the
instantaneous and perfect response of expression and gesture, — all these were the
denotements of genius ; and, above all
these, and not to be mistaken in its irradiation of the interior spirit of that extraordinary creature, was a voice of perfect music — rich, sonorous, flexible, vibrant, copious in volume, yet delicate as a silver thread
— a voice

> " Like the whisper of the woods
> In prime of even, when the stars are few."

It did not surprise that such a woman

should truly act Juliet. Much though there be in a personality that is assumed, there is much more in the personality that assumes it. Golden fire in a porcelain vase would not be more luminous than was the soul of that actress as it shone through her ideal of Juliet. The performance did not stop short at the interpretation of a poetic fancy. It was amply and completely that — but it was more than that, being also a living experience. The subtlety of it was only equalled by its intensity, and neither was surpassed except by its reality. The moment she came upon the scene all eyes followed her, and every imaginative mind was vaguely conscious of something strange and sad — a feeling of perilous suspense — a dark presentiment of impending sorrow. In that was felt at once the presence of a nature to which the experience of Juliet would be possible ; and thus the conquest of human sympathy was effected at the outset — by a condition, and without the exercise of a single effort. Fate no less than art participated in the result. Though it was the music of Shakespeare that flowed from the harp, it was the hand of living genius that smote the strings ; it was the soul of a great woman that bore its vital testimony to the power of the universal passion.

Never was poet truer to the highest truth of spiritual life than Shakespeare is when he invests with ineffable mournfulness — shadowy as twilight, vague as the remembrance of a dream — those creatures of his fancy who are preordained to suffering and a miserable death.   Never was there sounded a truer note of poetry than that which thrills in Othello's, "If it were now to die," or sobs in Juliet's "Too early seen unknown, and known too late."   It was the exquisite felicity of Adelaide Neilson's acting of Juliet that she glided into harmony with that tragical undertone, and, with seemingly a perfect unconsciousness of it — whether prattling to the old nurse, or moving, sweetly grave and softly demure, through the stately figures of the minuet — was already marked off from among the living, already overshadowed by a terrible fate, already alone in the bleak loneliness of the broken heart.   Striking the keynote thus, the rest followed in easy sequence.   The ecstasy of the wooing scene, the agony of the final parting from Romeo, the forlorn tremor and passionate frenzy of the terrible night before the burial, the fearful awak-

ening, the desperation, the paroxysm, the
death-blow that then is mercy and kindness,
— all these were in unison with the spirit
at first denoted, and through these was
naturally accomplished its prefigured doom.
If clearly to possess a high purpose, to follow it directly, to accomplish it thoroughly,
to adorn it with every grace, to conceal
every vestige of its art, and to cast over
the art that glamour of poetry which en-
nobles while it charms, and while it dazzles
also endears, — if this is greatness in acting,
then was Adelaide Neilson's Juliet a great
embodiment. It never will be forgotten.
Its soft romance of tone, its splendour of
passion, its sustained energy, its beauty of
speech, and its poetic fragrance are such
as fancy must always cherish and memory
cannot lose. Placing this embodiment beside Imogen and Viola, it was easy to understand the secret of her extraordinary
success. She satisfied for all kinds of persons the sense of the ideal. To youthful
fancy she was the radiant vision of love
and pleasure ; to grave manhood, the image
of all that chivalry should honour and
strength protect ; to woman, the type of
noble goodness and constant affection ; to
the scholar, a relief from thought and care ;

to the moralist, a spring of tender pity — that loveliness, however exquisite, must fade and vanish. Childhood, mindful of her kindness and her frolic, scattered flowers at her feet ; and age, that knows the thorny pathways of the world, whispered its silent prayer and laid its trembling hands in blessing on her head. She sleeps beneath a white marble cross in Brompton cemetery, and all her triumphs and glories have dwindled to a handful of dust.

NOTE ON CYMBELINE. — Genest records productions of Shakespeare's *Cymbeline*, in London, as follows: Haymarket, November 8, 1744; Covent Garden, April 7, 1746; Drury Lane, November 28, 1761; Covent Garden, December 28, 1767; Drury Lane, December 1, 1770; Haymarket, August 9, 1782; Covent Garden, October 18, 1784; Drury Lane, November 21, 1785, and January 29 and March 20, 1787; Covent Garden, May 13, 1800, January 18, 1806, June 3, 1812, May 29, 1816, and June 2, 1825; and Drury Lane, February 9, 1829; Imogen was represented, successively, by Mrs. Pritchard, Miss Bride, Mrs. Yates, Mrs. Barry, Mrs. Bulkley, Miss Younge, Mrs. Jordan, Mrs. Siddons, Mrs. Pope, Miss Smith, Mrs. H. Johnston Miss Stephens, Miss Foote, and Miss Phillips. Later representatives of it were Sally Booth, Helen Faucit, and Laura Addison.

IV.

EDWIN BOOTH.

THERE was a great shower of meteors on the night of November 13, 1833, and on that night, near Baltimore, Maryland, was born the most famous tragic actor of America in this generation, Edwin Booth. No other American actor of this century has had a rise so rapid or a career so early and continuously brilliant as that of Edwin Booth. His father, the renowned Junius Brutus Booth, had hallowed the family name with distinction and romantic interest. If ever there was a genius upon the stage the elder Booth was a genius. His wonderful eyes, his tremendous vitality, his electrical action, his power to thrill the feelings and easily and inevitably to awaken pity and terror, — all these made him a unique being and obtained for him a reputation with old-time audiences distinct from that of all other men. He was followed as a marvel, and even now the mention of his

name stirs, among those who remember
him, an enthusiasm such as no other theatrical memory can evoke. His sudden death
(alone, aboard a Mississippi river steamboat, November 30, 1852) was pathetic, and
the public thought concerning him thenceforward commingled tenderness with passionate admiration. When his son Edwin
began to rise as an actor the people everywhere rejoiced and gave him an eager wel-
come. With such a prestige he had no
difficulty in making himself heard, and
when it was found that he possessed the
same strange power with which his father
had conquered and fascinated the dramatic
world the popular exultation was unbounded.

Edwin Booth went on the stage in 1849
and accompanied his father to California
in 1852, and between 1852 and 1856 he
gained his first brilliant success. The early
part of his California life was marked by
hardship and all of it by vicissitude, but his
authentic genius speedily flamed out, and
long before he returned to the Atlantic sea-
board the news of his fine exploits had
cleared the way for his conquest of all hearts.
He came back in 1856-57, and from that
time onward his fame continually increased.
He early identified himself with two of the

most fascinating characters in the drama
— the sublime and pathetic Hamlet and
the majestic, romantic, picturesque, tender,
and grimly humorous Richelieu. He first
acted Hamlet in 1854 ; he adopted Richelieu
in 1856 ; and such was his success with
the latter character that for many years
afterward he made it a rule (acting on
the sagacious advice of the veteran New
Orleans manager, James H. Caldwell), always to introduce himself in that part
before any new community. The popular
sentiment toward him early took a romantic turn and the growth of that sentiment
has been accelerated and strengthened by
every important occurrence of his private
life. In July 1860 he was married to a
lovely and interesting woman, Miss Mary
Devlin, of Troy, and in February 1863 she
died. In 1867 he lost the Winter Garden
theatre, which was burnt down on the
night of March 22, that year, after a performance of John Howard Payne's *Brutus*.
He had accomplished beautiful revivals of
Hamlet, *Othello*, *The Merchant of Venice*,
and other plays at the Winter Garden, and
had obtained for that theatre an honourable
eminence ; but when in 1869 he built and
opened Booth's Theatre in New York, he

proceeded to eclipse all his previous efforts
and triumphs.   The productions of *Romeo
and Juliet*, *Othello*, *Richelieu*, *Hamlet*, *A
Winter's Tale*, and *Julius Cæsar* were
marked by ample scholarship and magnificence.   When the enterprise failed and
the theatre passed out of Edwin Booth's
hands (1874) the play-going public endured
a calamity.   But the failure of the actor's
noble endeavour to establish a great theatre
in the first city of America, like every other
conspicuous event in his career, served but
to deepen the public interest in his welfare.
He has more than retrieved his losses since
then, and has made more than one triumphal march throughout the length and
breadth of the Republic, besides acting in
London and other cities of Great Britain,
and gaining extraordinary success upon the
stage of Germany.   To think of Edwin Booth
is immediately to be reminded of those leading events in his career, while to review
them, even in a cursory glance, is to perceive that, notwithstanding calamities and
sorrows, notwithstanding a bitter experience of personal bereavement and of the
persecution of envy and malice, Edwin
Booth has ever been a favourite of fortune.
    The bust of Booth as Brutus and that of

John Gilbert as Sir Peter, standing side by
side in the Players' Club, stir many memories and prompt many reflections. Gilbert
was a young man of twenty-three, and had
been six years on the stage, before Edwin
Booth was born; and when, at the age of
sixteen, Booth made his first appearance
(September 10, 1849, at the Boston Museum,
as Tressil to his father's Richard), Gilbert
had become a famous actor. The younger
man, however, speedily rose to the higher
level of the best dramatic ability as well as
the best theatrical culture of his time; and
it is significant of the splendid triumph of
tragic genius, and of the advantage it possesses over that of comedy in its immediate
effect upon mankind, that when the fine
and exceptional combination was made
(May 21, 1888, at the Metropolitan Opera
House, New York), for a performance of
Hamlet for the benefit of Lester Wallack,
Edwin Booth acted Hamlet, with John
Gilbert for Polonius, and Joseph Jefferson
for the first Grave-digger. Booth has had
his artistic growth in a peculiar period in
the history of dramatic art in America.
Just before his time the tragic sceptre was
in the hands of Edwin Forrest, who never
succeeded in winning the intellectual part of

the public, but was constantly compelled to dominate a multitude that never heard any sound short of thunder and never felt anything till it was hit with a club. The bulk of Forrest's great fortune was gained by him with *Metamora*, which is rant and fustian. He himself despised it and deeply despised and energetically cursed the public that forced him to act in it. Forrest's best powers, indeed, were never really appreciated by the average mind of his fervent admirers. He lived in a rough period and he had to use a hard method to subdue and please it. Edwin Booth was fortunate in coming later, when the culture of the people had somewhat increased, and when the old sledge-hammer style was going out, so that he gained almost without an effort the refined and fastidious classes. As long ago as 1857, with all his natural grace, refinement, romantic charm, and fine bearing, his impetuosity was such that even the dullest sensibilities were aroused and thrilled and astonished by him, — and so it happened that he also gained the multitude. To think of these things is to realise the steady advance of the stage in the esteem of the best people, and to feel grateful that we do not live in " the palmy days " —

those raw times that John Brougham used to call the days of light houses and heavy gas bills.

Mrs. Asia Booth Clarke, wife of the distinguished and excellent comedian John S. Clarke, wrote a life of her father, Junius Brutus Booth, in which she has recounted interesting passages in his career, and chronicled significant and amusing anecdotes of his peculiarities. He was on the stage from 1813 to 1852, in which latter year he died, aged fifty-six. In his youth he served for a while in the British navy, showed some talent for painting, learned the printer's trade, wrote a little, and dabbled in sculpture — all before he turned actor. The powerful hostility of Edmund Kean and his adherents drove him from the London stage, though not till after he had gained honours there, and he came to America in 1821, and bought a farm near Baltimore, where he settled, and where his son Edwin (the seventh of ten children) was born. That farm remained in the family till 1880, when for the first time it changed hands. There is a certain old cherry-tree growing upon it — remarkable among cherry-trees for being large, tall, straight, clean, and handsome — amid the boughs of which the youthful Edwin might often have been found in his juvenile days. It is a coincidence that Edwin L. Davenport and John McCullough, also honoured names in American stage history, were born on the same day in the same month with Edwin Booth, though in different years.

From an early age Edwin Booth was associated with his father in all the wanderings and strange and often sad adventures of that wayward man of genius, and no doubt the many sorrowful experiences of his youth deepened the gloom of his inherited temperament. Those who know him well are aware that he has great tenderness of heart and abundant playful humour ; that his mind is one of extraordinary liveliness, and that he sympathises keenly and cordially with the joys and sorrows of others ; and yet that he seems saturated with sadness, isolated from companionship, lonely and alone. It is this temperament, combined with a sombre and melancholy aspect of countenance, that has helped to make him so admirable in the character of Hamlet. Of his fitness for that part his father was the first to speak, when on a night many years ago, in Sacramento, they had dressed for Pierre and

Jaffier, in *Venice Preserved.* Edwin, as
Jaffier, had put on a close-fitting robe of
black velvet. "You look like Hamlet,"
the father said. The time was destined to
come when Edwin Booth would be accepted all over America as the greatest
Hamlet of the day. In the season of
1864–65, at the Winter Garden theatre,
New York, he acted that part for a hundred nights in succession, accomplishing a
feat then unprecedented in theatrical annals. Since then Henry Irving, in London,
has acted Hamlet two hundred consecutive
times in one season ; but this latter achievement, in the present day and in the capital
city of the world, was less difficult than
Edwin Booth's exploit, performed in turbulent New York in the closing months of
the terrible civil war.

The elder Booth was a short, spare, mus-
cular man, with a splendid chest, a symmetrical Greek head, a pale countenance, a
voice of wonderful compass and thrilling
power, dark hair, and blue eyes. His son's
resemblance to him is chiefly obvious in the
shape of the head and face, the arch and
curve of the heavy eyebrows, the radiant
and constantly shifting light of expression
that animates the countenance, the natural

grace of carriage, and the celerity of movement. Booth's eyes are dark brown, and seem to turn black in moments of excitement, and they are capable of conveying, with electrical effect, the most diverse meanings — the solemnity of lofty thought, the tenderness of affection, the piteousness of forlorn sorrow, the awful sense of spiritual surroundings, the woful weariness of despair, the mocking glee of wicked sarcasm, the vindictive menace of sinister purpose, and the lightning glare of baleful wrath. In range of facial expressiveness his countenance is thus fully equal to that of his father. The present writer saw the elder Booth but once, and then in a comparatively inferior part — Pescara, in Shiel's ferocious tragedy of *The Apostate*. He was a terrible presence. He was the incarnation of smooth, specious, malignant, hellish rapacity. His exultant malice seemed to buoy him above the ground. He floated rather than walked. His glance was deadly. His clear, high, cutting, measured tone was the exasperating note of hideous cruelty. He was acting a fiend then, and making the monster not only possible but actual. He certainly gave a greater impression of overwhelming power

than is given by Edwin Booth, and seemed
a more formidable and tremendous man.
But his face was not more brilliant than
that of his renowned son ; and in fact it
was, if anything, somewhat less splendid in
power of the eye.   There is a book about
him, called *The Tragedian*, written by
Thomas R. Gould, who also made a noble
bust of him in marble ; and those who never
saw him can obtain a good idea of what
sort of an actor he was by reading that
book.   It conveys the image of a greater
actor, but not a more brilliant one, than
Edwin Booth.   Only one man of our time
has equalled Edwin Booth in this singular
splendour of countenance — the great New
England orator Rufus Choate.   Had Choate
been an actor upon the stage — as he was
before a jury — with those terrible eyes of
his, and that passionate Arab face, he must
have towered fully to the height of the tradition of George Frederick Cooke.

The lurid flashes of passion and the vehement outbursts in the acting of Edwin
Booth are no doubt the points that most persons who have seen him will most clearly remember.   Through these a spectator naturally discerns the essential nature of an
actor.   The image of George Frederick

Cooke, pointing with his long, lean fore-finger and uttering Sir Giles's imprecation upon Marrall, never fades out of theatrical history. Garrick's awful frenzy in the storm scene of King Lear, Kean's colossal agony in the farewell speech of Othello, Macready's heartrending yell in *Werner*, Junius Booth's terrific utterance of Richard's "What do they i' the north?" Forrest's hyena snarl when, as Jack Cade, he met Lord Say in the thicket, or his volumed cry of tempestuous fury when, as Lucius Brutus, he turned upon Tarquin under the black midnight sky — those are things never to be forgotten. Edwin Booth has provided many such great moments in acting, and the traditions of the stage will not let them die. To these no doubt we must look for illuminative manifestations of hereditary genius. Garrick, Henderson, Cooke, Edmund Kean, Junius Booth, and Edwin Booth are names that make a natural sequence in one intellectual family. Could we but see them together, we should undoubtedly find them, in many particulars, kindred. Henderson flourished in the school of nature that Garrick had created — to the discomfiture of Quin and all the classics. Cooke had seen Henderson act, and was thought to resemble him. Edmund Kean worshipped the memory of Cooke and repeated many of the elder tragedian's ways. So far, indeed, did he carry his homage that when he was in New York in 1824 he caused Cooke's remains to be taken from the vault beneath St. Paul's church and buried in the church-yard, where a monument, set up by Kean and restored by his son Charles, by Sothern, and by Edwin Booth, still marks their place of sepulture. That was the occasion when, as Dr. Francis records, in his book on old New York, Kean took the index finger of Cooke's right hand, and he, the doctor, took his skull, as relics. " I have got Cooke's style in acting," Kean once said, " but the public will never know it, I am so much smaller." It was not the imitation of a copyist ; it was the spontaneous devotion and direction of a kindred soul. The elder Booth saw Kean act, and although injured by a rivalry that Kean did not hesitate to make malicious, admired him with honest fervour. " I will yield Othello to him," he said, " but neither Richard nor Sir Giles." Forrest thought Edmund Kean the greatest actor of the age, and copied him, especially in Othello. Pathos, with

all that it implies, seems to have been
Kean's special excellence. Terror was the
elder Booth's. Edwin Booth may be less
than either, but he unites attributes of
both.

In the earlier part of his career Edwin
Booth was accustomed to act Sir Giles Overreach, Sir Edward Mortimer, Pescara, and
a number of other parts of the terrific order,
that he has since discarded. He was fine
in every one of them. The first sound of
his voice when, as Sir Edward Mortimer,
he was heard speaking off the scene, was
eloquent of deep suffering, concentrated
will, and a strange, sombre, formidable
character. The sweet, exquisite, icy, infernal joy with which, as Pescara, he told his
rival that there should be "music" was
almost comical in its effect of terror : it
drove the listener across the line of tragical
tension and made him hysterical with the
grimness of a deadly humour. His swift
defiance to Lord Lovell, as Sir Giles, and
indeed the whole mighty and terrible action
with which he carried that scene — from
" What, are you pale ? " down to the grisly
and horrid viper pretence and reptile spasm
of death — were simply tremendous. This
was in the days when his acting yet re-

tained the exuberance of a youthful spirit,
before "the philosophic mind" had checked
the headlong currents of the blood or curbed
imagination in its lawless flight. And those
parts not only admitted of bold colour and
extravagant action but demanded them.
Even his Hamlet was touched with that
elemental fire. Not alone in the great
junctures of the tragedy — the encounters
with the ghost, the parting with Ophelia,
the climax of the play-scene, the slaughter of poor old Polonius in delirious mis-
take for the king, and the avouchment to
Laertes in the graveyard — was he brilliant and impetuous ; but in almost everything that quality of temperament showed
itself, and here, of course, it was in excess.
He no longer hurls the pipe into the flies
when saying "Though you may fret me,
you can not play upon me" ; but he used
to do so then, and the rest of the performance was kindred with that part of it.
He needed, in that period of his development, the more terrible passions to express. Pathos and spirituality and the
mountain air of great thought were yet to
be. His Hamlet was only dazzling — the
glorious possibility of what it has since
become. But his Sir Giles was a consum-

mate work of genius — as good then as it
ever afterward became, and better than
any other that has been seen since, not
excepting that of E. L. Davenport. And
in all kindred characters he showed himself a man of genius. His success was
great. The admiration that he inspired
partook of zeal that almost amounted to
craziness. When he walked in the streets
of Boston in 1857 his shining face, his
compact figure, and his elastic step drew
every eye, and people would pause and
turn in groups to look at him.

The actor is born but the artist must be
made, and the actor who is not an artist
only half fulfils his powers. Edwin Booth
had not been long upon the stage before he
showed himself to be an actor. During
his first season he played Cassio in *Othello,*
Wilford in *The Iron Chest,* and Titus in
The Fall of Tarquin, and he played them
all auspiciously well. But his father, not
less wise than kind, knew that the youth
must be left to himself to acquire experience, if he was ever to become an artist,
and so left him in California, "to rough
it," and there, and in the Sandwich Islands
and Australia, he had four years of the most
severe training that hardship, discipline,

labour, sorrow, and stern reality can furnish. When he came east again, in the autumn of 1856, he was no longer a novice but an educated, artistic tragedian, still crude in some things, though on the right road, and in the fresh, exultant vigour, if not yet the full maturity, of extraordinary powers. He appeared first at Baltimore, and after that made a tour of the south, and during the ensuing four years he was seen in many cities all over the country. In the summer of 1860 he went to England, and acted in London, Liverpool, and Manchester, but he was back again in New York in 1862, and from September 21, 1863 to March 23, 1867 he managed what was known as the Winter Garden theatre, and incidentally devoted himself to the accomplishment of some of the stateliest revivals of standard plays that have ever been made in America. On February 3, 1869 he opened Booth's Theatre and that he managed for five years. In 1876 he made a tour of the south, which, so great was the enthusiasm his presence aroused, was nothing less than a triumphal progress. In San Francisco, where he filled an engagement of eight weeks, the receipts exceeded $96,000, a result at that time unprecedented on the dramatic stage.

The circumstances of the stage and of the lives of actors have greatly changed since the generation went out to which such men as Junius Booth and Augustus A. Addams belonged. No tragedian would now be so mad as to put himself in pawn for drink, as Cooke is said to have done, nor be found scraping the ham from the sandwiches provided for his luncheon, as Junius Booth was, before going on to play Shylock. Our theatre has no longer a Richardson to light up a pan of red fire, as that old showman once did, to signalise the fall of the screen in *The School for Scandal*. The eccentrics and the taste for them have passed away. It seems really once to have been thought that the actor who did not often make a maniac of himself with drink could not be possessed of the divine fire. That demonstration of genius is not expected now, nor does the present age exact from its favourite players the performance of all sorts and varieties of parts. Forrest was the first of the prominent actors to break away from the old usage in this latter particular. During the most prosperous years of his life, from 1837 to 1850, he acted only about a dozen parts, and most of them were old. The

only new parts that he studied were Claude
Melnotte, Richelieu, Jack Cade, and Mor-
daunt, the latter in the play of *The Patri-
cian's Daughter*, and he " recovered "
Marc Antony, which he particularly liked.
Edwin Booth, who had inherited from his
father the insanity of intemperance, conquered that utterly, many years ago, and
nobly and grandly trod it beneath his feet;
and as he matured in his career, through
acting every kind of part, from a dandy
negro up to Hamlet, he at last made choice
of the characters that afford scope for his
powers and his aspirations, and so settled
upon a definite, restricted repertory. His
characters were Hamlet, Macbeth, Lear,
Othello, Iago, Richard the Second, Richard the Third, Shylock, Cardinal Wolsey,
Benedick, Petruchio, Richelieu, Lucius
Brutus, Bertuccio, Ruy Blas, and Don
Cæsar de Bazan. These he acted in customary usage, and to these he occasionally added Marcus Brutus, Antony, Cassius,
Claude Melnotte, and the Stranger. The
range thus indicated is extraordinary; but
more extraordinary still was the evenness of
the actor's average excellence throughout
the breadth of that range.

Booth's tragedy is better than his elegant comedy. There are other actors who equal or surpass him in Benedick or Don Cæsar. The comedy in which he excels is that of silvery speciousness and bitter sarcasm, as in portions of Iago and Richard the Third and the simulated madness of Lucius Brutus, and the comedy of grim drollery, as in portions of Richelieu — his expression of those veins being wonderfully perfect. But no other actor who has trod the American stage in our day has equalled him in certain attributes of tragedy that are essentially poetic. He is not at his best, indeed, in all the tragic parts that he acts ; and, like his father, he is an uneven actor in the parts to which he is best suited. No person can be said to know Edwin Booth's acting who has not seen him play the same part several times. His artistic treatment will generally be found adequate, but his mood or spirit will continually vary. He cannot at will command it, and when it is absent his performance seems cold. This characteristic is, perhaps, inseparable from the poetic temperament. Each ideal that he presents is poetic ; and the suitable and adequate presentation of it, therefore, needs poetic warmth and glamour. Booth never goes

behind his poet's text to find a prose image
in the pages of historic fact. The spectator who takes the trouble to look into his
art will find it, indeed, invariably accurate as to historic basis, and will find that
all essential points and questions of scholarship have been considered by the actor.
But this is not the secret of its power
upon the soul. That power resides in its
charm, and that charm consists in its
poetry. Standing on the lonely ramparts
of Elsinore, and with awe-stricken, preoc-
cupied, involuntary glances questioning the
star-lit midnight air, while he talks with
his attendant friends, Edwin Booth's Hamlet is the simple, absolute realisation of
Shakespeare's haunted prince, and raises no
question, and leaves no room for inquiry,
whether the Danes in the Middle Ages
wore velvet robes or had long flaxen hair.
It is dark, mysterious, melancholy, beautiful — a vision of dignity and of grace,
made sublime by suffering, made weird and
awful by " thoughts beyond the reaches of
our souls." Sorrow never looked more
wofully and ineffably lovely than his sorrow
looks in the parting scene with Ophelia,
and frenzy never spoke with a wilder glee
of horrid joy and fearful exultation than is

heard in his tempestuous cry of delirium, "Nay, I know not: is it the king?"

An actor who is fine only at points is not, of course, a perfect actor. The remark of Coleridge about the acting of Edmund Kean, that it was like "reading Shakespeare by flashes of lightning," has misled many persons as to Kean's art. Macready bears a similar testimony. But the weight of evidence will satisfy the reader that Kean was, in fact, a careful student and that he never neglected any detail of his art. This is certainly true of Edwin Booth. In the level plains that lie between the mountain-peaks of expression he walks with as sure a footstep and as firm a tread as on the summit of the loftiest crag or the verge of the steepest abyss. In 1877–78, in association with the present writer, he prepared for the press an edition of fifteen of the plays in which he acts, and these were published for the use of actors. There is not a line in either of those plays that he has not studiously and thoroughly considered; not a vexed point that he has not scanned; not a questionable reading that he has not, for his own purposes in acting, satisfactorily settled. His Shakespearean scholarship is extensive and sound, and it is no less minute than ample. His stage business has been arranged, as stage business ought to be, with scientific precision. If, as king Richard the Third, he is seen to be abstractedly toying with a ring upon one of his fingers, or unsheathing and sheathing his dagger, those apparently capricious actions would be found to be done because they were illustrative parts of that monarch's personality, warranted by the text and context. Many years ago an accidental impulse led him, as Hamlet, to hold out his sword, hilt foremost, toward the receding spectre, as a protective cross — the symbol of that religion to which Hamlet so frequently recurs. The expedient was found to justify itself and he made it a custom. In the graveyard scene of this tragedy he directs that one of the skulls thrown up by the first clown shall have a tattered and mouldy fool's-cap adhering to it, so that it may attract attention, and be singled out from the others, as "Yorick's skull, the king's jester." These are little things ; but it is of a thousand little things that a dramatic performance is composed, and without this care for detail — which must be precise, logical, profound, vigilant, unerring, and at the same time always unobtrusive and seemingly involuntary — there can be neither cohesion, nor symmetry, nor an illusory image consistently maintained ; and all great effects would become tricks of mechanism and detached exploits of theatrical force.

The absence of this thoroughness in such acting as that of Edwin Booth would instantly be felt ; its presence is seldom adequately appreciated. We feel the perfect charm of the illusion in the great fourth act of *Richelieu* — one of the most thrilling situations, as Booth fills it, that ever were created upon the stage ; but we should not feel this had not the foreground of character, incident, and experience been prepared with consummate thoroughness. The character of Richelieu is one that the elder Booth could never act. He tried it once, upon urgent solicitation, but he had not proceeded far before he caught Joseph around the waist, and with that astonished friar in his arms proceeded to dash into a waltz, over which the curtain was dropped. He had no sympathy with the moonlight mistiness and lace-like complexity of that weird and many-fibred nature. It lacked for him the reality of the imagination, the

trumpet blare and tempest rush of active
passion. But Edwin Booth, coming after
Forrest, who was its original in America,
has made Richelieu so entirely his own that
no actor living can stand a comparison with
him in the character. Macready was the
first representative of the part, as everybody knows, and his performance of it was
deemed magnificent; but when Edwin
Booth acted it in London in 1880, old
John Ryder, the friend and advocate of
Macready, who had participated with him
in all his plays, said to the American tragedian, with a broken voice and·with tears in
his eyes, "You have thrown down my
idol." Two at least of those great moments
in acting that everybody remembers were
furnished by Booth in this character — the
defiance of the masked assailant, at Rouel,
and the threat of excommunication deliv-
ered upon Barradas. No spectator possessed of imagination and sensibility ever
saw, without utter forgetfulness of the
stage, the imperial entrance of that Richelieu into the gardens of the Louvre and into
the sullen presence of hostile majesty. The
same spell of genius is felt in kindred moments of his greater impersonations. His
Iago, standing in the dark street, with

sword in hand, above the prostrate bodies
of Cassio and Roderigo, and as the sudden impulse to murder them strikes his
brain, breathing out in a blood-curdling
whisper, "How silent is this town!" his
Bertuccio, begging at the door of the ban-
quet-hall, and breaking down in hysterics
of affected glee and maddening agony; his
Lear, at that supreme moment of intolerable torture when he parts away from Goneril and Regan, with his wild scream of
revenges that shall be the terrors of the
earth; his Richard the Third, with the
gigantic effrontery of his "Call him again,"
and with his whole matchless and wonderful utterance of the awful remorse speech
with which the king awakens from his last
earthly sleep — those, among many others,
rank with the best dramatic images that
ever were chronicled, and may well be cited
to illustrate Booth's invincible and splendid
adequacy at the great moments of his art.

Edwin Booth has been tried by some of
the most terrible afflictions that ever tested
the fortitude of a human soul. Over his
youth, plainly visible, impended the lowering cloud of insanity. While he was yet
a boy, and when literally struggling for life
in the semi-barbarous wilds of old Califor-

nia, he lost his beloved father, under circumstances of singular misery. In early manhood he laid in her grave the woman of his first love — the wife who had died in absence from him, herself scarcely past the threshold of youth, lovely as an angel and to all that knew her precious beyond expression. A little later his heart was well-nigh broken and his life was well-nigh blasted by the crime of a lunatic brother that for a moment seemed to darken the hope of the world. Recovering from that blow, he threw all his resources and powers into the establishment of the grandest theatre in the metropolis of America, and he saw his fortune of more than a million dollars, together with the toil of some of the best years of his life, frittered away. Under all trials he has borne bravely up, and kept the even, steadfast tenor of his course; strong, patient, gentle, neither elated by public homage nor imbittered by private grief. Such a use of high powers in the dramatic art, and the development and maintenance of such a character behind them, entitle him to the affection of his countrymen, proud equally of his goodness and his renown.

V.

MARY ANDERSON: HERMIONE: PERDITA.

ON November 25, 1875 an audience was assembled in one of the theatres of Louisville, Kentucky, to see "the first appearance upon any stage" of "a young lady of Louisville," who was announced to play Shakespeare's Juliet. That young lady was in fact a girl, in her sixteenth year, who had never received any practical stage training, whose education had been comprised in five years of ordinary schooling, whose observation of life had never extended beyond the narrow limits of a provincial city, who was undeveloped, unheralded, unknown, and poor, and whose only qualifications for the task she had set herself to accomplish were the impulse of genius and the force of commanding character. She dashed at the work with all the vigour of abounding and enthusiastic youth, and with all the audacity of complete inexperience. A rougher performance of Juliet

probably was never seen, but through all
the disproportion and turbulence of that
effort the authentic charm of a beautiful
nature was distinctly revealed. The sweetness, the sincerity, the force, the exceptional superiority and singular charm of that
nature could not be mistaken. The uncommon stature and sumptuous physical beauty
of the girl were obvious. Above all, her
magnificent voice — copious, melodious,
penetrating, loud and clear, yet soft and
gentle — delighted every ear and touched
every heart. The impersonation of Juliet
was not highly esteemed by judicious hearers ; but some persons who saw that performance felt and said that a new actress
had risen and that a great career had begun.
Those prophetic voices were right. That
" young lady of Louisville " was Mary Anderson.

It is seldom in stage history that the
biographer comes upon such a character as
that of Mary Anderson, or is privileged to
muse over the story of such a career as she
has had. In many cases the narrative of
the life of an actress is a narrative of talents
perverted, of opportunity misused, of failure, misfortune, and suffering. For one
story like that of Mrs. Siddons there are

many like that of Mrs. Robinson. For one
name like that of Charlotte Cushman or
that of Helen Faucit there are many like
that of Lucille Western or that of Matilda
Heron — daughters of sorrow and victims of
trouble. The mind lingers, accordingly,
impressed and pleased with a sense of sweet
personal worth as well as of genius and
beauty upon the record of a representative
American actress, as noble as she was brilliant, and as lovely in her domestic life as
she was beautiful, fortunate, and renowned
in her public pursuits. The exposition of
her nature, as apprehended through her
acting, constitutes the principal part of her
biography.

Mary Anderson, a native of California,
was born at Sacramento, July 28, 1859.
Her father, Charles Joseph Anderson, who
died in 1863, aged twenty-nine, and was
buried in Magnolia cemetery, Mobile, Ala-
bama, was an officer in the service of the
Southern Confederacy at the time of his
death, and he is said to have been a handsome and dashing young man. Her mother,
Marie Antoinette Leugers, was a native of
Philadelphia. Her earlier years were passed
in Louisville, whither she was taken in
1860, and she was there taught in a Roman

Catholic school and reared in the Roman
Catholic faith under the guidance of a
Franciscan priest, Anthony Miller, her
mother's uncle. She left school before she
was fourteen years old and she went upon
the stage before she was sixteen. She had
while a child seen various theatrical performances, notably those given by Edwin
Booth, and her mind had been strongly
drawn toward the stage under the influence
of those sights. The dramatic characters
that she first studied were male characters
— those of Hamlet, Wolsey, Richelieu, and
Richard III. — and to those she added
Schiller's Joan of Arc. She studied those
parts privately, and she knew them all and
knew them well. Professor Noble Butler,
of Louisville, gave her instruction in English
literature and elocution, and in 1874, at
Cincinnati, Charlotte Cushman said a few
encouraging words to her, and told her to
persevere in following the stage, and to
"begin at the top." George Vandenhoff
gave her a few lessons before she came out,
and then followed her début as Juliet, leading to her first regular engagement, which
began at Barney Macaulay's Theatre, Louisville, January 20, 1876. From that time
onward for thirteen years she was an ac-

tress, — never in a stock company but
always as a star, — and her name became
famous in Great Britain as well as America.
She had eight seasons of steadily increasing
prosperity on the American stage before
she went abroad to act, and she became a
favourite all over the United States.   She
filled three seasons at the Lyceum Theatre,
London (from September 1, 1883, to April
5, 1884 ; from November 1, 1884, to April
25, 1885 ; and from September 10, 1887, to
March 24, 1888), and her success there
surpassed, in profit, that of any American
actor who had appeared in England.   She
revived *Romeo and Juliet* with much splendour at the London Lyceum on November
1, 1884, and she restored *A Winter's Tale*
to the stage, bringing forward that comedy
on September 10, 1887, and carrying it
through the season.   She made several
prosperous tours of the English provincial
theatres, and established herself as a favourite actress in fastidious Edinburgh, critical
Manchester, and impulsive but exacting
Dublin.   The repertory with which she
gained fame and fortune included Juliet,
Hermione, Perdita, Rosalind, Lady Macbeth, Julia, Bianca, Evadne, Parthenia,
Pauline, The Countess, Galatea, Clarice,

Ion, Meg Merrilies, Berthe, and the Duchess de Torrenueva. She incidentally acted a few other parts, Desdemona being one of them. Her distinctive achievements were in Shakespearean drama. She adopted into her repertory two plays by Tennyson, *The Cup* and *The Falcon*, but never produced them. This record signifies the resources of mind, the personal charm, the exalted spirit, and the patient, wisely directed and strenuous zeal that sustained her achievements and justified her success.

Aspirants in the field of art are continually coming to the surface. In poetry, painting, sculpture, music, and in acting — which involves and utilises those other arts — the line of beginners is endless. Constantly, as the seasons roll by, these essayists emerge, and as constantly, after a little time, they disappear. The process is sequent upon an obvious law of spiritual life, — that all minds which are conscious of the art impulse must at least make an effort toward expression, but that no mind can succeed in the effort unless, in addition to the art impulse, it possesses also the art faculty. For expression is the predominant necessity of human nature. Out of this proceed forms and influences of beauty. These

react upon mankind, pleasing an instinct
for the beautiful, and developing the faculty
of taste.   Other and finer forms and influences of beauty ensue, civilisation is advanced, and thus finally the way is opened
toward that condition of immortal spiritual
happiness which this process of experience prefigures and prophesies.   But the
art faculty is of rare occurrence.   At long
intervals there is a break in the usual experience of stage failure, and some person
hitherto unknown not only takes the field
but keeps it.   When Garrick came out, as
the Duke of Gloster, in the autumn of 1741,
in London, he had never been heard of, but
within a brief time he was famous.   " He
at once decided the public taste," said
Macklin ; and Pope summed up the victory
in the well-known sentence, " That young
man never had an equal, and will never
have a rival."   Tennyson's line furnishes
the apt and comprehensive comment—
" The many fail, the one succeeds."   Mary
Anderson in her day furnished the most
conspicuous and striking example, aside
from that of Adelaide Neilson, to which it
is possible to refer of this exceptional experience.   And yet, even after years of trial
and test, it is doubtful whether the excel-

lence of that remarkable actress was entirely comprehended in her own country. The provincial custom of waiting for foreign authorities to discover our royal minds is one from which many inhabitants of America have not yet escaped. As an actress, indeed, Mary Anderson was, probably, more popular than any player on the American stage excepting Edwin Booth or Joseph Jefferson ; but there is a difference between popularity and just and comprehensive intellectual recognition. Many actors get the one ; few get the other.

Much of the contemporary criticism that is lavished upon actors in this exigent period — so bountifully supplied with critical observations, so poorly furnished with creative art — touches only upon the surface. Acting is measured with a tape and the chief demand seems to be for form. This is right, and indeed is imperative, whenever it is certain that the actor at his best is one who never can rise above the high-water mark of correct mechanism. There are cases that need a deeper method of inquiry and a more searching glance. A wise critic, when this emergency comes, is something more than an expert who gives an opinion upon a professional exploit. The special piece of work may contain technical flaws, and yet there may be within it a soul worth all the "icily regular and splendidly null" achievements that ever were possible to proficient mediocrity. That soul is visible only to the observer who can look through the art into the interior spirit of the artist, and thus can estimate a piece of acting according to its inspirational drift and the enthralling and ennobling personality out of which it springs. The acting of Mary Anderson, from the first moment of her career, was of the kind that needs that deep insight and broad judgment, — aiming to recognise and rightly estimate its worth. Yet few performers of the day were so liberally favoured with the monitions of dulness and the ponderous patronage of self-complacent folly.

Conventional judgment as to Mary Anderson's acting expressed itself in one statement — "she is cold." There could not be a greater error. That quality in Mary Anderson's acting — a reflex from her spiritual nature — which produced upon the conventional mind the effect of coldness was in fact distinction, the attribute of being exceptional. The judgment that she was cold was a resentful judgment, and was given in

a spirit of detraction. It proceeded from an
order of mind that can never be content
with the existence of anything above its
own level. "He hath," said Iago, speaking of Cassio, "a daily beauty in his life
that makes me ugly." Those detractors
did not understand themselves as well as
the wily Italian understood himself, and
they did not state their attitude with such
precision; in fact, they did not state it at
all, for it was unconscious with them and
involuntary. They saw a being unlike themselves, they vaguely apprehended the presence of a superior nature, and that they
resented. The favourite popular notion is
that all men are born free and equal; which
is false. Free and equal they all are, undoubtedly, in the eye of the law. But every
man is born subject to heredity and circumstance, and whoever will investigate his life
will perceive that he never has been able to
stray beyond the compelling and constrain-
ing force of his character — which is his
fate. All men, moreover, are unequal.
To one human being is given genius; to
another, beauty; to another, strength; to
another, exceptional judgment; to another,
exceptional memory; to another, grace
and charm; to still another, physical ugli-

ness and spiritual obliquity, moral taint, and every sort of disabling weakness. To the majority of persons Nature imparts mediocrity, and it is from mediocrity that the derogatory denial emanates as to the superior men and women of our race. A woman of the average kind is not difficult to comprehend. There is nothing distinctive about her. She is fond of admiration ; rather readily censorious of other women ; charitable toward male rakes ; and partial to fine attire. The poet Wordsworth's formula, "Praise, blame, love, kisses, tears, and smiles," comprises all that is essential for her existence, and that bard has himself precisely described her, in a grandfatherly and excruciating couplet, as

> " A creature not too bright and good
> For human nature's daily food."

Women of that sort are not called "cold." The standard is ordinary and it is understood. But when a woman appears in art whose life is not ruled by the love of admiration, whose nature is devoid of vanity, who looks with indifference upon adulation, whose head is not turned by renown, whose composure is not disturbed by flattery, whose simplicity is not marred by wealth, who does not go into theatrical hysterics and offer that condition of artificial delirium as the mood of genius in acting, who above all makes it apparent in her personality and her achievements that the soul can be sufficient to itself and can exist without taking on a burden of the fever or dulness of other lives, there is a flutter of vague discontent among the mystified and bothered rank and file, and we are apprised that she is "cold." That is what happened in the case of Mary Anderson.

What are the faculties and attributes essential to great success in acting? A sumptuous and supple figure that can realise the ideals of statuary; a mobile countenance that can strongly and unerringly express the feelings of the heart and the workings of the mind; eyes that can awe with the majesty or startle with the terror or thrill with the tenderness of their soul-subduing gaze; a voice, deep, clear, resonant, flexible, that can range over the wide compass of emotion and carry its meaning in varying music to every ear and every heart; intellect to shape the purposes and control the means of mimetic art; deep knowledge of human nature; delicate intuitions; the skill to listen as

well as the art to speak; imagination to
grasp the ideal of a character in all its conditions of experience; the instinct of the
sculptor to give it form, of the painter to
give it colour, and of the poet to give it
movement; and, back of all, the temperament of genius — the genialised nervous
system — to impart to the whole artistic
structure the thrill of spiritual vitality.
Mary Anderson's acting revealed those
faculties and attributes, and those observers who realised the poetic spirit, the moral
majesty, and the isolation of mind that she
continually suggested felt that she was an
extraordinary woman. Such moments in
her acting as that of Galatea's mute supplication at the last of earthly life, that of
Juliet's desolation after the final midnight
parting with the last human creature whom
she may ever behold, and that of Hermione's despair when she covers her face and
falls as if stricken dead, were the eloquent
denotements of power, and in those and
such as those — with which her art abounded
— was the fulfilment of every hope that her
acting inspired and the vindication of every
encomium that it received.

Early in her professional career, when
considering her acting, the present essayist

quoted as applicable to her those lovely lines
by Wordsworth : —

"The stars of midnight shall be dear
  To her, and she shall lean her ear
    In many a secret place
  Where rivulets dance their wayward round,
And beauty born of murmuring sound
    Shall pass into her face."

In the direction of development thus indicated she steadily advanced. Her affilia-
tions were with grandeur, purity, and
loveliness. An inherent and passionate
tendency toward classic stateliness increased in her more and more. Characters of the statuesque order attracted her
imagination — Ion, Galatea, Hermione —
but she did not leave them soulless. In the
interpretation of passion and the presentation of its results she revealed the striking
truth that her perceptions could discern
those consequences that are recorded in
the soul and in comparison with which the
dramatic entanglements of visible life are
puny and evanescent. Though living in
the rapid stream of the social world she
dwelt aloof from it. She thought deeply,
and in mental direction she took the pathway of intellectual power. It is not sur-

prising that the true worth of such a
nature was not accurately apprehended.
Minds that are self-poised, stately, irre-
sponsive to human weakness, unconventional, and self-liberated from allegiance
to the commonplace are not fully and instantly discernible, and may well perplex
the smiling glance of frivolity; but they are
permanent forces in the education of the
human race. Mary Anderson retired from
the stage, under the pressure of extreme
fatigue, in the beginning of 1889 and en-
tered upon a matrimonial life on June 17,
1890. It is believed that her retirement
is permanent. The historical interest at-
taching to her dramatic career justifies the
preservation of this commemorative essay.

There is so much beauty in the comedy
of *A Winter's Tale* — so much thought,
character, humour, philosophy, sweetly
serene feeling and loveliness of poetic
language — that the public ought to feel
obliged to any one who successfully restores
it to the stage, from which it usually is ban-
ished. The piece was written in the maturity of Shakespeare's marvellous powers,
and indeed some of the Shakespearean
scholars believe it to be the last work that
fell from his hand. Human life, as depicted

in *A Winter's Tale*, shows itself like what
it always seems to be in the eyes of patient,
tolerant, magnanimous experience — the
eyes "that have kept watch o'er man's
mortality" — for it is a scene of inexpli-
cable contrasts and vicissitudes, seemingly
the chaos of caprice and chance, yet always,
in fact, beneficently overruled and guided
to good ends.   Human beings are shown in
it as full of weakness ; often as the puppets
of laws that they do not understand and of
universal propensities and impulses into
which they never pause to inquire ; almost
always as objects of benignant pity.   The
woful tangle of human existence is here
viewed with half-cheerful, half-sad toler-
ance, yet with the hope and belief that all
will come right at last.   The mood of the
comedy is pensive but radically sweet.
The poet is like the forest in Emerson's
subtle vision of the inherent exultation of
nature : —

> " Sober, on a fund of joy,
>   The woods at heart are glad."

Mary Anderson doubled the characters of
Hermione and Perdita.   This had not been
conspicuously done until it was done by
her, and her innovation, in that respect,

was met with grave disapproval. The
moment the subject is examined, however,
objection to that method of procedure is
dispelled. Hermione, as a dramatic person, disappears in the middle of the
third act of Shakespeare's comedy and
comes no more until the end of the piece,
when she emerges as a statue. Her character has been entirely expressed and her
part in the action of the drama has been
substantially fulfilled before she disappears.
There is no intermediate passion to be
wrought to a climax, nor is there any
intermediate mood, dramatically speaking,
to be sustained. The dramatic environment, the dramatic necessities, are vastly
unlike, for example, those of Lady Macbeth
— one of the hardest of all parts to play
well, because exhibited intermittently, at
long intervals, yet steadily constrained by
the necessity of cumulative excitement.
The representative of Lady Macbeth must
be identified with that character, whether
on the stage or off, from the beginning of
it to the end. Hermione, on the contrary,
is at rest from the moment when she faints
upon receiving information of the death of
her boy. A lapse of sixteen years is
assumed, and then, standing forth as a

statue, she personifies majestic virtue and victorious fortitude. When she descends from the pedestal she silently embraces Leontes, speaks a few pious, maternal and tranquil lines (there are precisely seven of them in the original, but Mary Anderson added two, from "All's Well"), and embraces Perdita, whom she has not seen since the girl's earliest infancy. This is their only meeting, and little is sacrificed by the use of a substitute for the daughter in that scene. Perdita's brief apostrophe to the statue has to be cut, but it is not missed in the representation. The resemblance between mother and daughter heightens the effect of illusion, in its impress equally upon fancy and vision ; and a more thorough elucidation is given than could be provided in any other way of the spirit of the comedy. It was a judicious and felicitous choice that the actress made when she selected those two characters, and the fact that her impersonation of them carried a practically disused Shakespearean comedy through a season of one hundred and fifty nights at the Lyceum Theatre in London furnishes an indorsement alike of her wisdom and her ability. She played in a stage version of the piece, in five acts, containing thirteen scenes, arranged by herself.

While Mary Anderson was acting those two parts in London the sum of critical opinion seemed to be that her performance of Perdita was better than her performance of Hermione; but beneath that judgment there was, apparently, the impression that Hermione is a character fraught with superlatively great passions, powers, and qualities, such as are only to be apprehended by gigantic sagacity and conveyed by herculean talents and skill. Those vast attributes were not specified, but there was a mysterious intimation of their existence — as of something vague, formidable, and mostly elusive. But in truth Hermione, although a stronger part than Perdita, is neither complex, dubious, nor inaccessible; and Mary Anderson, although more fascinating in Perdita, could and did rise, in Hermione, to a noble height of tragic power — an excellence not possible for her, nor for anybody, in the more juvenile and slender character.

Hermione has usually been represented as an elderly woman and by such an actress as is technically called "heavy." She ought to be represented as about thirty

years of age at the beginning of the piece,
and forty-six at the end of it. Leontes is
not more than thirty-four at the opening,
and he would be fifty at the close. He
speaks, in his first scene, of his boyhood as
only twenty-three years gone, when his
dagger was worn " muzzled, lest it should
bite its master " — at which time he may
have been ten years old ; certainly not
more, probably less. His words, toward
the end of act third, " so sure as this
beard's gray," refer to the beard of Antigonus, not to his own. He is a young man
when the play begins, and Polixenes is
about the same age, and Hermione is a young
woman. Antigonus and Paulina are mid-
dle-aged persons in the earlier scenes and
Paulina is an elderly woman in the statue
scene — almost an old woman, though not
too old to be given in marriage to old
Camillo, the ever-faithful friend. In Mary
Anderson's presentation of *A Winter's
Tale* those details received thoughtful consideration and correct treatment.

In Hermione is seen a type of the celestial nature in woman — infinite love, infinite
charity, infinite patience. Such a nature
is rare ; but it is possible. it exists, and
Shakespeare, who depicted everything, did

not omit to portray that. To comprehend
Hermione the observer must separate her,
absolutely and finally, from association
with the passions. Mrs. Jameson acutely
and justly describes her character as exhibiting " dignity without pride, love without
passion, and tenderness without weakness."
That is exactly true. Hermione was not
easily won, and the best thing known about
Leontes is that at last she came to love
him and that her love for him survived his
cruel and wicked treatment, chastened him,
reinstated him, and ultimately blessed him.
Hermione suffers the utmost affliction that
a good woman can suffer. Her boy dies,
heart-broken, at the news of his mother's
alleged disgrace. Her infant daughter is
torn from her breast and cast forth to per-
ish. Her husband becomes her enemy and
persecutor. Her chastity is assailed and
vilified. She is subjected to the bitter in-
dignity of a public trial. It is no wonder
that at last her brain reels and she falls as
if stricken dead. The apparent anomaly is
her survival for sixteen years, in lonely
seclusion, and her emergence, after that,
as anything but a forlorn shadow of her
former self. The poet Shelley has recorded
the truth that all great emotions either kill

themselves or kill those who feel them. It
is here, however, that the exceptional temperament of Hermione supplies an explanatory and needed qualification. Her emotions are never of a passionate kind. Her
mind predominates. Her life is in the
affections and therefore it is one of thought.
She sees clearly the facts of her experience
and condition, and she knows exactly how
those facts look in the eyes of others. She
is one of those persons who possess a keen
and just prescience of events, who can look
far into the future and discern those resultant consequences of the present which,
under the operation of inexorable moral
law, must inevitably ensue. Self-poised in
the right and free from the disturbing force
of impulse and desire, she can await the
justice of time, she can live, and she can
live in the tranquil patience of resignation.
True majesty of the person is dependent on
repose of the soul, and there can be no
repose of the soul without moral rectitude
and a far-reaching, comprehensive, wise
vision of events. Mary Anderson embodied
Hermione in accordance with that ideal.
By the expression of her face and the tones
of her voice, in a single speech, the actress
placed beyond question her grasp of the
character : —

"Good my lords,
I am not prone to weeping, as our sex
Commonly are — the want of which vain dew
Perchance shall dry your pities — but I have
That honourable grief lodged here, which
    burns
Worse than tears drown."

The conspicuous, predominant, convincing artistic beauty in Mary Anderson's impersonation of Hermione was her realisation
of the part, in figure, face, presence, demeanour, and temperament. She did not
afflict her auditor with the painful sense of
a person struggling upward toward an un-
attainable identity. She made you conscious of the presence of a queen. This,
obviously, is the main thing — that the individuality shall be imperial, not merely
wearing royal attire but being invested with
the royal authenticity of divine endowment
and consecration. Much emphasis has been
placed by Shakespeare upon that attribute
of innate grandeur. Leontes, at the opening of the trial scene, describes his accused
wife as "the daughter of a king," and in
the same scene her father is mentioned as
the Emperor of Russia. The gentleman
who, in act fifth, recounts to Autolycus the
meeting between Leontes and his daughter

Perdita especially notes " the majesty of
the creature, in resemblance of the mother."
Hermione herself, in the course of her vindication — expressed in one of the most
noble and pathetic strains of poetical eloquence in our language — names herself " a
great king's daughter," therein recalling
those august and piteous words of Shakespeare's Katharine : —

" We are a Queen, or long have thought so,
      certain
   The daughter of a king."

Poor old Antigonus, in his final soliloquy,
recounting the vision of Hermione that had
come upon him in the night, declares her to
be a woman royal and grand not by descent
only but by nature : —

" I never saw a vessel of like sorrow,
   So filléd and so becoming. In pure white
      robes,
   Like very sanctity, she did approach."

   That image Mary Anderson embodied,
and therefore the ideal of Shakespeare was
made a living thing — that glorious ideal,
in shaping which the great poet " from all
that are took something good, to make a
perfect woman."   Toward Polixenes, in

the first scene, her manner was wholly
gracious, delicately playful, innocently kind,
and purely frank. Her quiet archness at
the question, "Will you go yet?" struck
exactly the right key of Hermione's mood.
With the baby prince Mamillius her frolic
and banter, affectionate, free, and gay,
were in a happy vein of feeling and
humour. Her simple dignity, restraining
both resentment and grief, in face of the
injurious reproaches of Leontes, was entirely
noble and right, and the pathetic words,
"I never wished to see you sorry, now I
trust I shall," could not have been spoken
with more depth and intensity of grieved
affection than were felt in her composed
yet tremulous voice. The entrance, at the
trial scene, was made with the stateliness
natural to a queenly woman, and yet with
a touch of pathos — the cold patience of despair. The delivery of Hermione's defen-
sive speeches was profoundly earnest and
touching. The simple cry of the mother's
breaking heart, and the action of veiling
her face and falling like one dead, upon the
announcement of the prince's death, were
perfect denotements of the collapse of a
grief-stricken woman. The skill with which
the actress, in the monument scene — which

is all repose and no movement — contrived
nevertheless to invest Hermione with steady
vitality of action, and to imbue the crisis
with a feverish air of suspense, was in a
high degree significant of the personality of
genius. For such a performance of Hermione Shakespeare himself has provided
the sufficient summary and encomium : —

" Women will love her, that she is a woman
    More worth than any man ; men that she is
    The rarest of all women."

It is one thing to say that Mary Anderson
was better in Perdita than in Hermione,
and another thing to say that the performance of Perdita was preferred. Everybody
preferred it — even those who knew that it
was not the better of the two ; for everybody
loves the sunshine more than the shade.
Hermione means grief and endurance.
Perdita means beautiful youth and happy
love. It does not take long for an observer
to choose between them. Suffering is not
companionable. By her impersonation of
Hermione the actress revealed her knowledge of the stern truth of life, its trials,
its calamities, and the possible heroism of
character under its sorrowful discipline.
Into that identity she passed by the force

of her imagination. The embodiment was majestic, tender, pitiable, transcendent, but its colour was the sombre colour of pensive melancholy and sad experience. That performance was the higher and more significant of the two. But the higher form of art is not always the most alluring — never the most alluring when youthful beauty smiles and rosy pleasure beckons another way. All hearts respond to happiness. By her presentment of Perdita the actress became the glittering image and incarnation of glorious youthful womanhood and fascinating joy. No exercise of the imagination was needful to her in that. There was an instantaneous correspondence between the part and the player. The embodiment was as natural as a sunbeam. Shakespeare has left no doubt about his meaning in Perdita. The speeches of all around her continually depict her fresh and piquant loveliness, her innate superiority, her superlative charm; while her behaviour and language as constantly show forth her nobility of soul. One of the subtlest side lights thrown upon the character is in the description of the manner in which Perdita heard the story of her mother's death — when "attentiveness wounded" her "till, from one sign of dolour to another, she did bleed tears." And of the fibre of her nature there is perhaps no finer indication than may be felt in her comment on old Camillo's worldly view of prosperity as a vital essential to the permanence of love : —

"I think affliction may subdue the cheek,
   But not take in the mind."

In the thirty-seven plays of Shakespeare there is no strain of the poetry of sentiment and grace essentially sweeter than that which he has put into the mouth of Perdita ; and poetry could not be more sweetly spoken than it was by Mary Anderson in that delicious scene of the distribution of the flowers. The actress evinced comprehension of the character in every fibre of its being, and she embodied it with the affluent vitality of splendid health and buoyant temperament — presenting a creature radiant with goodness and happiness, exquisite in natural refinement, piquant with archness, soft, innocent, and tender in confiding artlessness, and, while gleeful and triumphant in beautiful youth, gently touched with an intuitive pitying sense of the thorny aspects of this troubled world. The giving of the flowers completely be-

witched her auditors. The startled yet
proud endurance of the king's anger was
in an equal degree captivating. Seldom has
the stage displayed that rarest of all combi-
nations, the passionate heart of a woman
with the lovely simplicity of a child. Nothing could be more beautiful than she was
to the eyes that followed her lithe figure
through the merry mazes of her rustic
dance — an achievement sharply in contrast
with her usually statuesque manner. It
"makes old hearts fresh" to see a spectacle of grace and joy, and that spectacle
they saw then and will not forget. The
value of those impersonations of Hermione
and Perdita, viewing them as embodied in-
terpretations of poetry was great, but they
possessed a greater value and a higher significance as denotements of the guiding
light, the cheering strength, the elevating
loveliness of a noble human soul. They
embodied the conception of the poet, but at
the same time they illumined an actual incarnation of the divine spirit. They were
like windows to a sacred temple, and
through them you could look into the soul
of a true woman — always a realm where
thoughts are gliding angels, and feelings are
the faces of seraphs, and sounds are the
music of the harps of heaven.

VI.

IT has sometimes been thought that the acting of Henry Irving is seen at its best in those impersonations of his that derive their vitality from the grim, ghastly, and morbid attributes of human nature. That he is a unique actor, and distinctively a great actor, in Hamlet, Mathias, Eugene Aram, Louis XI., Lesurque, and Dubosc, few judges will deny. His performances of those parts have shown him to be a man of weird imagination, and they have shown that his characteristics, mental and spiritual, are sombre. Accordingly, when it was announced that he would play Dr. Primrose — Goldsmith's simple, virtuous, homely, undramatic village-preacher, the *Vicar of Wakefield*, — a doubt was felt as to his suitability for the part and as to the success of his endeavour. He played Dr. Primrose, and he gained in that character some of the brightest laurels of his profes-

sional career. The doubt proved unwar-
ranted. More than one competent observer
of that remarkable performance has granted
it an equal rank with the best of Henry Irving's achievements ; and now, more clearly
than before, it is perceived that the current
of his inspiration flows as freely from the
silver spring of goodness as from the dark
and troubled fountain of human misery.

On the first night of *Olivia*, at the Lyceum Theatre (it was May 27, 1885, when
the present writer happened to be in London), Henry Irving's performance of Dr.
Primrose was fettered by a curb of con-
straint.   The actor's nerves had been
strained to a high pitch of excitement and
he was obviously anxious. His spirit, accordingly, was not fully liberated into the
character. He advanced with cautious care
and he executed each detail of his design
with precise accuracy. To various auditors, for that reason, the work seemed a
little Methodistical ; and drab is a colour
at which the voice of the scoffer is apt to
scoff. But the impersonation of Dr. Primrose soon became equally a triumph of
expression and of ideal ; not only flowing
out of goodness, but flowing smoothly and
producing the effect of nature. It was not

absolutely and identically the Vicar that
Goldsmith has drawn, for its personality
was unmarked by either rusticity or strong
humour; but it was a kindred and higher
type of the simple truth, the pastoral sweetness, the benignity, and the human tenderness of that delightful original. To invest goodness with charm, to make virtue
piquant, and to turn common events of
domestic life to exquisite pathos and noble
exaltation was the actor's purpose. It was
accomplished; and Dr. Primrose, thitherto
an idyllic figure, existent only in the cham-
bers of fancy, is henceforth as much a deni-
zen of the stage as Luke Fielding or Jesse
Rural; a man not merely to be read of,
as one reads of Uncle Toby and Parson
Adams, but to be known, remembered, and
loved.

Wills's drama of *Olivia*, based upon an
episode in Goldsmith's story, is one of extreme simplicity. It may be described as
a series of pictures displaying the consequences of action rather than action itself.
It contains an abundance of incident, but
the incident is mostly devoid of inherent
dramatic force and therefore is such as must
derive its chief effect from the manner in
which it is treated by the actors who repre-

sent the piece. Nevertheless, the piece was found to be, during its first three acts, an expressive, coherent, interesting play. It tells its story clearly and entirely, not by narrative but by the display of characters in their relations to each other. Its language, flavoured here and there with the phraseology of the novel, is consistently appropriate. The fourth and last act is feeble. Nobody can sympathise with "the late remorse of love" in a nature so trivial as that of Thornhill, and the incident of the reconciliation between Olivia and her husband, therefore, goes for nothing. It is the beautiful relation between the father and his daughter that animates the play. It is paternal love that thrills its structure with light, warmth, colour, sincerity, moral force, and human significance. Opinion may differ as to the degree of skill with which Wills selected and employed the materials of Goldsmith's story; but nobody can justly deny that he wrought for the stage a practical dramatic exposition of the beauty and sanctity of the holiest relation that is possible in human life; and to have done that is to have done a noble thing.

Many persons appear to think that criticism falls short of its duty unless it wounds

and hurts.   Goldsmith himself observed
that fact.   It was in the story of *The
Vicar of Wakefield* that he made his playful suggestion that a critic should always
take care to say that the picture would
have been better if the painter had taken
more pains.   Wills probably heard more
than enough for his spiritual welfare about
the faults of his piece ; yet there is really
nothing weak in the play except the conclusion.   It is not easy to suggest, however, in what way the fourth act could be
strengthened, unless it were by a recasting
and renovation of the character of Squire
Thornhill.   But the victory was gained, in
spite of a feeble climax.   Many persons
also appear to think that it is a sort of sacrilege to lay hands upon the sacred ark of a
classic creation.   Dion Boucicault, per-
ceiving this when he made a play about
Clarissa Harlowe, felt moved to depre-
cate anticipated public resentment of the
liberties that he had taken with Richardson's novel.   Yet it is difficult to see why
the abundant details of that excellent though
protracted narrative should not be curtailed,
in order to circumscribe its substance within
the limits of a practical drama.   Jefferson
was blamed for condensing and slightly

changing the comedy of *The Rivals*. Yet
the author, who probably knew something
about his work, deemed it a wretchedly
defective piece, and expressed the liveliest
regret for having written it. Wills did
not reproduce Goldsmith's Vicar upon the
stage: in some particulars he widely di-
verged from it — and his work, accordingly, may be censured. Yet *The Vicar
of Wakefield* is far from being a faultless
production, such as a divinity should be
supposed to hedge. Critical students are
aware of this. It is not worth while to
traverse the old ground. The reader who
will take the trouble — and pleasure — to
refer to that excellent chapter on Goldsmith
in Dr. Craik's *History of English Literature*
will find the structural defects of the novel
specifically enumerated. If the dramatist
has ignored many details he has at least
extracted from the narrative the salient
points of a consistent, harmonious story.
The spectator can enjoy the play, whether
he has read the original or not. At the end
of its first act he knows the Vicar and his
family, their home, their way of life, their
neighbours, the two suitors for the two girls,
the motives of each and every character,
and the relations of each to all ; and he sees,

what is always touching in the spectacle of
actual human life, the contrasted states of
circumstance and experience surrounding
and enmeshing all. After this preparation
the story is developed with few and rapid
strokes. Two of the pictures were poems.
At the end of act first the Vicar, who has
been apprised of the loss of his property,
imparts this sad news to his family. The
time is the gloaming. The chimes are
sounding in the church-tower. It is the
hour of evening prayer. The gray-haired
pastor calls his loved ones around him, in
his garden, and simply and reverently tells
them of their misfortune, which is to be
accepted submissively, as Heaven's will.
The deep religious feeling of that scene, the
grouping, the use of sunset lights and shadows, the melody of the chimes, the stricken
look in the faces of the women and children, the sweet gravity of the Vicar — instinct with the nobleness of a sorrow not yet
become corrosive and lachrymose, as is the
tendency of settled grief — and, over all,
the sense of blighted happiness and an
uncertain future, made up a dramatic as
well as a pictorial effect of impressive poetic
significance. In act second — which is pictorial almost without intermission — there

was a companion picture, when the Vicar
reads, at his fireside, a letter announcing
the restitution of his estate ; while his wife
and children and Mr. Burchell are assembled around the spinet singing an old song.
The repose with which Henry Irving made
that scene tremulous, almost painful, in its
suspense, was observed as one of the hap-
piest strokes of his art.   The face and
demeanour of Dr. Primrose, changing from
the composure of resignation to a startled
surprise, and then to almost an hysterical
gladness, presented a study not less instructive than affecting of the resources of acting.
Only two contemporary actors have presented anything kindred with Mr. Irving's
acting in that situation and throughout the
scene that is sequent on the discovery of
Olivia's flight — Jefferson in America and
Got in France.

Evil is restless and irresistibly prone to
action.   Goodness is usually negative and
inert.   Dr. Primrose is a type of goodness.
In order to invest him with piquancy and
dramatic vigour Henry Irving gave him
passion, and therewithal various attributes
of charming eccentricity.   The clergyman
thus presented is the fruition of a long life
of virtue.   He has the complete repose of

innocence, the sweet candour of absolute
purity, the mild demeanour of spontaneous, habitual benevolence, the supreme
grace of unconscious simplicity. But he
is human and passionate; he shows — in
his surroundings, in his quick sympathy
with natural beauty, and in his indicated
rather than directly stated ideals of conduct — that he has lived an imaginative
and not a prosaic life; he is vaguely and
pathetically superstitious; and while essentially grand in his religious magnanimity
he is both fascinating and morally formidable as a man. Those denotements point
at Henry Irving's ideal. For his method
it is less easy to find the right description.
His mechanical reiteration of the words
that are said to him by Sophia, in the
moment when the fond father knows that
his idolised Olivia has fled with her lover;
his collapse, when the harmless pistols are
taken from his nerveless hands; his de-
spairing cry, "If she had but died!"; his
abortive effort to rebuke his darling child
in the hour of her abandonment and misery, and the sudden tempest of passionate
affection with which the great tender heart
sweeps away that inadequate and paltry
though eminently appropriate morality, and

takes its idol to itself as only true love can do — those were instances of high dramatic achievement for which epithets are inadequate, but which the memory of the heart will always treasure.

It was said by the poet Aaron Hill, in allusion to Barton Booth, that the blind might have seen him in his voice and the deaf might have heard him in his visage. Such a statement made concerning an actor now would be deemed extravagant. But, turning from the Vicar to his cherished daughter, that felicitous image comes naturally into the mind. To think of Ellen Terry as Olivia will always be to recall one especial and remarkable moment of beauty and tenderness. It is not her distribution of the farewell gifts, on the eve of Olivia's flight — full although that was of the emotion of a good heart torn and tortured by the conflict between love and duty — and it is not the desperate resentment with which Olivia beats back her treacherous betrayer, when, at the climax of his baseness, he adds insult to heartless perfidy. Those, indeed, were made great situations by the profound sincerity and the rich, woman-like passion of the actress. But there was one instant, in the second act of the play, when the woman's heart has at length yielded to her lover's will, and he himself, momentarily dismayed by his own conquest, strives to turn back, that Ellen Terry made pathetic beyond description. The words she spoke are simply these, " But I said I would come ! " What language could do justice to the voice, to the manner, to the sweet, confiding, absolute abandonment of the whole nature to the human love by which it had been conquered ? The whole of that performance was astonishing, was thrilling, with knowledge of the passion of love. That especial moment was the supreme beauty of it. At such times human nature is irradiated with a divine fire, and art fulfils its purpose.

I

VII.

ON JEFFERSON'S AUTOBIOGRAPHY.

JOSEPH JEFFERSON has led a life of noble endeavour and has had a career of ample prosperity, culminating in honourable renown and abundant happiness. He was born in Philadelphia, February 20, 1829. He went on the stage when he was four years old and he has been on the stage ever since. His achievements as an actor have been recognised and accepted with admiration in various parts of the world; in Australia and New Zealand and in England, Scotland, and Ireland, as well as in the United States. Among English-speaking actors he is the foremost living representative of the art of eccentric comedy. He has not, of late years, played a wide range of parts, but, restricting himself to a few characters, and those of a representative kind, the manner in which he has acted them is a perfect manner — and it is this that has gained for him his distinctive eminence. Jefferson, however, is not simply and exclusively an actor. His mind is many sided. He has painted landscape pictures of a high order of merit, — pictures in which elusive moods and subtle sentiments of nature are grasped with imaginative insight and denoted and interpreted with a free, delicate, and luminous touch. He has also addressed the public as an author. He has written an easy, colloquial account of his own life, and that breezy, off-hand, expeditious work, — after passing it as a serial through their Century Magazine, — the Century Company has published in a beautiful volume. It is a work that, for the sake of the writer, will be welcomed everywhere, and, for its own sake as well as his, will everywhere be preserved.

Beginning a theatrical career nearly sixty years ago (1833), roving up and down the earth ever since, and seldom continuing in one place, Jefferson has had uncommon opportunities of noting the development of the United States and of observing, in both hemispheres, the changeful aspect of one of the most eventful periods in the history of the world. Actors, as a class, know nothing but the stage and see noth-

ing but the pursuit in which they are occupied.   Whoever has lived much among
them knows that fact, from personal observation.   Whoever has read the various and
numerous memoirs that have from time to
time been published by elderly members of
that profession must have been amused to
perceive that, while they conventionally agree
that "all the world's a stage," they are
enthusiastically convinced that the stage
is all the world.   Jefferson's book, although it contains much about the theatre,
shows him to be an exception in this respect, even as he is in many others.   He
has seen many countries and many kinds
of men and things, and he has long looked
upon life with the thoughtful gaze of a
philosopher as well as the wise smile of
a humourist. He can, if he likes, talk
of something besides the shop.   His account of his life "lacks form a little," and
his indifference to "accurate statistics" —
which he declares to be "somewhat tedious" — is now and then felt to be an
embarrassment.   One would like to know,
for instance, while reading about the primitive theatrical times, when actors sailed
the western rivers in flatboats, and shot
beasts and birds on the bank, precisely

the extent and limits of that period. Nor
is this the only queer aspect of the dramatic past that might be illumined. The
total environment of a man's life is almost equally important with the life itself
— being, indeed, the scenery amid which
the action passes — and a good method for
the writing of a biography is that which
sharply defines the successive periods of
childhood, youth, manhood, and age, and,
while depicting the development of the
individual from point to point, depicts also
the entire field through which he moves,
and the mutations, affecting his life, that
occur in the historic and social fabric
around him. Jefferson, while he has
painted vigorously and often happily, on
a large canvas, has left many spaces empty
and others but thinly filled. The reader
who accompanies him may, nevertheless,
with a little care, piece out the story so as
to perceive it as a sequent, distinct, harmonious, and rounded narrative. Meanwhile
the companionship of this heedless historian
is delightful — for whether as actor, painter,
or writer, Jefferson steadily exerts the
charm of a genial personality. You are as
one walking along a country road, on a
golden autumn day, with a kind, merry

companion, who knows all about the trees
that fringe your track and the birds that
flit through their branches, and who beguiles
the way with many a humorous tale and
many a pleasant remembrance, now im-
pressing your mind by the sagacity of his
reflections, now touching your heart by
some sudden trait of sentiment or pathos,
and always pleasing and satisfying you
with the consciousness of a sweet, human,
broad, charitable, piquant nature. Although
an autobiographer Jefferson is not ego-
tistical, and although a moralist he is not
a bore. There is a tinge of the Horatian
mood in him — for his reader often becomes
aware of that composed, sagacious, half-
droll, quizzical mind that indicates, with
grave gentleness, the folly of ambition, the
vanity of riches, the value of the present
hour, the idleness of borrowing trouble, the
blessing of the golden medium in fortune,
the absurdity of flatterers, and the comfort
of keeping a steadfast spirit amid the inevitable vicissitudes of this mortal state.

Jefferson has memories of a boyhood
that was passed in Washington, Baltimore,
and New York. He went to Chicago in
1838, when that place was scarcely more
than a village — making the journey from

New York to Buffalo in a canal-boat, and sailing thence, aboard a steamer, through the lakes of Erie, Huron, and Michigan. He travelled with his parents, and they gave dramatic performances, in which he assisted, in western towns. It was a time of poverty and hardship, but those ills were borne cheerfully — the brighter side of a hard life being kept steadily in view, and every comic incident of it being seen and appreciated. His father was a gentleman of the Mark Tapley temperament, who came out strong amid adverse circumstances, and the early disappearance from the book of that delightful person (who died in 1842, of yellow fever, at Mobile), is a positive sorrow. His mother, a refined and gentle lady, of steadfast character and of uncommon musical and dramatic talents and accomplishments, survived till 1849, and her ashes rest in Ronaldson's cemetery, in Philadelphia. Jefferson might have said much more about his parents, and especially about his famous grandfather, without risk of becoming tedious — for they were remarkably interesting people ; but he was writing his own life and not theirs, and he has explained that he likes not to dwell much upon domestic

matters. The story of his long ancestry of
actors, which reaches back to the days of
Garrick (for there have been five generations of the Jeffersons upon the stage), he
has not mentioned ; and the story of his
own young days is hurried rapidly to a conclusion. He was brought on the stage,
when a child, at the theatre in Washington,
D.C., by the negro comedian Thomas D.
Rice, who emptied him out of a bag ; and
thereupon, being dressed as " a nigger
dancer," in imitation of Rice, he performed
the antics of Jim Crow. He adverts to his
first appearance in New York and remembers his stage combat with Master Titus ;
and he thinks that Master Titus must remember it also, — since one of that boy's
big toes was nearly cut off in the fray.
That combat occurred at the Franklin theatre, September 30, 1837 — a useful fact
that the autobiographer cares not to mention. He speedily becomes a young man,
as the reader follows him through the first
three chapters of his narrative, — of which
there are seventeen, — and he is found to
be acting, as a stock player, in support of
James W. Wallack, Junius Brutus Booth,
W. C. Macready, and Mr. and Mrs. J. W.
Wallack, Jr. Upon the powers and peculi-

arities of those actors, and upon the traits
of many others who, like them, are dead
and gone (for there is scarcely a word in
the book about any of his living contempo-
raries), he comments freely and instruc-
tively. He was "barn-storming" in Texas
when the Mexican war began, and he followed in the track of the American army,
and acted in the old Spanish theatre in
Matamoras, in the spring of 1846; and,
subsequently, finding that this did no good,
he opened a stall there for the sale of coffee
and other refreshments, in the corner of a
gambling hell. He calls to mind the way of
domestic life and the every-day aspect of
houses, gardens, people, and manners in
Matamoras, and those he describes with
especial skill — deftly introducing the portraiture of a dusky, black-eyed, volatile
Mexican girl, to whom he lost, temporarily,
the light heart of youth, and whom he
thinks that he might have married had he
not deemed it prudent to journey northward
toward a cooler clime. In New Orleans,
at about that time, he first saw the then
young comedian John E. Owens: and he
records the fact that his ambition to
excel as an actor was awakened by the
spectacle of that rival's success. Owens

has had his career since then, — and a brilliant one it was, — and now he sleeps in peace.

After that experience Jefferson repaired to Philadelphia, and during the next ten years, from 1846 to 1856, he wrought in that city and in New York, Baltimore, Richmond, and other places, sometimes as a stock actor, sometimes as a star, and sometimes as a manager. He encountered various difficulties. He took a few serious steps and many comic ones. He was brought into contact with some individuals that were eminent and with some that were ludicrous. He crossed the Allegheny mountains in mid-winter, from Wheeling to Cumberland, in a cold stage-coach, and almost perished. He was a member of Burton's company at the Arch Street theatre, Philadelphia, and was one of the chorus in that great actor's revival of *Antigone* — which there is little doubt that the chorus extinguished. He was the low comedian in Joseph Foster's amphitheatre, where he sang *Captain Kidd* to fill up the "carpenter scenes," and where he sported amid the turbulent rhetorical billows of *Timour the Tartar* and *The Terror of the Road*. He acted in New York at the Franklin theatre and also at the Chatham. He managed theatres in Macon and Savannah, where he brought out the blithe Sir William Don; and one of the sprightliest episodes of his memoir is the chapter in which he describes that tall, elegant, nonchalant adventurer. Don was a Scotchman, born in 1826, who made his first appearance in America in November 1850 at the Broadway theatre, New York, and afterward drifted aimlessly through the provincial theatres. Don was married in 1857 to Miss Emily Sanders, and he died at Tasmania, March 19, 1862, and was buried at Hobartstown. Jefferson saw the dawn of promise in the career of Julia Dean, — when that beautiful girl was acting with him, in the stock — and afterwards he saw the noonday splendour of her prosperity; and he might have recalled, but that sad touches are excluded from his biography, her mournful decline. In 1853 he was stage manager of the Baltimore museum, for Henry C. Jarrett, and in 1854 he was manager of the Richmond theatre, for John T. Ford. Among the players whom he met, and who deeply influenced him, were James E. Murdoch, Henry Placide, Edwin Forrest, Edwin Adams, and Agnes Robertson. But the actor who most

affected the youth of Joseph Jefferson,
whose influence sank deepest into his heart
and has remained longest in his memory
and upon his style, was his half-brother,
Charles Burke: and certainly, as a serio-
comic actor, it may be doubted whether
Charles Burke ever was surpassed. That
comedian was born March 27, 1822, in Philadelphia, and he died in New York, November 10, 1854. Jefferson's mother, Cor-
nelia Frances Thomás, born in New York,
October 1, 1796, the daughter of French
parents, was married in her girlhood to the
Irish comedian Thomas Burke, who died
in 1824 ; and she contracted her second
marriage, with Jefferson's father, in
1826. Jefferson writes at his best in the
description of scenery, in the analysis of
character, and in the statement of artistic
principles. His portraiture of Murdoch, as
a comedian, is particularly clear and fine.
His account of Julia Dean's hit, as Lady
Priory, is excellent and will often be cited.
His portrayal of the reciprocal action of
Burton and Charles Burke, when they
were associated in the same piece, conveys
a valuable lesson. His anecdotes of Edwin
Forrest present that grim figure as yet
again the involuntary cause of mirth. It

often was so. Jefferson, however, draws
a veil of gentle charity over those misused
powers, that perverse will, that wasted life.
The most striking dramatic portraiture in
the book is that bestowed on Charles
Burke, William Warren, George Holland,
Tom Glessing, and Edwin Adams. Those
were men who lived in Jefferson's affections, and when he wrote about them he
wrote from the heart. The sketch of Glessing, whom everybody loved that ever
knew him, is in a touching strain of tender
remembrance.

Jefferson visited England and France
in 1856, but not to act. At that time he
saw the famous English comedians Comp-
ton, Buckstone, Robson, and Wright, and
that extraordinary actor, fine alike in
tragedy and comedy, the versatile Samuel
Phelps. In 1857 he was associated with
Laura Keene at her theatre in New York ;
and from that date onward his career has
been upon a high and sunlit path, visible to
the world. His first part at Laura Keene's
theatre was Dr. Pangloss. Then came
Our American Cousin, in which he gained
a memorable success as Asa Trenchard,
and in which Edward A. Sothern laid
the basis of that fantastic structure of

whim and grotesque humour that afterward became famous as Lord Dundreary.
Sothern, Laura Keene, and William Rufus
Blake, of course, gained much of Jefferson's attention at that time, and he
has not omitted to describe them. His account of Blake, however, does not impart an
adequate idea of the excellence of that comedian. In 1858 he went to the Winter Garden
theatre, and was associated with the late
Dion Boucicault. His characters then were
Newman Noggs, Caleb Plummer, and Salem
Scudder — in *Nicholas Nickleby*, *The Cricket
on the Hearth*, and *The Octoroon*. Mr.
Boucicault told him not to make Caleb
Plummer a solemn character at the beginning — a deliverance that Jefferson seems
to have cherished as one of colossal wisdom. He made a brilliant hit in Salem
Scudder, and it was then that he determined
finally to assume the position of a star.
"Art has always been my sweetheart,"
exclaims Jefferson, "and I have loved her
for herself alone." No observer can doubt
that who has followed his career. It was
in 1859 that he reverted to the subject of
Rip Van Winkle, as the right theme for his
dramatic purpose. He had seen Charles
Burke as Rip, and he knew the several

versions of Washington Irving's story that
had been made for the theatre by Burke,
Hackett, and Yates. The first Rip Van
Winkle upon the stage, of whom there is
any record in theatrical annals, was Thomas
Flynn (1804–1849). That comedian, the
friend of the elder Booth, acted the part
for the first time on May 24, 1828, at Albany. Charles B. Parsons, who afterward
acted in many theatres as Rip, and ultimately became a preacher, was, on that
night, the performer of Derrick. Jefferson's predecessors as Rip Van Winkle were
remarkably clever men — Flynn, Parsons,
Burke, Chapman, Hackett, Yates, and William Isherwood. But it remained for Jefferson to do with that character what no
one else had ever thought of doing — to
lift it above the level of the tipsy rustic
and make it the poetical type of the drifting and dreaming vagrant — half-haunted,
half-inspired, a child of the trees and the
clouds. Jefferson records that he was
lying on the hay in a barn in Paradise
Valley, Pennsylvania, in the summer of
1859, taking advantage of a rainy day to
read Washington Irving's *Life and Letters*,
when that plan came to him. It proved an
inspiration of happiness to thousands of

people all over the world. The comedian
made a play for himself, on the basis of
Charles Burke's play, but with one vital
improvement — he arranged the text and
business of the supernatural scene so that
Rip only should speak, while the ghosts
should remain silent. That stroke of
genius accomplished his object. The man
capable of that exploit in dramatic art
could not fail to win the world, because he
would at once fascinate its imagination while
touching its heart.

In 1861 Jefferson went to California
and thence to Australia, and in the latter
country he remained four years. He has
written a fine description of the entrance
to the harbour at Sydney. His accounts of
"the skeleton dance," as he saw it performed by the black natives of that land;
of his meeting with the haunted hermit in
the woods; of the convict audience at Tasmania, for whom he acted in *The Ticket-of-
Leave Man;* and of the entertainment furnished in a Chinese theatre, are compositions that would impart to any book the
interest of adventure and the zest of novelty.
Such pictures as those have a broad background; they are not circumscribed within
the proscenium frame. The man is seen

in those passages as well as the actor; and
he plays his part well, amid picturesque
surroundings of evil and peril, of tragedy
and of pathos. In Australia Jefferson
met Charles Kean and his wife (Ellen
Tree), of whom his sketches are boldly
drawn and his memories are pleasant. Mr.
and Mrs. Kean afterward made their farewell visit to the United States, beginning,
when they reached New York (from San
Francisco, in April 1865), with *Henry
VIII.*, and closing with *The Jealous Wife.*
In 1865 Jefferson went from Australia to
South America and passed some time in
Lima, where he saw much tropical luxury
and many beautiful ladies — an inspiriting
spectacle, fittingly described by him in
some of the most felicitous of his fervent
words. In June 1865 he reached London,
and presently he came forth, at the Adelphi,
as Rip Van Winkle, — having caused the
piece to be rewritten by Mr. Boucicault,
who introduced the colloquy of the children, paraphrased for it the recognition
scene between King Lear and Cordelia, and
kept Gretchen alive to be married to Derrick. Mr. Boucicault, however, had no
faith in the piece or the actor's plan, and
down to the last moment prophesied fail-

K

ure. Jefferson's success was unequivocal.
Friends surrounded him and in the gentle
and genial record that he has made of those
auspicious days some of the brightest
names of modern English literature sparkle
on his page. Benjamin Webster, Paul Bed-
ford, John Billington, John Brougham, and
Marie Wilton were among the actors who
were glad to be his associates. Robertson,
the dramatist, was his constant companion
— one of the most intellectual and one of the
wittiest of men. Planché, aged yet hearty
and genial (and no man had more in his
nature of the sweet spirit of the comrade),
speedily sought him. Charles Reade and
Anthony Trollope became his cronies; and
poor Artemas Ward arrived and joined the
party just as Jefferson was leaving it —
as bright a spirit, as kind a heart, and as
fine and quaint a humourist as ever cheered
this age — from which he vanished too soon
for the happiness of his friends and for
the fruition of his fame. "I was much
impressed," says the comedian, "with
Ward's genial manner; he was not in good
health, and I advised him to be careful lest
the kindness of London should kill him."
That advice was not heeded, and the kindness of London speedily ended Ward's
days.

Jefferson came home in 1866 and passed ten years in America — years of fame and fortune, whereof the record is smooth prosperity. Its most important personal incident was his second marriage, on December 20, 1867, at Chicago, to Miss Sarah Warren. In July 1873 he made a voyage to Europe, with his wife and William Warren, the comedian, and remained there till autumn. From November 1, 1875 to April 29, 1876 and from Easter 1877 until midsummer he was again acting in London, where he redoubled his former success. In October 1877 he returned home, and since then he has remained in America. The chronicle that he has written glides lightly over these latter years, only now and then touching on their golden summits. The manifest wish of the writer has been to people his pages as much as possible with the men and women of his artistic circle and knowledge who would be likely to interest the reader. Robert Browning, Charles Kingsley, and George Augustus Sala come into the picture, and there is a pleasing story of Browning and Longfellow walking arm in arm in London streets till driven into a cab by a summer shower, when Longfellow insisted on pass-

ing his umbrella through the hole in the
roof, for the protection of the cab-driver.
Jefferson lived for one summer in an
old mansion at Morningside, Edinburgh,
and he dwells with natural delight on his
recollections of that majestic city. He
had many a talk, at odd times, with the
glittering farceur Charles Mathews, about
dramatic art, and some of this is recorded
in piquant anecdotes. "By many," says
the amiable annalist, "he was thought to
be cold and selfish; I do not think he was
so." There is a kind word for Charles
Fechter, whose imitations of Frederick Le-
maitre, in *Belphegor, the Mountebank,* live
in Jefferson's remembrance as wonderfully graphic. There are glimpses of James
Wallack, Walter Montgomery, Peter Rich-
ings, E. A. Sothern, Laura Keene, James
G. Burnett, John Gilbert, Tyrone Power,
Lester Wallack, John McCullough, John T.
Raymond, Mr. and Mrs. Barney Williams,
John Drew (the elder), F. S. Chanfrau,
Charlotte Cushman, Mrs. Drake, and many
others; and the record incorporates two
letters, not before published, from John
Howard Payne, the author of *Home,
Sweet Home* — a melody that is the nat-
ural accompaniment of Jefferson's life.

There is a pretty picture of that ancient supper-room at No. 2 Bulfinch Place, Boston — Miss Fisher's kitchen — as it appeared when William Warren sat behind the mound of lobsters, at the head of the table, while the polished pewters reflected the cheerful light, and wit and raillery enlivened the happy throng, and many a face was wreathed with smiles that now is dark and still forever. In one chapter Jefferson sets forth his views upon the art of acting ; and seldom within so brief a compass will so many sensible reflections be found so simply and tersely expressed. The book closes with words of gratitude for many blessings, and with an emblematic picture of a spirit resigned to whatever vicissitudes of fortune may yet be decreed.

Jefferson's memoir is a simple message to simple minds. It will find its way to thousands of readers to whom a paper by Addison or an essay by Hume would have no meaning. It will point for them the moral of a good life. It will impress them with the spectacle of a noble actor, profoundly and passionately true to the high art by which he lives, bearing eloquent testimony to its beauty and its worth, and to the fine powers and sterling virtues of the good men and women with whom he has been associated in its pursuit. It will display to them — and to all others who may chance to read it — a type of that absolute humility of spirit which yet is perfectly compatible with a just pride of intellect. It will help to preserve interesting traits of famous actors of an earlier time, together with bright stories that illumine the dry chronicle of our theatrical history. And, in its simple record of the motives by which he has been impelled, and the artistic purposes that he has sought to accomplish, it will remain an eloquent, vital, indestructible memorial to the art and the character of a great comedian, when the present reality of his exquisite acting shall have changed to a dim tradition and a fading memory of the past.

VIII.

ON JEFFERSON'S ACTING.

FIFTY years from now the historian of
the American stage, if he should be
asked to name the actor of this period who
was most beloved by the people of this generation, will answer that it was Joseph
Jefferson. Other actors of our time are
famous, and they possess in various degrees
the affection of the public. Jefferson is
not only renowned but universally beloved. To state the cause of this effect is
at once to explain his acting and to do it
the honour to which it is entitled. That
cause can be stated in a single sentence.
Jefferson is at once a poetic and a human
actor, and he is thus able to charm all
minds and to win all hearts. His success, therefore, is especially important not
to himself alone but to the people.

Public taste is twofold. It has a surface
liking, and it has a deep, instinctive, natural
preference. The former is alert, capricious,

incessant, and continually passes from fancy to fancy. It scarcely knows what it wants, except that it wants excitement and change. Those persons in the dramatic world who make a point to address it are experimental speculators, whose one and only object is personal gain, and who are willing and ready to furnish any sort of entertainment that they think will please a passing caprice, and thereby will turn a penny for themselves. To judge the public entirely by this surface liking is to find the public what Tennyson once called it — a many-headed beast. With that animal every paltry and noxious thing can be made, for a time, to flourish ; and that fact leads observers who do not carefully look beneath the surface to conclude that the public is always wrong. But the deep preference of the public comes into the question, and observers who are able to see and to consider that fact presently perceive that the artist, whether actor or otherwise, who gives to the public, not what it says it wants but what it ought to have, is in the long run the victor. The deep preference is for the good thing, the real thing, the right. It is not intelligent. It does not go with thinking and reasoning. It does not pretend to have grounds of belief. It simply responds. But upon the stage the actor who is able to reach it is omnipotent. Jefferson conspicuously is an actor who appeals to the deep, instinctive, natural preference of humanity, and who reaches it, arouses it, and satisfies it. Throughout the whole of his mature career he has addressed the nobler soul of humanity and given to the people what they ought to have ; and the actor who is really able to do that naturally conquers everything. It is not a matter of artifice and simulation ; it is a matter of being genuine and not a sham.

Still further, Jefferson has aroused and touched and satisfied the feelings of the people, not by attempting to interpret literature but by being an actor. An actor is a man who acts. He may be an uneducated man, deficient in learning and in mental discipline, and yet a fine actor. The people care not at all for literature. They do not read it, and they know nothing about it until it is brought home to their hearts by some great interpreter of it. What they do know is action. They can see and they can feel, and the actor who makes them see and feel can do anything with them that he pleases. It is his privilege and his responsibility. Jefferson is one of those artists (and they are few) who depend for their effects not upon what authors have written but upon impersonation. He takes liberties with the text. It would not perhaps be saying too much to say that he does not primarily heed the text at all. He is an actor ; and speaking with reference to him and to others like him it would perhaps be well if those persons who write criticisms upon the stage would come to a definite conclusion upon this point and finally understand that an actor must produce his effects on the instant by something that he does and is, and not by rhetoric and elocution, and therefore that he should not be expected to repeat every word of every part, or to be a translator of somebody else, but that he must be himself. If we want the full, literal text of Shakespeare we can stop at home and read it. What we want of the actor is that he should give himself ; and the true actor does give himself. The play is the medium. A man who acts Romeo must embody, impersonate, express, convey, and make evident what he knows and feels about love. He need not trouble himself about Shakespeare. That great

poet will survive; while if Romeo, being
ever so correct, bores the house, Romeo
will be damned.   Jefferson is an actor
who invariably produces effect, and he produces it by impersonation, and by impersonation that is poetic and human.

Jefferson's performance of Acres conspicuously exemplifies the principles that
have been stated here.   He has not hesi-
tated to alter the comedy of *The Rivals*,
and in his alteration of it he has improved
it.   Acres has been made a better part for
an actor, and a more significant and sympathetic part for an audience.   You could
not care particularly for Acres if he were
played exactly as he is written.   You might
laugh at him, and probably would, but he
would not touch your feelings.   Jefferson
embodies him in such a way that he
often makes you feel like laughing and cry-
ing at the same moment, and you end with
loving the character, and storing it in your
memory with such cherished comrades of
the fancy as Mark Tapley and Uncle Toby.
There is but little human nature in Acres
as Sheridan has drawn him, and what there
is of human nature is coarse; but as
embodied by Jefferson, while he never
ceases to be comically absurd, he becomes

fine and sweet, and wins sympathy and inspires affection, and every spectator is glad
to have seen him and to remember him. It
is not possible to take that sort of liberty
with every author. You can do it but seldom with Shakespeare; never in any but
his juvenile plays. But there are authors
who can be improved by that process, and
Sheridan — in *The Rivals*, not in *The
School for Scandal* — is one of them. And
anyway, since it ought to be felt, known,
understood, and practically admitted that
an actor is something more than a telegraph
wire, that his personal faculty and testimony enter into the matter of embodiment
and expression, Jefferson's rare excellence and great success as Acres should
teach a valuable lesson, correcting that pernicious habit of the critical mind which
measures an actor by the printed text of a
play-book and by the hide-bound traditions
of custom on the stage. Jefferson has
had a royal plenitude of success as an actor,
chiefly with the part of Rip Van Winkle,
but also with the characters of Caleb Plummer, Bob Brierly, Dr. Pangloss, Dr. Olla-
pod, Mr. Golightly, and Hugh de Brass.
The reason of that success cannot be found
in conventional adherence to stage customs
and critical standards.

Jefferson has gained his great power over the people — of which his great fame is the shadow — by giving himself in his art — his own rich and splendid nature and the crystallised conclusions of his experience. As an artist, when it comes to execution, he leaves nothing to chance. The most seemingly artless of his proceedings is absolutely defined in advance, and never is what heedless observers call impulsive and spontaneous. But his temperament is free, fluent, opulent, and infinitely tender; and when the whole man is aroused, this flows into the moulds of literary and dramatic art and glorifies them. When you are looking at Jefferson as Acres in the duel scene in *The Rivals*, you laugh at him, but almost you laugh through your tears. When you see Jefferson as Rip Van Winkle confronting the ghosts on the lonely mountain-top at midnight, you see a display of imaginative personality quite as high as that of Hamlet in tremulous sensibility to supernatural influence, although wholly apart from Hamlet in altitude of intellect and in anguish of experience. The poetry of the impersonation, though, is entirely consonant with Hamlet, and that is the secret of Jefferson's exceptional hold upon the heart and the imagination of his time. The public taste does not ask Jefferson to trifle with his art. Its deep, spontaneous, natural preference feels that he is a true actor, and so yields to his power, and enjoys his charm, and is all the time improved and made fitter to enjoy it. He has reached as great a height as it is possible to reach in his profession. He could if he chose play greater parts than he has ever attempted ; he could not give a better exemplification than he gives, in his chosen and customary achievement, of all that is distinctive, beautiful, and beneficent in the art of the actor.

IX.

JEFFERSON AND FLORENCE IN OLD COMEDY.

A REVIVAL of *The Heir at Law* was
accomplished in the New York season
of 1890, with Joseph Jefferson in the character of Dr. Pangloss and William James
Florence in that of Zekiel Homespun. That
play dates back to 1797, a period in which
a sedulous deference to conventionality prevailed in the British theatre, as to the
treatment of domestic subjects ; and, although the younger Colman wrote in a
more flexible style than was possessed by
any other dramatist of the time, excepting
Sheridan, he was influenced to this extent
by contemporary usage, that often when he
became serious he also became artificial and
stilted. The sentimental part of *The Heir
at Law* is trite in plan and hard in expression. Furthermore that portion of it which,
in the character of Dr. Pangloss, satirises
the indigent, mercenary, disreputable private tutors who constituted a distinct and

pernicious class of social humbugs in Colman's day, has lost its direct point for the
present age, through the disappearance of
the peculiar type of imposture against
which its irony was directed. Dr. Pangloss, nevertheless, remains abstractly a
humorous personage; and when he is embodied by an actor like Jefferson, who can
elucidate his buoyant animal spirits, his
gay audacity, his inveterate good-nature,
his nimble craft, his jocular sportiveness,
his shrewd knowledge of character and of
society, and his scholar-like quaintness, he
becomes a delightful presence; for his
mendacity disappears in the sunshine of
his humour; his faults seem venial; and
we entertain him much as we do the infinitely greater and more disreputable character of Falstaff, — knowing him to be a
vagabond, but finding him a charming companion, for all that. This is one great relief
to the hollow and metallic sentimentality
of the piece. Persons like Henry More-
land, Caroline Dormer, and Mr. Steadfast
would be tiresome in actual life; they
belong, with Julia and Falkland and Pere-
grine and Glenroy, to the noble army of
the bores, and they are insipid on the stage;
but the association of the sprightly and

jocose Pangloss with those drab-tinted and preachy people irradiates even their constitutional platitude with a sparkle of mirth. They shine, in spite of themselves.

Colman's humour is infectious and penetrating. In that quality he was original and affluent. As we look along the line of the British dramatists for the last hundred years we shall find no parallel to his felicity in the use of comic inversion and equivoke, till we come to Gilbert. Though he was tedious while he deferred to that theatrical sentimentality which was the fashion of his day (and against which Goldsmith, in *She Stoops to Conquer*, was the first to strike), he could sometimes escape from it; and when he did escape he was brilliant. In *The Heir at Law* he has not only illumined it by the contrast of Dr. Pangloss but by the unctuous humour and irresistible comic force of the character of Daniel Dowlas, Lord Duberly. Situations in a play, in order to be invested with the enduring quality of humour, must result from such conduct as is the natural and spontaneous expression of comic character. The idea of the comic parvenu is ancient. It did not originate with Colman. His application of it, however, was novel and his treat-

ment of it — taking fast hold of the elemental springs of mirth — is as fresh to-day
as it was a hundred years ago. French
minds, indeed, and such as subscribe to
French notions, would object that the
means employed to elicit character and
awaken mirth are not scientifically and
photographically correct, and that they are
violent. Circumstances, they would say,
do not so fall out that a tallow-chandler is
made a lord. The Christopher Sly expedient, they would add, is a forced expedient. Perhaps it is. But English art sees
with the eyes of the imagination and in
dramatic matters it likes to use colour and
emphasis. Daniel Dowlas, as Lord Duberly, is all the droller for being a retired
tallow-chandler, ignorant, greasy, conventional, blunt, a sturdy, honest, ridiculous
person, who thinks he has observed how
lords act and who intends to put his gained
knowledge into practical use. We shall
never again see him acted as he was acted
by Burton, or by that fine actor William
Rufus Blake, or even by John Gilbert —
who was of rather too choleric a temperament and too fine a texture for such an
oily and stupidly complacent personage.
But whenever and however he is acted he

will be recognised as an elemental type of absurd human nature made ludicrous by comic circumstances; and he will give rich and deep amusement.

It is to be observed, in the analysis of this comedy, that according to Colman's intention the essential persons in it are all, at heart, human. The pervasive spirit of the piece is kindly. Old Dowlas, restricted to his proper place in life, is a worthy man. Dick Dowlas, intoxicated by vanity and prosperity, has no harm in him, and he turns out well at last. Even Dr. Pangloss —although of the species of rogue that subsists by artfully playing upon the weakness of human vanity — is genial and amiable; he is a laughing philosopher; he gives good counsel; he hurts nobody; he is but a mild type of sinner — and the satirical censure that is bestowed upon him is neither merciless nor bitter. Pangloss, in Milk Alley, spinning his brains for a subsistence, might be expected to prove unscrupulous; but the moraliser can imagine Pangloss, if he were only made secure by permanent good fortune, leading a life of blameless indolence and piquant eccentricity. From that point of view Jefferson formed his ideal of the character; and, indeed, his

treatment of the whole piece denoted an
active practical sympathy with that gentle
view of the subject. He placed before his
audience a truthful picture of old English
manners ; telling them, in rapid and cheery
action, Colman's quaint story — in which
there is no malice and no bitterness, but in
which simple virtue proves superior to
temptation, and integrity is strong amid
vicissitudes — and leaving in their minds,
at the last, an amused conviction that
indeed "Nature hath framed strange fel-
lows in her time." His own performance
was full of nervous vitality and mental
sparkle, and of a humour deliciously quaint
and droll. Dr. Panglo_s, as embodied by
Jefferson, is a man who always sees the
comical aspect of things and can make you
see it with him, and all the while can be
completely self-possessed and grave without
ever once becoming slow or heavy. There
was an air of candour, of ingenuous simplicity, of demure propriety, about the
embodiment, that made it inexpressibly
funny. There was no effort and no distortion. The structure of the impersonation
tingled with life, and the expression of it —
in demeanour, movement, facial play, into-
nation and business — was clear and crisp,

with that absolute precision and beautiful
finish for which the acting of Jefferson has
always been distinguished. He is probably
the only American comedian now left, excepting John S. Clarke, who knows all the
traditional embellishments that have gone
to the making of this part upon the stage
— embellishments fitly typified by the bank-
note business with Zekiel Homespun; a
device, however, that perhaps suggests a
greater degree of moral obliquity in Dr.
Pangloss than was intended by the author.
It was exceedingly comical, though, and it
served its purpose. Jefferson has had
the character of Pangloss in his repertory
for almost forty years. He first acted it in
New York as long ago as 1857, at Laura
Keene's theatre, when that beautiful woman
played Cicely and when Duberly was represented by the lamented James G. Burnett.
It takes the playgoer a long way back, to
be thinking about this old piece and the
casts that it has had upon the American
stage. *The Heir at Law* was a great favourite in Boston thirty years ago and more,
when William Warren was in his prime
and could play Dr. Pangloss with the best
of them, and when Julia Bennett Barrow
was living and acting, who could play Cicely

in a way that no later actress has excelled.
John E. Owens as Pangloss will never be for-
gotten. It was a favourite part with John
Brougham. And the grotesque fun of John
S. Clarke in that droll character has been
recognised on both sides of the Atlantic.

In Jefferson's impersonation of Dr.
Pangloss the predominant beauty was spontaneous and perfectly graceful identification with the part. The felicity of the apt
quotations seemed to be accidental. The
manner was buoyant, but the alacrity of
the mind was more nimble than the celerity
of the body, and those wise and witty
comments that Pangloss makes upon life,
character, and manners flowed naturally
from a brain that was in the vigour and repose of intense animation. The actor was
completely merged in the character, which
nevertheless his judgment dominated and
his will directed. No other representative
of Pangloss has quite equalled Jefferson
in the element of authoritative and convincing sincerity. His demure sapience was of
the most intense order and it arose out of
great mental excitement. No other actor
of the part has equalled him in softness and
winning charm of humour. His embodiment of Dr. Pangloss has left in the mem-

ory of his time an image of eccentric character not less lovable than ludicrous.

With Zekiel Homespun, an actor who is true to the author's plan will produce the impression of an affectionate heart, virtuous principles, and absolute honesty of purpose, combined with rustic simplicity. Florence easily reached that result. His preservation of a dialect was admirably exact. The soul of the part is fraternal love, and when Zekiel finds that his trusted friend has repulsed him and would wrong his sister, there is a fine flash of noble anger in the pride and scorn with which he confronts this falsehood and dishonour. Florence in days when he used to act the Irish Emigrant proved himself the consummate master of simple pathos. He struck that familiar note again in the lovely manner of Zekiel toward his sister Cicely, and his denotement of the struggle between affection and resentment in the heart of the brother when wounded by the depravity of his friend was not less beautiful in the grace of art than impressive in simple dignity and touching in passionate fervour. In point of natural feeling Zekiel Homespun is a stronger part than Dr. Pangloss, although not nearly so complex nor so difficult to act.

The sentiments by which it is animated awaken instant sympathy and the principles that impel it command universal respect. No actor who has attempted Zekiel Homespun in this generation on the American stage has approached the performance that was given by Florence, in conviction, in artless sweetness, in truth of passion, and in the heartfelt expression of the heart.

Purists customarily insist that the old comedies are sacred; that no one of their celestial commas or holy hyphens can be omitted without sin; and that the alteration of a sentence in them is sacrilege. The truth stands, however, without regard to hysterics: and it is a truth that the old comedies owe their vitality mostly to the actors who now and then resuscitate them. No play of the past is ever acted with scrupulous fidelity to the original text. The public that saw the *Heir-at-Law* and the *Rivals*, when Jefferson and Florence acted in them, saw condensed versions, animated by a living soul of to-day, and therefore it was impressed. The one thing indispensable on the stage is the art of the actor.

X.

ON THE DEATH OF FLORENCE.

THE melancholy tidings of the death of
Florence came suddenly (he died in
Philadelphia, after a brief illness, November 19, 1891), and struck the hearts of his
friends not simply with affliction but with
dismay.   Florence was a man of such vigorous and affluent health that the idea of
illness and death was never associated with
him.   Whoever else might go, he at least
would remain, and for many cheerful years
he would please our fancy and brighten our
lives.   His spirit was so buoyant and brilliant that it seemed not possible it could
ever be dimmed.   Yet now, in a moment,
his light was quenched and there was darkness on his mirth.   We shall hear his
pleasant voice no more and see no more
the sunshine of a face that was never seen
without joy and can never be remembered
without sorrow.   The loss to the public
was great.   Few actors within the last

forty years have stood upon a level with Florence in versatility and charm. His gentleness, his simplicity, his modesty, his affectionate fidelity, his ready sympathy, his inexhaustible patience, his fine talents — all those attributes united with his spontaneous drollery to enshrine him in tender affection.

William James Florence, whose family name was Conlin, was born in Albany, July 26, 1831. When a youth he joined the Murdoch Dramatic Association, and he early gave evidence of extraordinary dramatic talent. On December 9, 1849 he made his first appearance on the regular stage, at the Marshall theatre in Richmond, Virginia, where he impersonated Tobias, in *The Stranger*. After that he met with the usual vicissitudes of a young player. He was a member of various stock companies — notably that of W. C. Forbes, of the Providence museum, and that of the once-popular John Nickinson, of Toronto and Quebec — the famous Havresack of his period. Later he joined the company at Niblo's theatre, New York, under the management of Chippendale and John Sefton, appearing there on May 8, 1850. He also acted at the Broadway, under Marshall's man-

agement, and in 1852 he was a member
of the company at Brougham's Lyceum.
On January 1, 1853 he married Malvina
Pray, sister of the wife of Barney Williams ; and in that way those two Irish
comedians came to be domestically associated.

At that time Florence wrote several plays,
upon Irish and Yankee subjects, then very
popular, and he began to figure as a star —
his wife standing beside him.   They appeared at Purdy's National theatre, June
8, 1853, and then, and for a long time afterward, they had much popularity and success.   Florence had composed many songs
of a sprightly character (one of them, called
Bobbing Around, had a sale of more than
100,000 copies), and those songs were sung
by his wife, to the delight of the public.
The Irish drama served his purpose for
many years, but he varied that form of
art by occasional resort to burlesque and
by incursions into the realm of melodrama.
One of his best performances was that of
O'Bryan, in John Brougham's play of
Temptation, or the Irish Emigrant, with
which he often graced the stage of the Winter Garden.   In that he touched the extremes
of gentle humour and melting pathos.   He

was delightfully humorous, also, in *Handy Andy*, and in all that long line of Irish characters that came to our stage with Tyrone Power and the elder John Drew. He had exceptional talent for burlesque, and that was often manifested in his early days. *Fra Diavolo, Beppo, Lallah Rookh, The Lady of the Lions*, and *The Colleen Bawn*, were among the burlesques that he produced, and with those he was the pioneer.

Engagements were filled by Mr. and Mrs. Florence, at the outset of their starring tour, in many cities of the republic, and everywhere they met with kindness and honour. Among the plays written by Florence were *The Irish Princess, O'Neil the Great, The Sicilian Bride, Woman's Wrongs, Eva*, and *The Drunkard's Doom*. On April 2, 1856 Mr. and Mrs. Florence sailed for England, and presently they appeared at Drury Lane theatre, where they at once stepped into favour. The performance of the *Yankee Gal* by Mrs. Florence aroused positive enthusiasm — for it was new, and Mrs. Florence was the first American comic actress that had appeared upon the English stage. More than two hundred representations of

it were given at that time. Florence used
to relate that his fortunes were greatly
benefited by his success in London, and
he habitually spoke with earnest gratitude
of the kindness that he received there.
From that time onward he enjoyed almost
incessant prosperity. A tour of the English provincial cities followed his London
season. He acted at Manchester, Liverpool, Edinburgh, Glasgow, Belfast, and
Dublin, and both his wife and himself became favourites — so that their songs were
sung and whistled in the streets, wherever
they went.

Returning to the United States Mr. and
Mrs. Florence renewed their triumphs, all
over the land. In 1861 Florence played some
of Burton's characters in Wallack's theatre — among them being Toodle and Cuttle.
At a later period he made it a custom to
lease Wallack's theatre during the summer, and there he produced many burlesques. In 1863, at the Winter Garden,
he offered *The Ticket-of-Leave Man* and
acted Bob Brierly, which was one of the
best exploits of his life. In 1867 Wallack's
old theatre being then called the Broadway and managed by Barney Williams, he
brought to that house the comedy of *Caste*

and presented it with a distribution of the
parts that has not been equalled. The
actors were Mrs. Chanfrau, Mrs. Gilbert,
Mrs. Florence, William Davidge, Owen
Marlowe, Edward Lamb, and Florence —
who played George D'Alroy. In 1868 he
presented *No Thoroughfare* and enacted
Obenreizer, — a performance that established his rank among the leading actors
of the time. In 1876 he made a remarkable hit as the Hon. Bardwell Slote in the
play of *The Mighty Dollar*, by Benjamin
E. Woolff. That was the last important
new play that he produced. During the
last fifteen years of his life he offered selec-
tions from his accepted repertory. For a
time he was associated with Jefferson — to
whom he brought a strength that was deeply
valued and appreciated, equally by that
famous actor and by the public — acting Sir
Lucius O'Trigger in *The Rivals* and Zekiel
Homespun in *The Heir-at-Law.*

The power of Florence was that of impersonation. He was imaginative and sympathetic; his style was flexible; and he had
an unerring instinct of effect. The secret
of his success lay in his profound feeling,
guided by perfect taste and perfect self-con-
trol. He was an actor of humanity, and he

diffused an irresistible charm of truth and gentleness. His place was his own and it can never be filled.

An Epitaph.

Here Rest the Ashes of
WILLIAM JAMES FLORENCE,
Comedian.

His Copious and Varied Dramatic Powers, together with the Abundant Graces of his Person, combined with Ample Professional Equipment and a Temperament of Peculiar Sensibility and Charm, made him one of the Best and Most Successful Actors of his Time, alike in Comedy and in Serious Drama. He ranged easily from Handy Andy to Bob Brierly, and from Cuttle to Obenreizer. In Authorship, alike of Plays, Stories, Music, and Song, he was Inventive, Versatile, Facile, and Graceful. In Art Admirable; in Life Gentle; he was widely known, and he was known only to be loved.

He was Born in Albany, N.Y.,
July 26, 1831.
He Died in Philadelphia, Penn.,
November 19, 1891.

———

By Virtue cherished, by Affection mourned,
By Honour hallowed and by Fame adorned,
Here FLORENCE sleeps, and o'er his sacred
    rest
Each word is tender and each thought is
    blest.
Long, for his loss, shall pensive Mem'ry
    show,
Through Humour's mask, the visage of her
    woe,
Day breathe a darkness that no sun dispels,
And Night be full of whispers and farewells ;
While patient Kindness, shadow-like and
    dim,
Droops in its loneliness, bereft of him,
Feels its sad doom and sure decadence
    nigh, —
For how should Kindness live, when he
    could die !

The eager heart, that felt for every grief,
The bounteous hand, that loved to give
    relief,

The honest smile, that blessed where'er it
    lit,
The dew of pathos and the sheen of wit,
The sweet, blue eyes, the voice of melting
    tone,
That made all hearts as gentle as his own,
The Actor's charm, supreme in royal thrall,
That ranged through every field and shone
    in all —
For these must Sorrow make perpetual
    moan,
Bereaved, benighted, hopeless, and alone?
Ah, no; for Nature does no act amiss,
And Heaven were lonely but for souls like
    this.

M

XI.

HENRY IRVING AND ELLEN TERRY IN THE MERCHANT OF VENICE.

IN his beautiful production of *The Merchant of Venice* Henry Irving restored the fifth act, the jailer scene, and the casket scenes in full, and the piece was acted with strict fidelity to Shakespeare. With Ellen Terry for Portia that achievement became feasible. With an ordinary actress in that character the comedy might be tedious — notwithstanding its bold and fine contrasts of character, its fertility of piquant incident, and its lovely poetry. Radiant with her fine spirit and beautiful presence, and animated and controlled in every fibre by his subtle and authoritative intellect, judiciously cast and correctly dressed and mounted, Henry Irving's revival of *The Merchant of Venice* captured the public fancy ; and in every quarter it was sincerely felt and freely proclaimed that here, at last, was the perfection of stage display. That suc-

cess has never faded. The performance
was round, symmetrical, and thorough
— every detail being kept subordinate to
intelligent general effect, and no effort being made toward overweening individual
display.

Shakespeare's conception of Shylock has
long been in controversy. Burbage, who
acted the part in Shakespeare's presence,
wore a red wig and was frightful in form
and aspect. The red wig gives a hint of
low comedy, and it may be that the great
actor made use of low comedy expedients
to cloak Shylock's inveterate malignity and
sinister purpose. Dogget, who played the
part in Lord Lansdowne's alteration of
Shakespeare's piece, turned Shylock into
farce. Macklin, when he restored the original play to the stage — at Drury Lane,
February 14, 1741 — wore a red hat, a
peaked beard, and a loose black gown,
playing Shylock as a serious, almost a tragic
part, and laying great emphasis upon a display of revengeful passion and hateful
malignity. So terrible was he, indeed, that
persons who saw him on the stage in that
character not infrequently drew the infer-
ence and kept the belief that he was
personally a monster. His look was iron-

visaged; the cast of his manners was re-
lentless and savage. Quin said that his
face contained not lines but cordage. In
portraying the contrasted passions of joy
for Antonio's losses and grief for Jessica's
elopement he poured forth all his fire.
When he whetted his knife, in the trial
scene, he was silent, grisly, ominous, and fatal. No human touch, no hint of race-maj-
esty or of religious fanaticism, tempered the
implacable wickedness of that hateful ideal.
Pope, who saw that Shylock, hailed it as "the
Jew that Shakespeare drew" — and Pope,
among other things, was one of the editors
of Shakespeare. Cooke, who had seen
Macklin's Shylock, and also those of Henderson, King, Kemble, and Yates, adopted,
maintained, and transmitted the legend of
Macklin. Edmund Kean, who worshipped
Cooke, was unquestionably his imitator in
Shylock; but it seems to have been Edmund
Kean who, for the first time, gave prom-
inence to the Hebraic majesty and fanatical
self-consecration of that hateful but colossal
character. Jerrold said that Kean's Shylock was like a chapter of Genesis. Macready — whose utterance of "Nearest his
heart" was the blood-curdling keynote of his
whole infernal ideal — declared the part to

be "composed of harshness," and he saw
no humanity in the lament for the loss of
Leah's ring, but only a lacerated sense
of the value of that jewel. Brooke, a great
Shylock, concurred with Kean's ideal and
made the Jew orientally royal, the avenger
of his race, having "an oath in heaven,"
and standing on the law of "an eye for an
eye." Edwin Forrest, the elder Wallack,
E. L. Davenport, Edwin Booth, Bogumil
Davison, and Charles Kean steadily kept
Shylock upon the stage, — some walking in
the religious track and some leaving it.
But the weight of opinion and the spirit
and drift of the text would justify a presentment of the Jew as the incarnation not
alone of avarice and hate, but of the stern,
terrible Mosaic law of justice. That is the
high view of the part, and in studying
Shakespeare it is safe to prefer the high
view.

There must be imagination, or pathos, or
weirdness, or some form of humour, or a
personal charm in the character that awakens the soul of Henry Irving and calls forth
his best and finest powers. There is little
of that quality in Shylock. But Henry Irving took the high view of him. This Jew
"feeds fat the ancient grudge" against

Antonio — until the law of Portia, more
subtle than equitable, interferes to thwart
him; but also he avenges the wrongs that
his " sacred nation " has suffered. His ideal
was right, his grasp of it firm, his execution
of it flexible with skill and affluent with intellectual power. If memory carries away
a shuddering thought of his baleful gaze
upon the doomed Antonio and of his horrid
cry of the summons " Come, prepare ! "
it also retains the image of a father convulsed with grief — momentarily, but sincerely — and of a man who at least can remember that he once loved. It was a most
austere Shylock, inveterate of purpose, vindictive, malignant, cruel, ruthless; and yet
it was human. No creature was ever more
logical and consistent in his own justification. By purity, sincerity, decorum, fanaticism, the ideal was aptly suggestive of such
men as Robert Catesby, Guy Fawkes, and
John Felton — persons who, with prayer on
their lips, were nevertheless capable of hideous cruelty. The street scene demands
utterance, not repression. The Jew raves
there, and no violence would seem exces-
sive. Macklin, Kean, Cooke, and the elder
Booth, each must have been terrific at that
point. Henry Irving's method was that

of the intense passion that can hardly
speak — the passion that Kean is said to
have used so grandly in giving the curse of
Junius Brutus upon Tarquin.   But, there
was just as much of Shylock's nature in
Henry Irving's performance as in any performance that is recorded.   The lack was
overwhelming physical power — not men-
tality and not art.   At "No tears but of
my shedding" Henry Irving's Shylock took
a strong clutch upon the emotions and created an effect that will never be forgotten.

Ellen Terry's Portia long ago became a
precious memory.   The part makes no appeal to the tragic depths of her nature, but
it awakens her fine sensibility, stimulates
the nimble play of her intellect, and cordially promotes that royal exultation in the
affluence of physical vitality and of spiritual freedom that so often seems to lift her
above the common earth.   There have been
moments when it seemed not amiss to apply
Shakespeare's own beautiful simile to the
image of queen-like refinement, soft womanhood, and spiritualised intellect that this
wonderful actress presented — "as if an
angel dropped down from the clouds."
Her Portia was stately, yet fascinating; a
woman to inspire awe and yet to capti-

vate every heart. Nearer to Shakespeare's
meaning than that no actress can ever go.
The large, rich, superb manner never in-
validated the gentle blandishments of her
sex. The repressed ardour, the glowing
suspense, the beautiful modesty and candour with which she awaited the decision
of the casket scene, showed her to be
indeed all woman, and worthy of a true
man's love. Here was no paltering of a
puny nature with great feelings and a great
experience. And never in our day has the
poetry of Shakespeare fallen from human
lips in a strain of such melody — with such
teeming freedom of felicitous delivery and
such dulcet purity of diction.

XII.

JOHN McCULLOUGH IN SEVERAL CHARACTERS.

THERE is no greater gratification to the intellect than the sense of power and completeness in itself or the perception of power and completeness in others. Those attributes were in John McCullough's acting and were at the heart of its charm. His repertory consisted of thirty characters, but probably the most imposing and affecting of his embodiments was Virginius. The massive grandeur of adequacy in that performance was a great excellence. The rugged, weather-beaten plainness of it was full of authority and did not in the least detract from its poetic purity and ideal grace. The simplicity of it was like the lovely innocence that shines through the ingenuous eyes of childhood, while its majesty was like the sheen of white marble in the sunlight. It was a very high, serious, noble work ; yet, — although, to his immeasura-

ble credit, the actor never tried to apply a
"natural" treatment to artificial conditions
or to speak blank verse in a colloquial manner, — it was made sweetly human by a
delicate play of humour in the earlier scenes,
and by a deep glow of paternal tenderness
that suffused every part of it and created an
almost painful sense of sincerity.   Common
life was not made commonplace life by
McCullough, nor blank verse depressed to
the level of prose.   The intention to be real
— the intention to love, suffer, feel, act, de-
fend, and avenge, as a man of actual life
would do — was obvious enough, through
its harmonious fulfilment; yet the realism
was shorn of all triteness, all animal excess,
all of those ordinary attributes which are
right in nature, and wrong because obstruc-
tive in the art that is nature's interpretation.

Just as the true landscape is the harmonious blending of selected natural effects, so
the true dramatic embodiment is the crystal-
lization of selected attributes in any given
type of human nature, shown in selected
phases of natural condition.   McCullough
did not present Virginius brushing his hair
or paying Virginia's school-bills; yet he
suggested him, clearly and beautifully, in

the sweet domestic repose and paternal benignity of his usual life — making thus a
background of loveliness, on which to throw,
in lines of living light, the terrible image of
his agonising sacrifice.   And when the inevitable moment came for his dread act of
righteous slaughter it was the moral grandeur, the heart-breaking paternal agony, and
the overwhelming pathos of the deed that
his art diffused — not the "gashed stab,"
the blood, the physical convulsion, the re-
volting animal shock.   Neither was there
druling, or dirt, or physical immodesty, or
any other attribute of that class of the natural concomitants of insanity, in the subsequent delirium.

A perfect and holy love is, in one aspect
of it, a sadder thing to see than the profoundest grief.   Misery, at its worst, is at
least final : and for that there is the relief
of death.   But love, in its sacred exaltation, — the love of the parent for the child,
— is so fair a mark for affliction that one can
hardly view it without a shudder of apprehensive dread.   That sort of love was personified in McCullough's embodiment of
Virginius, and that same nameless thrill
of fear was imparted by its presence, —
even before the tragedian, with an exquis-

ite intuition of art, made Virginius convey
his vague presentiment, not admitted but
quickly thrust aside, of some unknown
doom of peril and agony. There was, in
fact, more heart in that single piece of acting than in any hundred of the most
pathetic performances of the "natural"
school; and all the time it was maintained
at the lofty level of classic grace. It would
be impossible to overstate the excellence of
all that McCullough did and said, in the
forum scene — the noble severity of the
poise, the grace of the outlines, the terrible
intensity of the mood, the heartrending
play of the emotions, the overwhelming
delirium of the climax. Throughout the
subsequent most difficult portraiture of
shattered reason the actor never, for an
instant, lost his steadfast grasp upon sympathy and inspiration. Every heart knew
the presence of a nature that could feel all
that Virginius felt and suffer and act all
that Virginius suffered and acted; and,
beyond this, in his wonderful investiture
of the mad scenes with the alternate va-
cancy and lamentable and forlorn anguish
of a special kind of insanity, every judge
of the dramatic art recognised the govern-
ing touch of a splendid intellect, imperial

over all its resources and instruments of art.

Virginius as embodied by McCullough was a man of noble and refined nature ; lovely in life ; cruelly driven into madness ; victorious over dishonour, by a deed of terrible heroism ; triumphant over crime, even in forlorn and pitiable dethronement and ruin ; and, finally, released by the celestial mercy of death. And this was shown by a poetic method so absolute that Virginius, while made an actual man to every human heart, was kept a hero to the universal imagination, whether of scholar or peasant, and a white ideal of manly purity and grace to that great faculty of taste which is the umpire and arbiter of the human mind.

The sustained poetic exaltation of that embodiment, its unity as a grand and sympathetic personage, and its exquisite simplicity were the qualities that gave it vitality in popular interest, and through those it will have permanence in theatrical history. There were many subtle beauties in it. The illimitable tenderness, back of the sweet dignity, in the betrothal of Virginia to Icilius ; the dim, transitory, evanescent touch of presentiment, in the forecasting of the festival joys that are to succeed the war; the self-abnegation and simple homeliness of grief for the dead Dentatus; the alternate shock of freezing terror and cry of joy, in the camp scene — closing with that potent repression and thrilling outburst, "Prudence, but no patience!" — a situation and words that call at once for splendid manliness of self-command and an ominous and savage vehemence; the glad, saving, comforting cry to Virginia, "Is she here?" — that cry which never failed to precipitate a gush of joyous tears; the rapt preoccupation and the exquisite music of voice with which he said, "I never saw thee look so like thy mother, in all my life"; the majesty of his demeanour in the forum; the look that saw the knife; the mute parting glance at Servia; the accents of broken reason, but unbroken and everlasting love, that called upon the name of the poor murdered Virginia; and then the last low wail of the dying father, conscious and happy in the great boon of death — those, as McCullough gave them, were points of impressive beauty, invested with the ever-varying light and shadow of a delicate artistic treatment, and all the while animated with passionate sincerity. The perfect finish of the performance, indeed, was little less than marvellous, when viewed with reference to the ever-increasing volume of power and the evident reality of afflicting emotion with which the part was carried. If acting ever could do good the acting of McCullough did. If ever dramatic art concerns the public welfare it is when such an ideal of manliness and heroism is presented in such an image of nobility.

In Lear and in Othello, — as in Virginius, — the predominant quality of McCullough's acting was a profound and beautiful sincerity. His splendidly self-poised nature — a solid rock of truth, which enabled him, through years of patient toil, to hold a steadfast course over all the obstacles that oppose and amid all the chatter that assails a man who is trying to accomplish anything grand and noble in art — bore him bravely up in those great characters, and made him, in each of them, a stately type of the nobility of the human soul. As the Moor, his performance was well-nigh perfect. There was something a little fantastic, indeed, in the facial style that he used ; and that blemish was enhanced by the display of a wild beast's head on the back of one of Othello's robes. The tendency of that sort of ornamentation — however consonant it may be deemed with the barbaric element in the Moor — is to suggest him as heedful of appearances, and thus to distract regard from his experience to his accessories. But the spirit was true. Simplicity, urged almost to the extreme of barrenness, would not be out of place in Othello, and McCullough, in his treatment of the part, testified to his practical appreciation of that truth. His ideal of Othello combined manly tenderness, spontaneous magnanimity, and trusting devotion, yet withal a volcanic ground-swell of passion, that early and clearly displayed itself as capable of delirium and ungovernable tempest. His method had the calm movement of a summer cloud, in every act and word by which this was shown. For intensity and for immediate, adequate, large, and overwhelming response of action to emotion, that performance has not been surpassed. There were points in it, though, at which the massive serenity of the actor's temperament now and then deadened the glow of feeling and depressed him to undue calmness; he sometimes recovered too suddenly and fully from a tempest of emotion — as at the agonising appeal to

Iago, "Give me a living reason she's dis-
loyal"; and he was not enough delirious in
the speech about the sybil and the handker-
chief. On the other hand, once yielded to
the spell of desecrated feeling, his mood
and his expression of it were immeasurably
pathetic and noble. Those two great ebulli-
tions of despair, "O, now forever," and
"Had it pleased heaven," could not be
spoken in a manner more absolutely heart-
broken or more beautifully simple than
the manner that was used by him. In
his obvious though silent suffering at the
disgrace and dismissal of Cassio; in the
dazed, forlorn agony that blended with
his more active passion throughout the
scene of Iago's wicked conquest of his
credulity; in his occasional quick relapses
into blind and sweet fidelity to the old belief in Desdemona; in his unquenchable
tenderness for her, through the delirium
and the sacrifice; and in the tone of soft,
romantic affection — always spiritualised,
never sensual — that his deep and loving
sincerity diffused throughout the work,
was shown the grand unity of the embodiment; a unity based on the simple passion
of love. To hear that actor say the one
supreme line to Iago, "I am bound to thee

N

forever," was to know that he understood
and felt the meaning of the character, to its
minutest fibre and its profoundest depth.

There were touches of fresh and aptly
illustrative " business " in the encounter of
Othello and Iago, in the great scene of the
third act. The gasping struggles of Iago
heightened the effect of the Moor's fury,
and the quickly suppressed impulse and
yell of rage with which he finally bounded
away made an admirable effect of nature.
In the last scene McCullough rounded his
performance with a solemn act of sacrifice.
There was nothing animal, nothing barbaric, nothing insane, in the slaughter of
Desdemona. It was done in an ecstasy of
justice, and the atmosphere that surrounded
the deed was that of awe and not of horror.

For the character of King Lear McCullough possessed the imposing stature, the
natural majesty, the great reach of voice,
and the human tenderness that are its basis
and equipment. No actor of Lear can ever
satisfy a sympathetic lover of the part unless he possesses a greatly affectionate heart,
a fiery spirit, and, — albeit the intellect must
be shown in ruins, — a regal mind. Within
that grand and lamentable image of shat-

tered royalty the man must be noble and
lovable. Nothing that is puny or artificial
can ever wear the investiture of that colossal sorrow. McCullough embodied Lear
as, from the first, stricken in mind —
already the unconscious victim of incip-
ient decay and dissolution; not mad but
ready to become so. There is a subtle
apprehensiveness all about the presence of
the king, in all the earlier scenes. He
diffuses disquietude and vaguely presages
disaster, and the observer looks on him
with solicitude and pain. He is not yet
decrepit but he will soon break; and the
spectator loves him and is sorry for him
and would avert the destiny of woe that is
darkly foreshadowed in his condition. Mc-
Cullough gave the invectives — as they
ought to be given — with the impetuous
rush and wild fury of the avalanche; and
yet they were felt to come out of agony as
well as out of passion. The pathos of those
tremendous passages is in their chaotic disproportion; in their lawlessness and lack
of government; in the evident helplessness
of the poor old man who hurls them forth
from a breaking heart and a distracted
mind. He loves, and he loathes himself for
loving: every fibre of his nature is in hor-

rified revolt against such lack of reverence, gratitude, and affection toward such a monarch and such a father as he knows himself to have been.   The feeling that McCullough poured through those moments of splendid yet pitiable frenzy was overwhelming in its intense glow and in its towering and incessant volume.   There was remarkable subtlety, also, in the manner in which that feeling was tempered.   In Lear's meeting with Goneril after the curse you saw at once the broken condition of an aged, infirm, and mentally disordered man, who had already forgotten his own terrible words.   "We'll no more meet, no more see one another" is a line to which McCullough gave its full eloquence of abject mournfulness and forlorn desolation.   Other denotements of subtlety were seen in his sad preoccupation with memories of the lost Cordelia, while talking with the Fool.   "I did her wrong" was never more tenderly spoken than by him.   They are only four little words ; but they carry the crushing weight of eternal and hopeless remorse.   It was in this region of delicate, imaginative touch that McCullough's dramatic art was especially puissant.   He was the first actor of Lear to discriminate be-

tween the agony of a man while going mad
and the careless, volatile, fantastic condition — afflicting to witness, but no longer
agonising to the lunatic himself — of a man
who has actually lapsed into madness.
Edwin Forrest — whose Lear is much ex-
tolled, often by persons who, evidently,
never saw it — much as he did with the
part, never even faintly suggested such a
discrimination as that.

To one altitude of Lear's condition it is
probably impossible for dramatic art to rise
— the mood of divine philosophy, warmed
with human tenderness, in which the dazed
but semi-conscious vicegerent of heaven
moralises over human life. There is a
grandeur in that conception so vast that
nothing short of the rarest inspiration of
genius can rise to it. The deficiences of
McCullough's Lear were found in the analysis of that part of the performance. He
had the heart of Lear, the royalty, the
breadth ; but not all of either the exalted
intellect, the sorrow-laden experience, or
the imagination — so gorgeous in its disor-
der, so infinitely pathetic in its misery.

His performance of Lear signally exemplified, through every phase of passion, that
temperance which should give it smoothness.

The treatment of the curse scene, in particular, was extraordinarily beautiful for the low, sweet, and tender melody of the voice, broken only now and then — and rightly broken — with the harsh accents of wrath. Gentleness never accomplished more, as to taste and pathos, than in McCullough's utterance of " I gave you all," and " I'll go with you." The rallying of the broken spirit after that, and the terrific outburst, " I'll not weep," had an appalling effect. The recognition of Cordelia was simply tender, and the death scene lovely in pathos and solemn and affecting in tragic climax.

Throughout *Othello* and *King Lear* Mc-Cullough's powers were seen to be curbed and guided, not by a cold and formal design but by a grave and sweet gentleness of mind, always a part of his nature, but more and more developed by the stress of experience, by the reactionary subduing influence of noble success, and by the definite consciousness of power. He found no difficulty in portraying the misery of Othello and of Lear, because this is a form of misery that flows out of laceration of the heart, and not from the more subtle wounds that are inflicted upon the spirit through the imagination. There was no brooding

over the awful mysteries of the universe,
nor any of that corroding, haunted gloom
that comes of an over-spiritualised state of
suffering, longing, questioning, doubting
humanity. Above all things else Othello
and Lear are human ; and the human heart,
above all things else, was the domain of that
actor.

The character of Coriolanus, though high
and noble, is quite as likely to inspire resentment as to awaken sympathy. It contains many elements and all of them are
good ; but chiefly it typifies the pride of intellect. This, in itself a natural feeling and
a virtuous quality, practically becomes a
vice when it is not tempered with charity for
ignorance, weakness, and the lower orders
of mind. In the character of Coriolanus it
is not so tempered, and therefore it vitiates
his greatness and leads to his destruction.
Much, of course, can be urged in his defence.
He is a man of spotless honour, unswerving
integrity, dauntless courage, simple mind,
straightforward conduct, and magnanimous
disposition. He is always ready to brave
the perils of battle for the service of his
country. He constantly does great deeds
— and would continue constantly to do
them — for their own sake and in a spirit

of total indifference alike to praises and
rewards. He exists in the consciousness
of being great and has no life in the opinions of other persons. He dwells in "the
cedar's top" and "dallies with the wind
and scorns the sun." He knows and he
despises with active and immitigable contempt the shallowness and fickleness of
the multitude. He is of an icy purity,
physical as well as mental, and his nerves
tingle with disgust of the personal unclean-
liness of the mob. "Bid them wash their
faces," he says — when urged to ask the
suffrages of the people — "and keep their
teeth clean." "He rewards his deeds with
doing them," says his fellow-soldier Comin-
ius, "and looks upon things precious as the
common muck of the world." His aristocracy does not sit in a corner, deedless and
meritless, brooding over a transmitted name
and sucking the orange of empty self-con-
ceit: it is the aristocracy of achievement
and of nature — the solid superiority of
having done the brightest and best deeds
that could be done in his time and of being
the greatest man of his generation. It is as
if a Washington, having made and saved a
nation, were to spurn it from him with his
foot, in lofty and by no means groundless

contempt for the ignorance, pettiness, meanness, and filth of mankind.   The story of
Coriolanus, as it occurs in Plutarch, is
thought to be fabulous, but it is very far
from being fabulous as it stands transfigured
in the stately, eloquent tragedy of Shakespeare.   The character and the experience
are indubitably representative.   It was some
modified form of the condition thus shown
that resulted in the treason and subsequent
ruin of Benedict Arnold.   Pride of intellect
largely dominated the career of Aaron Burr.
More than one great thinker has split on
that rock, and gone to pieces in the surges
of popular resentment.   "No man," said
Dr. Chapin, in his discourse over the coffin
of Horace Greeley, "can lift himself above
himself."   He who repudiates the humanity
of which he is a part will inevitably come
to sorrow and ruin.   It is perfectly true that
no intellectual person should in the least depend upon the opinions of others — which,
in the nature of things, exist in all stages
of immaturity, mutability, and error — but
should aim to do the greatest deeds and
should find reward in doing them : yet always the right mood toward humanity is gentleness and not scorn.   "Thou, my father,"
said Matthew Arnold, in his tribute to one

of the best men of the century, "wouldst
not be saved alone." To enlighten the
ignorant, to raise the weak, to pity the
frail, to disregard the meanness, ingrati-
tude, misapprehension, dulness, and petty
malice of the lower orders of humanity —
that is the wisdom of the wise ; and that is
accordant with the moral law of the universe, from the operation of which no man
escapes. To study, in Shakespeare, the
story of Coriolanus is to observe the viola-
tion of that law and the consequent retribution.

>   "Battles, and the breath
>   Of stormy war and violent death"

fill up the first part of the tragedy as it
stands in Shakespeare, and that portion is
also much diversified with abrupt changes
of scene ; so that it has been found expedient to alter the piece, with a view to its
more practical adaptation to the stage.
While however it is not acted· in strict
accordance with Shakespeare its essential
parts are retained and represented. Many
new lines, though, occur toward the close.
McCullough used the version that was used
by Forrest, who followed in the footsteps
of Cooper, the elder Vandenhoff, and James

R. Anderson. There is, perhaps, an excess
of foreground — a superfluity of fights and
processions — by way of preparing for the
ordeal through which the character of Coriolanus is to be displayed. Yet when Hecuba
at last is reached the interest of the situation makes itself felt with force. The massive presence and stalwart declamation of
Edwin Forrest made him superb in this
character; but the embodiment of Coriolanus by McCullough, while equal to its
predecessor in physical majesty, was superior to it in intellectual haughtiness and
in refinement. An actor's treatment of
the character must, unavoidably, follow
the large, broad style of the historical
painter. There is scant opportunity afforded in any of the scenes allotted to
Coriolanus for fine touches and delicate
shading. During much of the action the
spectator is aware only of an imperial
figure that moves with a mountainous
grace through the fleeting rabble of Roman
plebeians and Volscians, dreadful in war,
loftily calm in peace, irradiating the conscious superiority of power, dignity, worth,
and honourable renown. McCullough filled
that aspect of the part as if he had been
born for it. His movements had the splen-

did repose not merely of great strength but of intellectual poise and native mental supremacy. The " I must be found " air of Othello was again displayed, in ripe perfection, through the Roman toga. His declamation was as fluent and as massively graceful as his demeanour. If this actor had not the sonorous, clarion voice of John Kemble, he yet certainly suggested the tradition of the stately port and dominating step of that great master of the dramatic art. He looked Coriolanus, to the life. More of poetic freedom might have been wished, in the decorative treatment of the person — a touch of wildness in the hair, a tinge of imaginative exaltation in the countenance, an air of mischance in the gashes of combat. Still the embodiment was correct in its superficial conventionality ; and it certainly possessed affecting grandeur. Whenever there was opportunity for fine treatment, moreover, the actor seized and filled it, with the easy grace of unerring intuition and spontaneity. The delicacy of vocalism, the movement, the tone of sentiment, and the manliness of condition — the royal fibre of a great mind — in the act of withdrawal from the senate, was right and beautiful. It is difficult not to over-emphasise the

physical symbols of mental condition, in
the street scene with "the voices"; but
there again the actor denoted a fine spiritual
instinct.   To a situation like that of the
banishment he proved easily equal : indeed,
he gave that magnificent outburst of scorn
with tremendous power : but it was in the pathetic scene with Volumnia and Virgilia that
he reached the summit of the Shakespearean
conception.   The deep heart as well as the
imperial intellect of Coriolanus must then
speak.   It is, for the distracted son, a moment
of agonised and pathetic conflict : for McCullough it was a moment of perfect adequacy
and consummate success.   The stormy utterance of revolted pride and furious disgust,
in the denial of Volumnia's request — the
tempestuous outburst, "I will not do it"
— made as wild, fiery, and fine a moment
in tragic acting as could be imagined ; but
the climax was attained in the pathetic
cry —

"The gods look down, and this unnatural
    scene
  They laugh at."

XIII.

CHARLOTTE CUSHMAN.

MAKING, one summer day, a pilgrimage to the grave of Charlotte Cushman, I was guided to the place of her rest by one of the labourers employed about the cemetery, who incidentally pronounced upon the deceased a comprehensive and remarkable eulogium. "She was," he said, "considerable of a woman, for a play-actress." Well — she was. The place of her sepulture is on the east slope of the principal hill in Mount Auburn. Hard by, upon the summit of the hill, stands the gray tower that overlooks the surrounding region and constantly symbolises, to eyes both far and near, the perpetual peace of which it is at once guardian and image. All around the spot tall trees give shade and music, as the sun streams on their branches and the wind murmurs in their leaves. At a little distance, visible across green meadows and the river Charles, — full and calm between

its verdant banks, — rise the "dreaming
spires" of Cambridge. Further away,
crowned with her golden dome, towers old
Boston, the storied city that Charlotte
Cushman loved. Upon the spot where her
ashes now rest the great actress stood, and,
looking toward the city of her home and
heart, chose that to be the place of her
grave; and there she sleeps, in peace, after
many a conflict with her stormy nature and
after many sorrows and pains. What terrific ideals of the imagination she made to
be realities of life! What burning eloquence of poesy she made to blaze! What
moments of pathos she lived! What moods
of holy self-abnegation and of exalted
power she brought to many a sympathetic
soul! Standing by her grave, on which the
myrtle grows dense and dark, and over
which the small birds swirl and twitter in
the breezy silence, remembrance of the
busy scenes of brilliant life wherein she
used to move — the pictured stage, the
crowded theatre, the wild plaudits of a delighted multitude — came strongly on the
mind, and asked, in perplexity and sadness, what was the good of it all. To her
but little. Fame and wealth were her cold
rewards, after much privation and labour;

but she found neither love nor happiness, and the fullest years of her life were blighted with the shadow of fatal disease and impending death. To the world, however, her career was of great and enduring benefit. She was a noble interpreter of the noble minds of the past, and thus she helped to educate the men and women of her time — to ennoble them in mood, to strengthen them in duty, to lift them up in hope of immortality. She did not live in vain. It is not likely that the American people will ever suffer her name to drift quite out of their remembrance: it is a name that never can be erased from the rolls of honourable renown.

Charlotte Cushman was born on July 23, 1816, and she died on February 12, 1876. Boston was the place of her birth and of her death. She lived till her sixtieth year and she was for forty years an actress. Her youth was one of poverty and the early years of her professional career were full of labour, trouble, heart-ache, and conflict. The name of Cushman signifies " crossbearer," and certainly Charlotte Cushman did indeed bear the cross, long before and long after, she wore the crown. At first she was a vocalist, but, having broken her

voice by misusing it, she was compelled to
quit the lyric and adopt the dramatic stage,
and when nineteen years old she came out,
at New Orleans, as Lady Macbeth. After
that she removed to New York and for the
next seven years she battled with adverse
fortune in the theatres of that city and of
Albany and Philadelphia. From 1837 to
1840 she was under engagement at the old
Park as walking lady and for general utility
business. "I became aware," she wrote,
"that one could never sail a ship by entering at the cabin windows; he must serve
and learn his trade before the mast. This
was the way that I would henceforth learn
mine."

Her first remarkable hits were made in
Emilia, Meg Merrilies, and Nancy — the
latter in *Oliver Twist*. But it was not till
she met with Macready that the day of her
deliverance from drudgery really dawned.
They acted together in New York in 1842
and 1843, and in Boston in 1844, and in the
autumn of the latter year Miss Cushman
went to England, where, after much effort,
she obtained an opening in London, at the
Princess's, and in 1845 made her memorable success as Bianca. "Since the first
appearance of Edmund Kean, in 1814,"

o

said a London journal of that time, "never
has there been such a *début* on the stage
of an English theatre." Her engagement
lasted eighty-four nights (it was an engagement to act with Edwin Forrest), and she
recorded its result in a letter to her mother,
saying: "All my successes put together
since I have been upon the stage would not
come near my success in London, and I
only wanted some one of you here to enjoy
it with me, to make it complete." She
acted Bianca, Emilia, Lady Macbeth, Mrs.
Haller, and Rosalind. A prosperous provincial tour followed, and then, in December, 1845, she came out at the Haymarket,
as Romeo, her sister Susan appearing as
Juliet. Her stay abroad lasted till the end
of the summer of 1849, and to that period
belongs her great achievement as Queen
Katharine.

From the fall of 1849 till the spring of
1852 Miss Cushman was in America, and
she was everywhere received with acclamation, gathering with ease both laurels and
riches. When she first reappeared, October
8, 1849, at the old Broadway theatre, New
York — as Mrs. Haller — she introduced
Charles W. Couldock to our stage, on which
he has ever since maintained his rank as a

powerful and versatile actor. He acted the
Stranger and subsequently was seen in the
other leading characters opposite to her
own. Miss Cushman's repertory then included Lady Macbeth, Queen Katharine,
Meg Merrilies, Beatrice, Rosalind, Bianca,
Julia, Mariana, Katharine, the Countess,
Pauline, Juliana, Lady Gay Spanker, and
Mrs. Simpson. Her principal male characters then, or later, were Romeo, Wolsey,
Hamlet, and Claude Melnotte. In 1852 she
announced her intention of retiring from the
stage, and from that time till the end of her
days she wavered between retirement and
professional occupation. The explanation
of this is readily divined, in her condition.
There never was a time, during all those
years, when she was not haunted by dread
of the disease that ultimately destroyed her
life. From 1852 to 1857 she lived in England, and in the course of that period she
acted many times, in different cities. In
December 1854, when dining with the Duke
of Devonshire, at Brighton, she read *Henry
VIII.* to the Duke and his guests, and in
that way began her experience as a reader.
In the autumn of 1857 she acted at Burton's
theatre, New York, and was seen as Cardinal Wolsey, and in the early summer of

1858 she gave a series of "farewell" performances at Niblo's Garden — after which she again crossed the Atlantic and established her residence in Rome. In June 1860 the great actress came home again and passed a year in America. *Oliver Twist* was given at the Winter Garden in the spring of 1861, when Miss Cushman acted Nancy, and J. W. Wallack, Jr., J. B. Studley, William Davidge, and Owen Marlowe were in the company. In 1863, having come from Rome for that purpose, Miss Cushman acted in four cities, for the benefit of the United States Sanitary Commission, and earned for it $8267. The seven ensuing years were passed by her in Europe, but in October 1870 she returned home for the last time, and the brief remainder of her life was devoted to public readings, occasional dramatic performances, and the society of friends. She built a villa at Newport, which still bears her name. She gave final farewell performances, in the season of 1874–1875, in New York, Philadelphia, and Boston. Her final public appearance was made on June 2, 1875, at Easton, Pennsylvania, where she gave a reading. Her death occurred at the Parker House, in Boston, February 18, 1876, and she was buried from King's chapel.

There is a mournful pleasure in recalling the details of Miss Cushman's life and meditating upon her energetic, resolute, patient, creative nature. She was faithful, throughout her career, to high principles of art and a high standard of duty. Nature gave her great powers but fettered her also with great impediments. She conquered by the spell of a strange, weird genius and by hard, persistent labour. In this latter particular she is an example to every member of the dramatic profession, present or future. In what she was as a woman she could not be imitated — for her colossal individuality dwelt apart, in its loneliness, as well of suffering that no one could share as of an imaginative life that no one could fathom. Without the stage she would still have been a great woman, although perhaps she might have lacked an entirely suitable vehicle for the display of her powers. With the stage she gave a body to the soul of some of Shakespeare's greatest conceptions, and she gave soul and body both to many works of inferior origin. There is no likelihood that we shall ever see again such a creation as her Meg Merrilies. Her genius could embody the sublime, the beautiful, the terrible, and

with all this the humorous ; and it was
saturated with goodness. If the love of
beauty was intensified by the influence of
her art, virtue was also strengthened by
the force of her example and the inherent
dignity of her nature.

XIV.

ON THE DEATH OF LAWRENCE BARRETT.

[Obiit March 20, 1891.]

THE death of Lawrence Barrett was the
disappearance of one of the noblest figures of the modern stage.   During the
whole of his career, in a public life of
thirty-five years, he was steadily and continuously impelled by a pure and fine ambition and the objects that he sought to
accomplish were always the worthiest and
the best.   His devotion to the dramatic art
was a passionate devotion, and in an equal
degree he was devoted to a high ideal of
personal conduct.   Doctrines of expediency
never influenced him and indeed were
never considered by him.   He had early
fixed his eyes on the dramatic sceptre.   He
knew that it never could be gained except by the greatest and brightest of artistic achievements, and to them accordingly he consecrated his life.   Whenever
and wherever he appeared the community

was impressed with a sense of intellectual character, moral worth, and individual dignity. Many other dramatic efforts might be trivial. Those of Lawrence Barrett were always felt to be important. Most of the plays with which his name is identified are among the greatest plays in our language, and the spirit in which he treated them was that of exalted scholarship, austere reverence, and perfect refinement. He was profoundly true to all that is noble and beautiful, and because he was true the world of art everywhere recognised him as the image of fidelity and gave to him the high tribute of its unwavering homage. His coming was always a signal to arouse the mind. His mental vitality, which was very great, impressed even unsympathetic beholders with a sense of fiery thought struggling in its fetters of mortality and almost shattering and consuming the frail temple of its human life. His stately head, silvered with graying hair, his dark eyes deeply sunken and glowing with intense light, his thin visage pallid with study and pain, his form of grace and his voice of sonorous eloquence and solemn music (in compass, variety, and sweetness one of the few great voices of the current dramatic gen-

eration), his tremendous earnestness, his
superb bearing, and his invariable authority
and distinction — all those attributes united
to announce a ruler and leader in the realm
of the intellect. The exceeding tumult of
his spirit enhanced the effect of this mordant personality. The same sleepless energy that inspired Loyola and Lanfranc
burned in the bosom of this modern actor;
and it was entirely in keeping with the
drift of his character and the tenor of his
life that the last subject that occupied his
thoughts should have been the story of
Becket, the great prelate — whom he intended to represent, and to whom in mental qualities he was nearly allied. In losing
Lawrence Barrett the American stage lost
the one man who served it with an apostle's
zeal because he loved it with an apostle's
love.

The essential attributes that Lawrence
Barrett did not possess were enchantment
for the public and adequate and philosophic
patience for himself. He gained, indeed, a
great amount of public favour, and, — with
reference to an indisputable lack of universal sympathy and enthusiasm, — he was
learning to regard that as a natural consequence of his character which formerly he

had resented as the injustice of the world.
Men and women of austere mind do not fascinate their fellow-creatures. They impress
by their strangeness. They awe by their
majesty. They predominate by their power.
But they do not involuntarily entice. Lawrence Barrett, — although full of kindness
and gentleness, and, to those who knew
him well, one of the most affectionate and
lovable of men, — was essentially a man of
austere intellect; and his experience was
according to his nature. To some persons
the world gives everything, without being
asked to give at all. To others it gives only
what it must, and that with a kind of icy
reluctance that often makes the gift a bitter
one. Lawrence Barrett, who rose from an
obscure and humble position, — without
fortune, without friends, without favouring
circumstances, without education, without
help save that of his talents and his will, —
was for a long time met with indifference,
or frigid obstruction, or impatient dispar-
agement. He gained nothing without battle.
He had to make his way by his strength.
His progress involved continual effort and
his course was attended with continual controversy and strife. When at last it had to
be conceded that he was a great actor, the

concession was, in many quarters, grudgingly made. Even then detraction steadily followed him, and its voice — though impotent and immeasurably trivial — has not yet died away. There came a time when his worth was widely recognised, and from that moment onward he had much prosperity, and his nature expanded and grew calmer, sweeter, and brighter under its influence. But the habit of warfare had got into his acting, and more or less it remained there to the last. The assertive quality, indeed, had long since begun to die away. The volume of needless emphasis was growing less and less. Few performances on the contemporary stage are commensurate with his embodiments of Harebell and Gringoire, in softness, simplicity, poetic charm, and the gentle tranquillity that is the repose of a self-centred soul. But his deep and burning desire to be understood, his anxiety lest his effects should not be appreciated, his inveterate purpose of conquest, — that overwhelming solicitude of ambition often led him to insist upon his points, to over-elaborate and enforce them, and in that way his art to some extent defeated itself by the excess of its eager zeal. The spirit of beauty that the human race pursues is the spirit that is typified in Emerson's poem of *Forerunners* — the elusive spirit that all men feel and no man understands. This truth, undiscerned by him at first, had become the conviction of his riper years ; and if his life had been prolonged the autumn of his professional career would have been gentle, serene, and full of tranquil loveliness.

The achievement of Lawrence Barrett as an actor was great, but his influence upon the stage was greater than his achievement. Among the Shakespearian parts that he played were Hamlet, Macbeth, King Lear, Othello, Iago, Shylock, Leontes, Cassius, Wolsey, Richard III., Romeo, and Benedick. Outside of Shakespeare (to mention only a few of his impersonations) he acted Richelieu, Evelyn, Aranza, Garrick, Claude Melnotte, Rienzi, Dan'l Druce, Lanciotto, Hernani, King Arthur, and Ganelon. The parts in which he was superlatively fine, — and in some respects incomparable, — are Cassius, Harebell, Yorick, Gringoire, King Arthur, Ganelon, and James V., King of the Commons. In his time he had played hundreds of parts, ranging over the whole field of the drama, but as the years passed and the liberty of choice came more and

more within his reach, he concentrated his
powers upon a few works and upon a specific
line of expression. The aspect of human
nature and human experience that especially
aroused his sympathy was the loneliness of
beneficent intellectual grandeur, isolated
by its supremacy and pathetic in its isolation. He loved the character of Richelieu,
and if he had acted Becket, as he purposed
to do, in Tennyson's tragedy, he would
have presented another and a different type
of that same ideal — lonely, austere, passionate age, defiant of profane authority and
protective of innocent weakness against
wicked and cruel strength. His embodiment of Cassius, with all its intensity of
repressed spleen and caustic malevolence,
was softly touched and sweetly ennobled
with the majesty of venerable loneliness, —
the bleak light of pathetic sequestration
from human ties, without the forfeiture of
human love, — that is the natural adjunct
of intellectual greatness. He loved also the
character of Harebell, because in that he
could express his devotion to the beautiful,
the honest impulses of his affectionate heart,
and his ideal of a friendship that is too pure
and simple even to dream that such a thing
as guile can exist anywhere in the world.

Toward the expression, under dramatic conditions, of natures such as those, the development of his acting was steadily directed ; and, even if he fell short, in any degree, of accomplishing all that he purposed, it is certain that his spirit and his conduct dignified the theatrical profession, strengthened the stage in the esteem of good men, and cheered the heart and fired the energy of every sincere artist that came within the reach of his example. For his own best personal success he required a part in which, after long repression, the torrent of passion can break loose in a tumult of frenzy and a wild strain of eloquent words. The terrible exultation of Cassius, after the fall of Cæsar, the ecstasy of Lanciotto when he first believes himself to be loved by Francesca, the delirium of Yorick when he can no longer restrain the doubts that madden his jealous and wounded soul, the rapture of King James over the vindication of his friend Seyton, whom his suspicions have wronged — those were among his distinctively great moments, and his image as he was in such moments is worthy to live among the storied traditions and the bright memories of the stage.

Censure seems to be easy to most people,

and few men are rated at their full value while they are yet alive. Just as mountains seem more sublime in the vague and hazy distance, so a noble mind looms grandly through the dusk of death. So it will be with him. Lawrence Barrett was a man of high principle and perfect integrity. He never spoke a false word nor knowingly harmed a human being, in all his life. Although sometimes he seemed to be harsh and imperious, he was at heart kind and humble. Strife with the world, and in past times uncertainty as to his position, caused in him the assumption of a stern and frigid manner, but beneath that haughty reserve there was a great longing for human affection and a sincere humility of spirit. He never nurtured hostility. He had no memory for injuries; but a kindness he never forgot. His good deeds were as numerous as his days — for no day rolled over his head without its act of benevolence in one direction or another. He was as impulsive as a child. He had much of the woman in his nature, and therefore his views were impetuous, strong, and often strongly stated; but his sense of humour kept pace with his sensibility and so maintained the equilibrium of his mind. In

temperament he was sad, pensive, intro-
spective, almost gloomy; but he opposed
to that tendency an incessant mental activity and the force of a tremendous will.
In his lighter moods he was not only appreciative of mirth but was the cause of it.
His humour was elemental and whatever
aspect of life he saw in a comic light he
could set in that light before the eyes of
others.   He had been a studious reader for
many years and his mind was stored with
ample, exact, and diversified information.
He had a scholar's knowledge of Roman
history and his familiar acquaintance with
the character and career of the first Napo-
leon was extraordinary.   In acting he was
largely influenced by his studies of Edmund
Kean and by his association with Charlotte
Cushman.   For a few years after 1864 his
art was especially affected by that of Edwin
Booth; but the style to which he finally
gravitated was his own.   He was not so
much an impersonator as he was an interpreter of character, and the elocutionary
part of acting was made more conspicuous
and important by him than by any other
tragedian since the days of Forrest and
Brooke.

It was a beautiful life prematurely ended.

It was a brave, strong spirit suddenly called out of the world. To the dramatic profession the loss is irreparable. In the condition of the contemporary theatre there are not many hopeful signs. No doubt there will be bright days in the future, as there have been in the past. They go and they return. The stage declines and the stage advances. At present its estate is low. Few men like Lawrence Barrett remain for it to lose. Its main hope is in the abiding influence of such examples as he has left. The old theatrical period is fast passing away. The new age rushes on the scene, with youthful vigour and impetuous tumult. But to some of us, — who perhaps have not long to stay, and to whom, whatever be their fortune, this tumult is unsympathetic and insignificant, — the way grows darker and lonelier as we lay our garlands of eternal farewell upon the coffin of Lawrence Barrett.

P

XV.

HENRY IRVING AND ELLEN TERRY IN RAVENSWOOD.

MERIVALE'S play of *Ravenswood*, written in four acts, was acted in six. The first act consists of a single scene — an exterior, showing the environment of the chapel which is the burial place of the House of Ravenswood. A rockbound coast is visible, at some distance, together with the ruinous tower of Wolf's Crag — which is Ravenswood's sole remaining possession. This act presents the interrupted funeral of Alan Ravenswood, the father of Edgar, — introducing ten of the seventeen characters that are implicated in the piece, and skilfully laying the basis of the action by exhibiting the essential personalities of the story in strong contrast, and denoting their relations to each other. Each character is clearly and boldly drawn and with a light touch. The second act consists of three scenes — an antique library in the ancient manor-house of Ravenswood, a room in a roadside ale-house, and a room in the dilapidated tower of Wolf's Crag. This act rapidly develops the well-known story, depicting the climax of antagonism between the Lord Keeper Ashton and Edgar of Ravenswood and their subsequent reconciliation. The third act passes in a lovely, romantic, rural scene, which is called "the Mermaiden's Well," — a fairy-like place in the grounds of Ravenswood, — and in this scene Edgar and Lucy Ashton, who have become lovers, are plighted by themselves and parted by Lucy's mother, Lady Ashton. The fourth and last act shows a room at Ravenswood, wherein is portrayed the betrothal of Lucy to Bucklaw, culminating in Edgar's sudden irruption; and finally, it shows the desolate seaside place of the quicksand in which, after he has slain Bucklaw, Edgar of Ravenswood is engulfed. The house that Scott, when he wrote the novel, had in his mind as that of Sir William Ashton is the house of Winston, which still is standing, not many miles from Edinburgh. The tower of Wolf's Crag was probably suggested to him by Fast Castle, the ruin of which still lures the traveller's eye, upon the iron-ribbed and gloomy coast

of the North Sea, a few miles southeast
of Dunbar — a place, however, that Scott
never visited, and never saw except from
the ocean.   There is a beach upon that
coast, just above Cockburnspath, that might
well have suggested to him the quicksand
and the final catastrophe.   I saw it when
the morning sun was shining upon it and
upon the placid waters just rippling on its
verge; and even in the glad glow of a summer day it was grim with silent menace
and mysterious with an air of sinister
secrecy.   In the preparation of this piece
for the stage all the sources and associations of the subject were considered ; and
the pictorial setting, framed upon the right
artistic principle — that imagination should
transfigure truth and thus produce the
essential result of poetic effect — was elaborate and magnificent.   And the play is
the best one that ever has been made upon
this subject.

The basis of fact upon which Sir Walter
Scott built his novel of the *Bride of Lammermoor* is given in the introduction that
he wrote for it in 1829.   Janet Dalrymple,
daughter of the first Lord Stair and of his
wife Margaret Ross, had privately plighted
herself to Lord Rutherford.   Those lovers

had broken a piece of gold together, and
had bound themselves by vows the most
solemn and fervent that passion could
prompt. But Lord Rutherford was objec-
tionable to Miss Dalrymple's parents, who
liked not either his family or his politics.
Lady Stair, furthermore, had selected a
husband for her daughter, in the person of
David Dunbar, of Baldoon; and Lady Stair
was a woman of formidable character, set
upon having her own way and accustomed
to prevail.   As soon as she heard of Janet's
private engagement to Lord Rutherford she
declared the vow to be undutiful and un-
lawful and she commanded that it should
be broken.   Lord Rutherford, a man of
energy and of spirit, thereupon insisted
that he would take his dismissal only from
the lips of Miss Dalrymple herself, and he
demanded and obtained an interview with
her.   Lady Stair was present, and such was
her ascendency over her daughter's mind
that the young lady remained motionless
and mute, permitting her betrothal to Lord
Rutherford to be broken, and, upon her
mother's command, giving back to him the
piece of gold that was the token of her
promise.   Lord Rutherford was deeply
moved, so that he uttered curses upon Lady

Stair, and at the last reproached Janet in these words : " For you, madam, you will be a world's wonder." After this sad end of his hopes the unfortunate gentleman went abroad and died in exile. Janet Dalrymple and David Dunbar meanwhile were married — the lady " being absolutely passive in everything her mother commanded or advised." As soon, however, as the wedded pair had retired from the bridal feast hideous shrieks were heard to resound through the house, proceeding from the nuptial chamber. The door was thereupon burst open and persons entering saw the bridegroom stretched upon the floor, wounded and bleeding, while the bride, dishevelled and stained with blood, was grinning in a paroxysm of insanity. All she said was, " Take up your bonny bridegroom." About two weeks later she died. The year of those events was 1669. The wedding took place on August 24. Janet died on September 12. Dunbar recovered, but he would never tell what occurred in that chamber of horror, nor indeed would he permit any allusion to the subject. He did not long survive the tragic event, — having been fatally injured, by a fall from his horse, when riding between Leith and

Holyrood. He died on March 28, 1682.
The death of Lord Rutherford is assigned
to the year 1685. Such is the melancholy
story as it may be gathered from Scott's
preface. In writing his novel that great
master of the art of fiction, — never yet dis-
placed from his throne or deprived of his
sceptre, — adopted fictitious names, invented
fresh circumstances, amplified and elevated
the characters, judiciously veiled the locali-
ties, and advanced the period of those tragical incidents to about the beginning of the
eighteenth century. The delicate taste with
which he used his materials has only been
surpassed, in that beautiful composition, by
the affluent genius with which he vitalised
every part of his narrative. In no other of
his many books has he shown a deeper
knowledge than is revealed in that one of
the terrible passion of love and of the dark
and sinuous ways of political and personal
craft. When *The Bride of Lammermoor*
was first published no mention was made
in it of the true story upon which remotely
it had been based ; but by the time Scott
came to write the preface of 1829 other
writers had been less reticent, and some
account of the Dalrymple tragedy had got
into print, so that no reason existed for
further silence on that subject.

Sir Robert H. D. Elphinstone, writing in 1829, gave the tradition as follows: "When, after the noise and violent screaming in the bridal chamber comparative stillness succeeded and the door was forced, the window was found open, and it was supposed by many that the lover, Lord Rutherford, had, by the connivance of some of the servants, found means, during the bustle of the marriage feast, to secrete himself within the apartment, and that soon after the entry of the married pair, or at least as soon as the parents and others retreated and the door was made fast, he had come out from his concealment, attacked and desperately wounded the bridegroom, and then made his escape, by the window, through the garden. As the unfortunate bride never spoke after having uttered the words mentioned by Sir Walter, no light could be thrown on the matter by them. But it was thought that Dunbar's obstinate silence on the subject favoured the supposition of the chastisement having been inflicted by his rival. It is but fair to give the unhappy victim (who was, by all accounts, a most gentle and feminine creature) the benefit of an explanation on a doubtful point."

Merivale, in dealing with this story, gave

a conspicuous illustration of the essential dramatic faculty. The first act is the adroit expansion of a few paragraphs, in the second chapter of the novel, which are descriptive of the bleak, misty November morning when Alan Ravenswood was borne to the grave; but by the introduction of the Lord Keeper and of the village crones into that funeral scene he opened the whole subject, indicated all the essential antecedents of the story, and placed his characters in a posture of lively action. That the tone is sombre must be conceded, and people who think that the chief end of man is to grin might condemn the piece for that reason; but *Ravenswood* is a tragedy and not a farce, and persons who wish that their feelings may not be affected should avoid tragedies.

In the second act Ravenswood seeks Ashton at Ravenswood manor, intending to kill him in a duel, but his hand is stayed when he catches sight of Lucy Ashton's portrait. The incident of Edgar's rescue of Lucy is used in this scene. In a later scene Sir William Ashton and his daughter take refuge in Wolf's Crag, and the bewitchment of Ravenswood is accomplished. The quarrel between Edgar and Bucklaw

is then given, as a basis for the ensuing rivalry and deadly conflict between
them. In the third act there is a beautiful
love-scene between Edgar and Lucy, the
dialogue being especially felicitous in tenderness and grace and fraught with that
reverential quality, that condition of commingled ecstasy and nobleness, which is
always characteristic of the experience of
this passion in pure natures. Lady Ashton's interruption of their happiness and
the subsequent parting have a vigorous
dramatic effect. The character of Lucy
has been much strengthened, so that it
differs from that of the original precisely
as Desdemona differs from Ophelia ; and
the change is an improvement. The fourth
act opens with "a song of choristers heard
outside." The letters of Lucy and Edgar
have been intercepted. The lady has been
told that her lover is false. The suit of
Bucklaw has been urged. The authority
of the stern mother has prevailed over her
daughter's will. It is the old story. "The
absent are always wrong" — and Ravenswood is absent. Lucy Ashton yields to her
fate. The marriage contract between Lucy
and Bucklaw has just been signed when Ravenswood bursts into the group. From that

point the action is animated equally with celerity and passion. The misery of Ravenswood utters itself in a swift stream of burning words. The grief of Lucy ends tragically in a broken heart and sudden death. The fight between Bucklaw and Ravenswood clashes for a moment but is abruptly finished on the moonlit sands, and Edgar is seen to leap down from a rock and rush away toward the manor, where, as his dying foe has told him, the faithful and innocent Lucy lies dead. He disappears and comes no more; but his old servant takes up from the beach a single black plume — the feather of a raven — which the tide has washed ashore, and which is the last relic and emblem of the vanished master of Ravenswood.

The tragedy is kindred, as to its spirit, with *Romeo and Juliet,* and like that representative poem of love and death it is intensely passionate, sombre, and lamentable. The first and second acts of it pass in almost unrelieved shadow. It begins with a funeral; it incorporates the ingredients of misery, madness, and death; it culminates in a fatal duel; and it ends in a picture of mortal desolation, qualified only by a mute suggestion of spiritual happiness conveyed by the pictorial emblem of the promise of

immortality. It is a poetical tragedy, conceived in the spirit and written in the manner of the old masters of the poetic art.
The treatment of Scott's novel is marked
by scrupulous fidelity, not indeed to every
detail of that noble book, but to its essential quality and tone. The structure of the
play reproduces in action substantially the
structure of the original story. The scene
in which Edgar and Lucy avow their love
and pledge themselves to each other is
written with exquisite grace and profound
tenderness. The picture presented upon
the stage when the lovers are parted was
one of astonishing animation. The scene
of the interrupted wedding and of Lucy
Ashton's agony, distraction, and death was
one of intense power and dramatic effect.
The duel of Ravenswood and Bucklaw upon
the desolate, moon-lit sands was invested
with the excitement of suspense and with
weird horror. And the final exposition of
dramatic contrast, — when upon the wide,
bleak beach, with the waste of vacant sea beyond and the eastern heaven lit with the first
splendour of sunrise, the old man stooped
to take up the raven's feather, the last relic
of Ravenswood — was so entirely beautiful
that the best of words can but poorly indi-

cate its loveliness. For an audience able
to look seriously at a serious subject, and
not impatient of the foreground of gloom
in which, necessarily, the story is enveloped
at its beginning, this was a perfect work.
The student of drama must go back many
years to find a parallel to it, in interest of
subject, in balance, in symmetry, and in
sympathetic interpretation of character.

There is a quality of Hamlet in the character of Ravenswood. He is by nature a
man of a sad mind, and under the pressure
of afflicting circumstances his sadness has
become embittered. He takes life thought-
fully and with passionate earnestness. He
is a noble person, finely sensitive and absolutely sincere, full of kindness at heart, but
touched with gloom ; and his aspect and
demeanour are those of pride, trouble, self-
conflict — of an individuality isolated and
constrained by dark thoughts and painful experience. That is the mood in which Henry
Irving conceived and portrayed him. You
saw a picturesque figure, dark, strange, romantic — the gravity engendered by thought
and sorrow not yet marring the bronzed face
and the elastic movement of youth — and
this personality, in itself fascinating, was
made all the more pictorial by an investiture

of romance, alike in the scenery and the incidents through which it moved. Around
such a figure funereal banners well might
wave, and under dark and lowering skies
the chill wind of the sea might moan
through monastic ruins and crumbling bat-
tlements. Edgar of Ravenswood, standing
by his lonely hearth, beneath the groined
arches of his seaside tower, revealed by the
flickering firelight, looked the ideal of romantic manhood ; the incarnation of poetic
fancy and of predestinate disaster. Above
the story of *Ravenswood* there is steadily
and continuously impending, and ever growing darker and coming nearer, the vague
menace of terrible calamity. This element
of mystery and dread was wrought into the
structural fibre of Henry Irving's performance of the part, and consistently coloured
it. The face of Edgar was made to wear
that haunted look which, — as in the countenance of Charles the First, in Vandyke's
portraits, — may be supposed, and often
has been supposed, to foreshadow a violent
and dreadful death. His sudden tremor,
when at the first kiss of Lucy Ashton the
thunder is heard to break above his ruined
home, was a fine denotement of that subtle
quality ; and even through the happiness of

the betrothal scene there was a hint of this
black presentiment — just as sometimes on
a day of perfect sunshine there is a chill in
the wind that tells of approaching storm.
All this is warranted by the prophetic
rhymes which are several times spoken, beginning — " When the last lord of Ravenswood to Ravenswood shall ride." A crone,
Ailsie Gourlay by name, embodied with grim
and grisly vigour by Alice Marriott, — whose
ample voice and exact elocution, together
with her formidable stature and her faculty
of identification with the character that she
assumes and with the spirit of the story,
made her of great value to this play — hov-
ered around Ravenswood, and aided to keep
this presage of evil doom fitfully present
in the consciousness of its victim. Henry
Irving gave to the part its perfectly distinct
individuality, and in that respect made as
fine a showing as he has ever made of his
authority as an actor. There was never the
least doubt as to what Ravenswood is and
what he means. The peculiar elocution of
Henry Irving, when he is under the influence of great excitement, is not effective
upon all persons ; but those who like it
consider it far more touching than a more
level, more sonorous, and more accurate

delivery. He wrought a great effect in the
scene of the marriage-contract. Indeed, so
powerful, sincere, and true was the acting
upon all sides, at this point, that not until
the curtain began to descend was it remembered that we were looking upon a fiction
and not upon a fact. This points to the
peculiar power that Henry Irving and Ellen
Terry conspicuously possess — of creating
and maintaining a perfect illusion.

During the earlier scenes the character of
Lucy Ashton is chiefly marked by the qualities of sweetness and of glee. No one acquainted with the acting of Ellen Terry
would need to be told how well and with
what charming grace those qualities were
expressed by her. In the scene of the wooing, at the Mermaiden's Well, Lucy Ashton
was not a cold woman trying to make herself loved, — which is what most actresses
habitually proffer upon the stage, — but a
loving woman, radiant with the consciousness of the love that she feels and has inspired. Nothing could be imagined more
delicate, more delicious, more enchanting
than the high-bred distinction and soft
womanlike tone of that performance. The
character, at the climax of this scene, is
made to manifest decision, firmness, and

force; and the superb manner in which she
set the maternal authority at naught and
stood by her lover might seem to denote a
nature that no tyranny could subdue. Subdued, however, she is, and forced to believe
ill of her absent lover, and so the fatal
marriage contract is signed and the crash
follows. When Ellen Terry came on for
that scene the glee had all vanished; the
face was as white as the garments that en-
swathed her; and you saw a creature whom
the hand of death had visibly touched. The
stage has not at any time heard from any
lips but her own such tones of pathos as
those in which she said the simple words :—

"May God forgive you, then, and pity me —
  If God can pity more than mothers do."

It is not a long scene, and happily not, —
for the strain upon the emotion of the actress
was intense. The momentary wild merriment, the agony of the breaking heart, the
sudden delirium and collapse, were not for
an instant exaggerated. All was nature —
or rather the simplicity, fidelity, and grace
of art that make the effect of nature.

Beautiful scenery, painted by Craven,
framed the piece with appropriate magnificence. The several seaside pictures were

Q

admirably representative of the grandeur, the gaunt loneliness, and the glorious colour for which Scotland is so much loved.

The public gain in that production was a revival of interest in one of the most famous novels in the language; the possession of a scenical pageant that filled the eye with beauty and strongly moved the imagination; a play that is successful in the domain of romantic poetry; a touching exemplification of the great art of acting; and once again the presentment of that vast subject, — the relation of heart to heart, under the dominion of love, in human society, — that more absorbs the attention, affects the character, and controls the destiny of the human race than anything else that is beneath the sun.

XVI.

THE MERRY WIVES AND FALSTAFF.

SHAKESPEARE wrote *The Merry Wives of Windsor* in 1601, and during the Christmas holidays of that year it was presented upon the stage, before Queen Elizabeth and her court, at Windsor Castle. In 1602 it was published in London in quarto form, and in 1619 a reprint of that quarto was published there. The version that appears in the two quartos is considered by Shakespeare scholars to be spurious. The authentic text, no doubt, is that of the comedy as it stands in the first folio (1623). Shakespeare had written *Henry IV.* — both parts of it — and also *Henry V.*, when this comedy was acted, and therefore he had completed his portrait of Falstaff, whose life is displayed in the former piece and whose death is described in the latter. *Henry IV.* was first printed in 1598 (we know not when it was first acted), and it passed through five quarto editions prior to

the publication of it in the folio of 1623. In
the epilogue to the second part of that play
a promise is made that the story shall be
continued, " with Sir John in it," but it is
gravely doubted whether that epilogue was
written by Shakespeare. The continuation
of the story occurs in *Henry V.*, in which
Falstaff does not figure, although he is mentioned in it. Various efforts have been
made to show a continuity between the
several plays in which Falstaff is implicated, but the attempt always fails. The
histories contain the real Falstaff. The
Falstaff of the comedy is another and less
important man. If there really were a sequence of story and of time in the portraiture of this character the plays would stand
in the following order: 1, *Henry IV., Part
First;* 2, *The Merry Wives of Windsor;*
3, *Henry IV., Part Second;* 4, *Henry V.*
As no such sequence exists, or apparently
was intended, the comedy should be viewed
by itself. Its texture is radically different
from that of the histories. One of the
best Shakespeare editors, Charles Knight,
ventures the conjecture that *The Merry
Wives of Windsor* was written first. Shakespeare invented the chief part of the plot,
taking, however, a few things from Tarl-

ton's *Newes out of Purgatorie*, which in turn was founded on a story called *The Lovers of Pisa*. It is possible also that he may have derived suggestions from a German play by Duke Henry Julius of Brunswick — a contemporary, who died in 1611 — to which *The Merry Wives of Windsor* bears some resemblance, and of which he may have received an account from English actors who had visited Germany, as the actors of his time occasionally did.

Tradition declares that he wrote this comedy at the command of Queen Elizabeth, who had expressed a wish to see Falstaff in love. This was first stated by John Dennis, in the preface to an alteration of *The Merry Wives of Windsor* which was made by him, under the name of *The Comical Gallant, or the Amours of Sir John Falstaff*, and was successfully acted at Drury Lane theatre. That piece, which is paltry and superfluous, appeared in 1702. No authority was given by Dennis for his statement about Queen Elizabeth and Shakespeare's play. The tradition rests exclusively on his word. Rowe, Pope, Theobald, and other Shakespeare editors, have transmitted it to the present day, but it rests on nothing but supposition

and it is dubious.   Those scholars who accept the story of Dennis, and believe that
Shakespeare wrote the piece "to order"
and within a few days, usually fortify their
belief by the allegation that the comedy
falls short of Shakespeare's poetical standard, being written mostly in prose ; that it
degrades his great creation of Falstaff;
that it is, for him, a trivial production ;
and that it must have been written in
haste and without spontaneous impulse.   If
judgment were to be given on the quarto
version of *The Merry Wives*, that reasoning would commend itself as at least plausible ; but it is foolish as applied to the version
in the folio, where the piece is found to be
remarkable for nimbleness of invention,
strength and variety of natural character,
affluent prodigality of animal spirits, delicious quaintness, exhilarating merriment,
a lovely pastoral tone, and many touches of
the transcendent poetry of Shakespeare.
Dennis probably repeated a piece of idle
gossip that he had heard, the same sort of
chatter that in the present day constantly
follows the doings of theatrical people, —
and is not accurate more than once in a
thousand times. *The Merry Wives of Windsor* is a brilliant and delightful comedy,

quite worthy of its great author (though not
in his most exalted mood), who probably
wrote it because his mind was naturally
impelled to write it, and no doubt laboured
over it exactly as he did over his other writings : for we know, upon the testimony of
Ben Jonson, who personally knew him
and was acquainted with his custom as a
writer, that he was not content with the
first draught of anything, but wrote it a
second time, and a third time, before he
became satisfied with it. Dr. Johnson,
who had studied Shakespeare as carefully
as any man ever studied him, speaking of
The Merry Wives of Windsor, says that
"its general power — that power by which
all works of genius should finally be tried
— is such that perhaps it never yet had
reader or spectator who did not think it too
soon at an end." A comedy that deserves
such praise as this — which assuredly is
not misplaced — need not be dismissed as a
pot-boiler.

Knight's conjecture that *The Merry
Wives* was written before the histories
were written is a plausible conjecture, and
perhaps worthy of some consideration. It
is not easy to believe that Shakespeare,
after he had created Falstaff and thoroughly

drawn him, was capable of lessening the character and making it almost despicable with paltriness — as certainly it becomes in *The Merry Wives.* That is not the natural way of an artistic mind. But it is easier to credit the idea that the Falstaff of *The Merry Wives* was the first study of the character, although not first shown, which subsequently expanded into the magnificent humorous creation of the histories. Falstaff in the comedy is a fat man with absurd amorous propensities, who is befooled, victimised, and made a laughing-stock by a couple of frolicsome women, who are so much amused by his preposterous folly that they scarcely bestow the serious consideration of contempt and scorn upon his sensuality and insolence. No creature was ever set in a more ludicrous light or made more contemptible, — in a kindly, good-humoured way. The hysterical note of offended virtue is never sounded, nor is anywhere seen the averted face of shocked propriety. The two wives are bent on a frolic, and they will merrily punish this presumptuous sensualist — this silly, conceited, gross fellow, "old, cold, withered, and of intolerable entrails." If we knew no more of Falstaff

than the comedy tells us of him we should
by no means treasure him as we do now ;
but it is through the histories that we
learn to know and appreciate him, and it is
of the man portrayed there that we always
unconsciously think when, in his humiliat-
ing discomfiture, we hear him declare that
" wit may be made a Jack-a-lent when 'tis
upon ill employment." For the Falstaff
of the histories is a man of intellect,
wisdom, and humour, thoroughly experienced in the ways of the world, fascinating in his drollery, human, companionable,
infinitely amusing, and capable of turning
all life to the favour of enjoyment and
laughter — a man who is passionate in the
sentiment of comradeship, and who, with
all his faults (and perhaps because of some
of them, for faultless persons are too good
for this world), inspires affection. " Would
I were with him," cries the wretched Bardolph, " wheresome'er he is, either in
heaven or in hell." It is not Bardolph
only whose heart has a warm corner for
the memory of the poor old jovial sinner,
wounded to death by the falling off of
friendship — the implacable hardness of
new-born virtue in the regenerated royal
mind.

A comprehensive view of Falstaff — a view that includes the afflicting circumstances of his humiliation and of his forlorn and pathetic death not less than the roistering frolics and jocund mendacity of his life and character — is essential to a right appreciation of the meaning of him. Shakespeare is never a prosy moralist, but he constantly teaches you, if you have eyes to see and ears to hear, that the moral law of the universe, working continually for goodness and not for evil, operates in an inexorable manner. Yet it is not of any moral consideration that the spectator of Falstaff upon the stage ever pauses to think. It is the humour of the fat knight that is perceived, and that alone. The thoughtful friends of Falstaff, however, see more in him than this, and especially they like not to think of him in a deplorable predicament. The Falstaff of *The Merry Wives* is a man to laugh at; but he is not a man to inspire the comrade feeling, and still less is he a man to impress the intellect with the sense of a stalwart character and of illimitable jocund humour. Falstaff's friends — whose hearts are full of kindness for the old reprobate — have sat with him "in my Dolphin chamber, at the round table, by a sea-coal fire," and "have heard the chimes at midnight" in his society, and they know what a jovial companion he is — how abundant in knowledge of the world ; how radiant with animal spirits ; how completely inexhaustible in cheerfulness ; how copious in comic invective ; how incessantly nimble and ludicrous in wit and in waggery ; how strange a compound of mind and sensuality, shrewdness and folly, fidelity and roguery, brazen mendacity, and comic selfishness ! They do not like to think of him as merely a fat old fool, bamboozled by a pair of sprightly, not over-delicate women, far inferior to him in mental calibre, and made a laughing-stock for Fenton and sweet Anne Page, and the lads and lassies of Windsor, and the chattering Welsh parson. "Have I lived," cried Falstaff, in the moment of his discomfiture, "to stand at the taunt of one that makes fritters of English ? " He is a hard case, an inveterate sinner, as worthless as any man well could be, in the eyes of decorum and respectability ; but those who know him well grow to be fond of him, even if they feel that they ought to be ashamed of it, and they do not quite forgive the poet for making him contemptible.

You can find many other figures that will make you laugh, but you can find no other figure that makes you laugh with such good reason. It seems incredible that Shakespeare, with his all-embracing mind and his perfect instinct of art, should deliberately have chosen to lessen his own masterpiece of humour. For Shakespeare rejoiced in Falstaff, even while he respected and recorded the inexorable justice of the moral law that decrees and eventually accomplishes his destruction. There is no one of his characters whose history he has traced with such minute elaboration. The conception is singularly ample. You may see Falstaff, as Shallow saw him, when he was a boy and page to Thomas Mowbray, Duke of Norfolk; you may see him all along the current of his mature years; his highway robberies on Gadshill; his bragging narrative to Prince Henry; his frolicsome, paternal, self-defensive lecture to the prince; his serio-comic association with the ragamuffin recruits at Coventry; his adroit escape from the sword of Hotspur; his mendacious self-glorification over the body of Harry Percy; his mishaps as a suitor to Mrs. Ford and Mrs. Page ; his wonderfully humorous interviews with the Chief-Justice and with Prince John of Lancaster ; his junketings with Justice Shallow in Gloucestershire, and his rebuff and consternation at his first and last meeting with King Henry V. ; and finally you may see him, as Mrs. Quickly saw him, on his death-bed, when "'a cried out God ! God ! God ! three or four times," and when "his nose was as sharp as a pen, and 'a babbled o' green fields."

A good and faithful study of *King Henry IV.*, and especially of the second part of that play, is essential for a right appreciation of Falstaff. Those scenes with the Chief-Justice are unmatched in literature. The knight stands royally forth in them, clothed with his entire panoply of agile intellect, robust humour, and boundless comic effrontery. But the arrogant and expeditious Falstaff of *The Merry Wives* — so richly freighted with rubicund sensuality, so abundant in comic loquacity, and so ludicrous in his sorry plights — is a much less complex person, and therefore he stands more level than the real Falstaff does with the average comprehension of mankind. The American stage, accordingly, by which more than by the printed book he has become known to our people, has usually given its preference to the Falstaff of the comedy. *The Merry Wives* was first acted in New York on October 5, 1788 at the John Street theatre, with Harper as Falstaff. On April 1, 1807 it was produced at the old Park, and the Falstaff then was Jóhn E. Harwood. The same stage offered it again on January 15, 1829, with Hilson as Falstaff. A little later, about 1832, James H. Hackett took up the character of Falstaff, and from that time onward performances of *The Merry Wives* occurred more frequently in different cities of America. Nor was the historical play neglected. On August 7, 1848 a remarkably fine production of the comedy was accomplished at the Astor Place Opera-house, New York, with Hackett as Falstaff, who never in his time was equalled in that character, and has not been equalled since. Another Falstaff, however, and a remarkably good one, appeared at Burton's theatre on August 24, 1850, in the person of Charles Bass. On March 14, 1853 *The Merry Wives* was again given at Burton's theatre, and Burton himself played Falstaff, with characteristic humour ; but Bur-

ton never acted the part as it stands in
Henry IV. Hackett, who used both the
history (Part I.) and the comedy, continued
to act Falstaff almost to the end of his life
and Hackett did not die till 1871. A distinguished representative of Falstaff in the
early days of the American theatre — the
days of the renowned Chestnut in Philadelphia — was William Warren (1767–1832),
who came from England in 1796. In
recent years the part has been acted by
Benedict De Bar and by John Jack. The
latest Falstaff in America was that embodied
by Charles Fisher, who first assumed the
character on November 19, 1872, at Daly's
theatre, and whose performance was picturesque and humorous.

On the English stage the historical play
of *Henry IV.* was exceedingly popular in
Shakespeare's time. The first Falstaff, according to Malone, whom everybody has
followed as to this point, was John Heminge (1555–1630). After him came John
Lowin (1572–1654), who is thought to have
acted the part in the presence of Charles I.
His successor seems to have been Lacy,
who died in 1681. Next came Cartwright,
and in 1699 or 1700 the great Betterton
(1635–1710) assumed the fat knight, acting

him in both parts of the history and in the comedy. Genest records twenty-two revivals of the first part of *Henry IV.* upon the London stage, at five different theatres, between 1667 and 1826 ; fifteen revivals of the second part between 1720 and 1821 ; and sixteen revivals of *The Merry Wives of Windsor* between 1667 and 1811. Many English actors have played Falstaff since Betterton's time, an incomplete though sufficiently ample list of them comprising Estcourt, 1704 ; F. Bullock, 1713 ; J. Evans and J. Hall, 1715 ; Mills, 1716 ; Quin, "dignity and declamation," 1738 ; Berry, 1747 ; Love (whose true name was James Dance), 1762 ; Shuter, 1774 ; John Henderson, one of the greatest actors that ever lived, 1774 ; Mrs. Webb (once only), 1776 ; Ryder, 1786 ; Palmer, 1788 ; King, 1792 ; Fawcett, 1795 ; Stephen Kemble, who was so fat that he could play it without stuffing or bladder, 1802 ; Blissett, 1803 ; George Frederick Cooke, 1804 ; Bartley, 1812 ; Charles Kemble, 1824 ; Dowton, 1824 ; Elliston, 1826 ; and Samuel Phelps, 1846. The latest representative of Falstaff in England was H. Beerbohm-Tree, who, although a man of slender figure, contrived to simulate corpulence, and who

manifested in his acting a fine instinct
as to the meaning of the character and
considerable resources of art in its expression, although the predominant individuality and the copious luxuriance of
Falstaff's rosy and juicy humour were not
within his reach. Upon the American stage
the part is practically disused; and this is
a pity, seeing that a source of great enjoyment and one of the most suggestive and
fruitful topics that exist in association with
the study of human nature are thus in a
great degree sequestered from the public
mind. Still it is better to have no Falstaff
on the stage than to have it encumbered
with a bad one; and certainly for the peculiar and exacting play of *Henry IV.* there
are now no actors left: at least they are
not visible in America.

R

XVII.

ADA REHAN.

IN browsing over the fragrant evergreen pages of Cibber's delightful book about the stage, and especially in reflecting upon the beautiful and brilliant women who, drawn by his magic pencil, dwell there, perpetual, in life, colour, and charm, the reflective reader may perhaps be prompted to remember that the royal line of stage beauties is not extinct, and that stage heroines exist in the present day who are quite as well worthy of commemoration as any that graced the period of Charles the Second or of good Queen Anne. Our age, indeed, has no Cibber to describe their loveliness and celebrate their achievements; but surely if he were living at this hour that courtly, characteristic, and sensuous writer — who saw so clearly and could portray so well the peculiarities of the feminine nature — would not deem the period of Ellen Terry and Marie Wilton, of Ada

Rehan and Sarah Bernhardt and Genevieve
Ward, of Clara Morris and Jane Had-
ing, unworthy of his pen. As often as
fancy ranges over those bright names and
others that are kindred with them — a glittering sisterhood of charms and talents —
the regret must arise that no literary artist
with just the gallant spirit, the chivalry,
the sensuous appreciation, the fine insight,
and the pictorial touch of old Cibber is
extant to perpetuate their glory. The hand
that sketched Elizabeth Barry so as to
make her live forever in a few brief lines,
the hand that drew the fascinating and
memorable portrait of Susanna Mountfort
(" Down goes her dainty diving body to
the ground, as if she were sinking under
the conscious load of her own attractions ")
— what might it not have done to preserve
for the knowledge of future generations the
queens of the theatre who are crowned and
regnant to-day ! Cibber could have caught
and reflected the elusive charm of such an
actress as Ada Rehan. No touch less
adroit and felicitous than his can accomplish more than the suggestion of her peculiar allurement, her originality, and her fascinating because sympathetic and piquant
mental and physical characteristics.

Ada Rehan, born at Limerick, Ireland, on April 22, 1860, was brought to America when five years old, and at that time she lived and went to school in Brooklyn. No one of her progenitors was ever upon the stage, nor does it appear that she was predisposed to that vocation by early reading or training. Her elder sisters had adopted that pursuit, and perhaps she was impelled toward it by the force of example and domestic association, readily affecting her innate latent faculty for the dramatic art. Her first appearance on the stage was made at Newark, New Jersey, in 1873, in a play entitled *Across the Continent*, in which she acted a small part, named Clara, for one night only, to fill the place of a performer who had been suddenly disabled by illness. Her readiness and her positive talent were clearly revealed in that effort, and it was thereupon determined in a family council that she should proceed; so she was soon regularly embarked upon the life of an actress. Her first appearance on the New York stage was made a little later, in 1873, at Wood's museum (it became Daly's theatre in 1879), when she played a small part in a piece called *Thorough-bred*. During the seasons of 1873–74–75 she was

associated with the Arch Street theatre,
Philadelphia, — that being her first regular
professional engagement. (John Drew,
with whom, professionally, Ada Rehan
has been long associated, made his first
appearance in the same season, at the
same house.) She then went to Macaulay's theatre, Louisville, where she acted
for one season. From Louisville she went
to Albany, as a member of John W. Albaugh's company, and with that manager
she remained two seasons, acting sometimes
in Albany and sometimes in Baltimore.
After that she was for a few months with
Fanny Davenport. The earlier part of
her career involved professional endeav-
ours in company with the wandering stars,
and she acted in a variety of plays with
Edwin Booth, Adelaide Neilson, John Mc-
Cullough, Mrs. Bowers, Lawrence Barrett,
John Brougham, Edwin Adams, Mrs. Lan-
der, and John T. Raymond. From the first
she was devotedly fond of Shakespeare, and
all the Shakespearian characters allotted to
her were studied and acted by her with
eager interest and sympathy. While thus
employed in the provincial stock she enacted
Ophelia, Cordelia, Desdemona, Celia, Olivia,
and Lady Anne, and in each of those parts

she was conspicuously good.   The attention
of Augustin Daly was first attracted to her
in December 1877, when she was acting
at Albaugh's theatre in Albany, the play
being *Katharine and Petruchio* (Garrick's
version of the *Taming of the Shrew*), and
Ada Rehan appearing as Bianca ; and subsequently Daly again observed her as an
actress of auspicious distinction and marked
promise at the Grand Opera House, New
York, in April 1879.   Fanny Davenport
was then acting in that theatre in Daly's
strong American play of *Pique* — one of
the few dramas of American origin that
aptly reflect the character of American
domestic life — and Ada Rehan appeared
in the part of Mary Standish.   She was
immediately engaged under Daly's management, and in May 1879 she came forth
at the Olympic theatre, New York, as
Big Clemence in that author's version
of *L'Assommoir*.   On September 17, 1879,
Daly's theatre (which had been suspended
for about two years) was opened upon
its present site, the southwest corner of
Thirtieth Street and Broadway, and Ada
Rehan made her first appearance there,
enacting the part of Nelly Beers in a
play called *Love's Young Dream*.   The

opening bill on that occasion comprised
that piece, together with a comedy by Olive
Logan, entitled *Newport*. On September
30 a revival of *Divorce*, one of Daly's
most fortunate plays, was effected, and
Ada Rehan impersonated Miss Lu Ten
Eyck — a part originally acted (1873) by
Fanny Davenport. From that time to this
(1892) Ada Rehan has remained the leading lady at Daly's theatre; and there she
has become one of the most admired figures
upon the contemporary stage. In five professional visits to Europe, acting in London, Paris, Edinburgh, Dublin, Berlin, and
other cities, she pleased judicious audiences and augmented her renown. Daly
took his company of comedians to London
for the first time in 1884, where they fulfilled an engagement of six weeks at Toole's
theatre, beginning July 19. The second
visit to London was made two seasons later,
when they acted for nine weeks at the
Strand theatre, beginning May 27, 1886.
At that time they also played in the English provinces, and they visited Germany
— acting at Hamburg and at Berlin, where
they were much liked and commended.
They likewise made a trip to Paris. Their
third season abroad began at the Lyceum

theatre, London, May 3, 1888, and it included another expedition to the French capital, which was well rewarded. Ada Rehan at that time impersonated Shakespeare's Shrew. It was in that season also that she appeared at Stratford-upon-Avon, where Daly gave a performance (August 3, 1888) in the Shakespeare Memorial theatre, for the benefit of that institution. The fourth season of Daly's comedians in London began on June 10, 1890, at the Lyceum theatre, and lasted ten weeks; and this was signalised by Ada Rehan's impersonation of Rosalind. The fifth London season extended from September 9 to November 13, 1891.

This is an outline of her professional story; but how little of the real life of an actor can be imparted in a record of the surface facts of a public career! Most expressive, as a comment upon the inadequacy of biographical details, is the exclamation of Dumas, about Aimée Desclée: "Une femme comme celle-là n'a pas de biographie! Elle nous a émus, et elle en est morte. Voilà toute son historie!" Ada Rehan, while she has often and deeply moved the audience of her riper time, is happily very far from having died of it.

There is deep feeling beneath the luminous and sparkling surface of her art; but it is chiefly with mirth that she has touched the public heart and affected the public experience. Equally of her, however, as of her pathetic sister artist of the French stage, it may be said that such a woman has no history. In a civilisation and at a period wherein persons are customarily accepted for what they pretend to be, instead of being seen and understood for what they are, she has been content to take an unpretentious course, to be original and simple, and thus to allow her faculties to ripen and her character to develop in their natural manner. She has not assumed the position of a star, and perhaps the American community, although favourable and friendly toward her, may have been somewhat slow to understand her unique personality and her superlative worth. The moment a thoughtful observer's attention is called to the fact, however, he perceives how large a place Ada Rehan fills in the public mind, how conspicuous a figure she is upon the contemporary stage, and how difficult it is to explain and classify her whether as an artist or a woman. That blending of complexity with transparency always imparts to indi-

vidual life a tinge of piquant interest,
because it is one denotement of the temperament of genius.

The poets of the world pour themselves
through all subjects by the use of their
own words. In what manner they are
affected by the forces of nature — its influences of gentleness and peace or its vast
pageants of beauty and terror — those words
denote ; and also those words indicate the
action, upon their responsive spirits, of the
passions that agitate the human heart.
The actors, on the other hand, assuming
to be the interpreters of the poets, must
pour themselves through all subjects by the
use of their own personality. They are to
be estimated accordingly by whatever the
competent observer is able to perceive of
the nature and the faculties they reveal
under the stress of emotion, whether tragic
or comic. Perhaps it is not possible —
mind being limited in its function — for
any person to form a full, true, and definite summary of another human creature.
To view a dramatic performance with a
consciousness of the necessity of forming
a judicial opinion of it is often to see
one's own thought about it rather than
the thing itself. Yet, when all allowance

is made for difficulty of theme and for in-
firmity of judgment, the observer of Ada
Rehan may surely conclude that she has
a rich, tender, and sparkling nature, in
which the dream-like quality of sentiment
and the discursive faculty of imagination,
intimately blended with deep, broad, and
accurate perceptions of the actual, and
with a fund of keen and sagacious sense,
are reinforced with strong individuality
and with affluent and extraordinary vital
force. Ada Rehan has followed no traditions. She went to the stage not because
of vanity but because of spontaneous impulse ; and for the expression of every part
that she has played she has gone to nature
and not to precept and precedent. The
stamp of her personality is upon everything that she has done ; yet the thinker who
looks back upon her numerous and various
impersonations is astonished at their diversity. The romance, the misery, and the
fortitude of Kate Verity, the impetuous
passion of Katharine, the brilliant raillery
of Hippolyta, the enchanting womanhood of
Rosalind — how clear-cut, how distinct, how
absolutely dramatic was each one of those
personifications ! and yet how completely
characteristic each one was of this individual

actress ! Our works of art may be subject
to the application of our knowledge and
skill, but we ourselves are under the dominance of laws which operate out of the
inaccessible and indefinable depths of the
spirit. Alongside of most players of this
period Ada Rehan is a prodigy of original
force. Her influence, accordingly, has been
felt more than it has been understood, and,
being elusive and strange, has prompted
wide differences of opinion. The sense
that she diffuses of a simple, unselfish,
patient nature, and of impulsive tenderness
of heart, however, cannot have been missed
by anybody with eyes to see. And she
crowns all by speaking the English language with a beauty that has seldom been
equalled.

XVIII.

TENNYSON'S COMEDY OF THE FORESTERS.

"BESIDES, the King's name is a tower
of strength." Thousands of people
all over the world honour, and ought to
honour, every word that falls from the pen
of Alfred Tennyson. He is a very great
man. No poet since the best time of Byron
has written the English language so well —
that is to say, with such affluent splendour
of imagination; such passionate vigour;
such nobility of thought; such tenderness
of pathos; such pervasive grace, and so
much of that distinctive variety, flexibility,
and copious and felicitous amplitude which
are the characteristics of an original style.
No poet of the last fifty years has done
so much to stimulate endurance in the
human soul and to clarify spiritual vision
in the human mind. It does not signify
that now, at more than fourscore, his hand
sometimes trembles a little on the harp-
strings, and his touch falters, and his

music dies away. It is still the same harp and the same hand. This fanciful, kindly, visionary, drifting, and altogether romantic comedy of *Robin Hood* is not to be tried by the standard that its author reared when he wrote *Ulysses* and *Tithonus* and *The Passing of Arthur* — that imperial, unapproachable standard that no other poet has satisfied.

" Cold upon the dead volcano sleeps the gleam
     of dying day."

But though the passion be subdued and the splendour faded, the deep current of feeling flows on and the strong and tender voice can still touch the heart and charm the ear. That tide of emotion and that tone of melody blend in this play and make it beautiful. The passion is no longer that of *Enone* and *Lucretius* and *Guinevere* and *Locksley Hall* and *Maud* and *The Vision of Sin*. The thought is no longer that of *In Memoriam*, with its solemn majesty and infinite pathos. The music is no longer that of *The May Queen* and the *Talking Oak* and *Idle Tears*. But why should these be expected? He who struck those notes strikes now another ; and as we listen our wonder grows, and cannot help but grow, that a

bard of fourscore and upward should write
in such absolute sympathy with youth, love,
love, hope, happiness, and all that is free
and wandering and martial and active in
the vicissitudes of adventure, the exploits
of chivalry, and the vagabondish spirit of
gypsy frolic. The fact that he does write
in that mood points to the one illuminative
truth now essential to be remembered.
The voice to which we are privileged to
listen, perhaps for the last time, is the
voice of a great poet — by which is meant
a poet who is able, not through the medium
of intellect but through the medium of
emotion, to make the total experience of
mankind his own experience, and to express it not only in the form of art but
with the fire of nature. The element of
power, in all the expressions of such a
mind, will fluctuate ; but every one of its
expressions will be sincere and in a greater
or less degree will be vital with a universal and permanent significance. That virtue is in Alfred Tennyson's comedy of
Robin Hood, and that virtue will insure
for it an abiding endurance in affectionate
public esteem.

The realm into which this play allures
its auditor is the realm of *Ivanhoe* —

the far-off, romantic region of Sherwood
forest, in the ancient days of stout king
Richard the First. The poet has gone to
the old legends of Robin Hood and to the
ballads that have been made upon them,
and out of those materials — using them
freely, according to his fancy — he has
chosen his scene and his characters and
has made his story. It is not the England
of the mine and the workshop that he
represents, and neither is it the England of
the trim villa and the formal landscape;
it is the England of the feudal times — of
gray castle towers, and armoured knights,
and fat priests, and wandering minstrels,
and crusades and tournaments; England
in rush-strewn bowers and under green
boughs; the England in which Wamba
jested and Blondel sung. To enter into
that realm is to leave the barren world of
prose; to feel again the cool, sweet winds
of summer upon the brow of youth; to
catch, in fitful glimpses, the shimmer of
the Lincoln green in the sunlit, golden
glades of the forest, and to hear the merry
note of the huntsman commingled, far
away, with "horns of Elfland faintly blow-
ing." The appeal is made to the primitive,
elemental, poetical instinct of mankind :

and no detail of realism is obtruded, no
question of probability considered, no agony
of the sin-tortured spirit subjected to analysis, no controversy promoted and no
moral lesson enforced. For once the public is favoured with a serious poetical play,
which aims simply to diffuse happiness by
arousing sympathy with pleasurable scenes
and picturesque persons, with virtue that
is piquant and humour that is refined, with
the cheerful fortitude that takes adversity
with a smile, and with that final fortunate
triumph of good over evil which is neither
ensanguined with gore nor saddened with
tears, nor made acrid with bitterness. The
play is pastoral comedy, written partly in
blank verse and partly in prose, and cast
almost wholly out of doors — in the open
air and under the greenwood tree — and,
in order to stamp its character beyond
doubt or question, one scene of it is frankly
devoted to a convocation of fairies around
Titania, their queen.

The impulse that underlies this piece is
the old, incessant, undying aspiration, that
men and women of the best order feel, for
some avenue of escape, some relief, some
refuge, from the sickening tyranny of con-
vention and the commonplace, and from

the overwhelming mystery with which all
human life is haunted and oppressed.   A
man who walks about in a forest is not
necessarily free.   He may be as great a
slave as anybody.   But the exalted imagination dwells upon his way of life as eman-
cipated, breezy, natural, and right.   That
way, to the tired thinker, lie peace and
joy.   There, if anywhere — as he fancies —
he might escape from all the wrongs of the
world, all the problems of society, all the
dull business of recording, and analysing,
and ticketing mankind, all the clash of
selfish systems that people call history,
and all the babble that they call literature.
In that retreat he would feel the rain upon
his face, and smell the grass and the
flowers, and hear the sighing and whisper-
ing of the wind in the green boughs ; and
there would be no need to trouble himself
any more, whether about the past or the
future.   Every great intellect of the world
has felt that wild longing, and has recorded it — the impulse to revert to the
vast heart of Nature, that knows no doubt,
and harbours no fear, and keeps no regret,
and feels no sorrow, and troubles itself not
at all.   Matthew Arnold dreamily and perhaps austerely expressed it in *The Scholar*

Gypsy. Byron more humanly uttered it in four well-remembered lines, of *Childe Harold :*

" Oh, that the desert were my dwelling-place,
    With one fair spirit for my minister,
That I might all forget the human race,
    And, hating nothing, love but only her."

Robin Hood, as technical drama, is frail. Its movement, indeed, is not more indolent than that of its lovely prototypes in Shakespeare, *As You Like It* and *A Midsummer Night's Dream*. With all the pastorals Time ambles. But, on the other hand, Tennyson's piece is not a match for either of those Shakespearean works, in massiveness of dramatic signification or in the element of opportunity for the art of acting. Character, poetry, philosophy, humour, and suggestion it contains ; but it contains no single scene in which its persons can amply put forth their full histrionic powers with essentially positive dramatic effect. Its charm resides more in being than in doing, and therefore it is more a poem than a play, and perhaps more a picture than a poem. It is not one of those works that arouse, agitate, and impel. It aims only to create and sustain a pleased condition ; and that

aim it has accomplished.   No spectator will
be deeply moved by it, but no spectator will
look at it without delight.   While, however,
Robin Hood as a drama is frail, it is not destitute of the dramatic element.   It depicts a
central character in action, and it tells a
representative love story — a story in which
the oppressive persecutor of impoverished
age is foiled and discomfited, in which faithful affection survives the test of trial, and in
which days of danger end at last in days of
blissful peace.   Traces of the influence of
Shakespeare — exerted by his pastoral comedies and by the *Merry Wives of Windsor*
— are obvious in it.   There is no imitation;
there is only kinship.   The sources that
Scott explored for some of the material
used in *Ivanhoe* also announce themselves.
Many stories could be derived from the old
Robin Hood ballads.   The poet has only
chosen and rearranged such of their incidents as would suit his purpose — using
those old ballads with perfect freedom, but
also using them with faultless taste.

Robin Hood was born at Locksley, in the
county of Nottingham, about 1160, when
Henry the Second was king.   His true name
was Robert Fitzooth — a name that popular mispronunciation converted into Robin

Hood — and he was of noble lineage. Old records declare him to have been the Earl of Huntingdon. He was extravagant and adventurous, and for reasons that are unknown he preferred to live in the woods. His haunts were chiefly Sherwood Forest, in Nottinghamshire, and Barnsdale, in Yorkshire. Among his associates were William Scadlock, commonly called Scarlet; Much, a miller's son; Friar Tuck, a vagabond monk; and Little John, whose name was Nailor. Robin Hood and his band were kind to the poor; but they robbed the rich and they were specially hard on the clergy. There is a tradition that a woman named Maid Marian went with Robin into the forest, but nothing is known about her. Robin lived till the age of eighty-seven, and he might have lived longer but that a treacherous relative, the prioress of Kirkley — to whose care he had entrusted himself in order that he might be bled — allowed him to bleed to death. At the time indicated in Tennyson's comedy — the year 1194, which was the year of King Richard's return from captivity in Germany — he was thirty-four years old. It is the year of *Ivanhoe*, and in the play as in the novel, the evil agent is the usurper Prince John.

Fifteen characters take part in this comedy. Act first is called "The Bond and the Outlawry." The action begins in a garden before Sir Richard Lea's castle — or rather the dialogue begins there, by which the basis of the action is revealed. Maid Marian is Marian Lea, the daughter of Sir Richard. Walter Lea, the son of Sir Richard, has been captured by the Moors, and in order to pay the boy's ransom Sir Richard has borrowed a large sum of money from the Abbot of York. That debt must presently be paid; but Sir Richard does not see his way clear to its payment, and if he does not pay it he must forfeit his land. The Sheriff of Nottingham, a wealthy suitor for the hand of Marian, is willing to pay that debt, in case the girl will favour his suit. But Marian loves the Earl of Huntingdon and is by him beloved; and all would go well with those lovers, and with Sir Richard, but that the Earl of Huntingdon is poor. Poor though he be, however, he makes a feast, to celebrate his birthday, and to that festival Sir Richard and his daughter are bidden. Act first displays the joyous proceedings of that good meeting and the posture of those characters toward each other. The Sheriff

of Nottingham intrudes himself upon the
scene, accompanied by Prince John, who
is disguised as a friar. The Prince has
cast a covetous eye upon Marian, and,
although he outwardly favours the wish
of the Sheriff, he is secretly determined
to seize her for himself. The revellers
at Huntingdon's feast, unaware of the
Prince's presence, execrate his name, and
at length he retires, in a silent fury. Robin
gives to Marian a remarkable ring that he
has inherited from his mother. Later a
herald enters and reads a proclamation
from Prince John, declaring the Earl of
Huntingdon to be a felon, and commanding his banishment. Robin cannot forcibly
oppose that mandate, and he therefore determines to cast in his lot with Scarlet and
Friar Tuck and other "minions of the
moon," and thenceforward to live a free
and merry life under the green boughs of
Sherwood Forest. A year is supposed to
pass. Act second, called "The Flight of
Marian," begins with a song of the Foresters, in the deep wood — "There is no
land like England." That is a scene of
much gentle beauty, enhanced by Robin
Hood's delivery of some of the finest poetry
in the play, and also by the delicious music

of Sir Arthur Sullivan. Robin descants upon freedom, and upon the advantage of dwelling beneath the sky rather than beneath a groined roof that shuts out all the meaning of heaven. There is a colloquy between Little John, who is one of Robin's men, and Kate, who is Marian's maid. Those two are lovers who quarrel and make it up again, as lovers will. Kate has come to the forest, bringing word of the flight of her mistress. Prince John has tried to seize Marian, and that brave girl has repulsed and struck him; and she and her father have fled — intending to make for France, in which land the old knight expects to find a friend who will pay his debt and save his estate. While Robin is considering these things he perceives the approach of Prince John and the Sheriff of Nottingham, and, thereupon, he takes refuge in the hut of an old witch and disguises himself in some of her garments. Prince John and the Sheriff, who are in pursuit of Sir Richard and Marian, find Robin in this disguise, and for a time they are deceived by him; but soon they penetrate his masquerade and assail him — whereupon some of his people come to his assistance, and he is reinforced by Sir Richard Lea. Prince

John and his party are beaten and driven away. Sir Richard is exhausted, and Robin commits him to the care of the Foresters. Marian, arrayed as a boy, and pretending to be her brother Walter, has been present at this combat, as a spectator, and a sparkling scene of equivoke, mischief, and sentiment ensues between Marian and Robin. That scene Tennyson wrote and inserted for Ada Rehan, to whose vivacious temperament it is fitted, and whose action in it expressed with equal felicity the teasing temper of the coquette and the propitious fondness of the lover. Robin discovers Marian's identity by means of the ring that he gave her, and, after due explanation, it is agreed that she and her father will remain under his protection. Act third is called "The Crowning of Marian," and is devoted to pictures, colloquies, and incidents, now serious and now comical, showing the life of the Foresters and the humorous yet discriminative justice of their gypsy chief. Sir Richard Lea is ill and he cannot be moved. The outlaws crown Marian, with an oaken chaplet, and declare her to be their queen. Robin Hood vindicates his vocation, and in a noble speech on freedom

—deriving his similes from the giant oak
tree, as Tennyson has ever loved to do—
declares himself the friend of the poor and
the servant of the king, the absent Richard
of the Lion Heart, for whose return all
good men are eager. Various beggars,
friars, and other travellers are halted on
the road, in practical illustration of Robin's
doctrine; comic incidents from the old ballads are reproduced; and so the episode
ends merrily of these frolics in the wood.
At that point a delicious fairy pageant is introduced, presenting Queen Titania and her
elves and illustrating at once the grievance
of the fairies against the men whose heavy
feet have crushed their toads and bats and
flowers and mystic rings, and Marian's
dream of love. Sir Arthur Sullivan's music
is here again used, and again it is felt to
be characteristic, melodious, and uncom-
monly sweet and tender. Act fourth begins in a forest bower at sunrise. Marian
and Robin meet there and talk of Sir Richard and of his bond to the Abbot of York
—soon to fall due and seemingly to remain
unpaid. Robin has summoned the Abbot
and his justiciary to come into the forest
and to bring the bond. King Richard, un-
recognised, now arrives, and in submission

to certain laws of the woodland he engages
in an encounter of buffets, and prevails
over all his adversaries. At the approach
of the Abbot, however, fearing premature
recognition, the monarch will flit away;
but his gypsy friends compel him to accept
a bugle, upon which he is to blow a blast
when in danger. The Abbot and his fol-
lowers arrive, and Robin Hood offers the
money to redeem Sir Richard's bond; but,
upon a legal quibble, the Abbot declines to
receive it — preferring to seize the forfeited
land. Prince John and the Sheriff of Nottingham appear, and Robin and his Foresters form an ambuscade. Sir Richard
Lea has been brought in, upon his litter,
and Marian stays beside him. Prince John
attempts to seize her, but this time he is
frustrated by the sudden advent of King
Richard — from whose presence he slinks
away. The myrmidons of John, however,
attack the King, who would oppose them
single-handed; but Friar Tuck snatches
the King's bugle and blows a blast of summons — whereupon the Foresters swarm
into the field and possess it. John's fac-
tion is dispersed, Marian is saved, the
absent Walter Lea reappears, Sir Richard
is assured of his estate, the Abbot and the

Sheriff are punished, and Robin Hood and
Maid Marian may wed — for now the good
King Richard has come again to his own.

The lyrics in the piece possess the charm
of fluent and unaffected sweetness, and of
original, inventive, and felicitous fancy, and
some of them are tenderly freighted with
that indescribable but deeply affecting undertone of pathetic sentiment which is a
characteristic attribute of Tennyson's poetry.

The characters in the comedy were creatures of flesh and blood to the author, and
they come out boldly, therefore, on the stage.
Marian Lea is a woman of the Rosalind
order — handsome, noble, magnanimous,
unconventional, passionate in nature, but
sufficient unto herself, humorous, playful,
and radiant with animal spirits. Ada Rehan
embodied her according to that ideal. The
chief exaction of the part is simplicity —
which yet must not be allowed to degener-
ate into tameness. The sweet affection of
a daughter for her father, the coyness yet
the allurement of a girl for her lover, the
refinement of high birth, the blithe bearing
and free demeanour of a child of the woods,
and the predominant dignity of purity and
honour — those are the salient attributes of

the part. Ada Rehan struck the true note at the outset — the note of buoyant health, rosy frolic, and sprightly adventure — and she sustained it evenly and firmly to the last. Every eye was pleased with the frank, careless, cheerful beauty of her presence, and every ear was soothed and charmed with her fluent and expressive delivery of the verse. In this, as in all of the important representations that Ada Rehan has given, the delightful woman-quality was conspicuously present. She can readily impersonate a boy. No actress since Adelaide Neilson has done that so well. But the crowning excellence of her art was its expression of essential womanhood. Her acting was never trivial and it never obtruded the tedious element of dry intellect. It refreshed — and the spectator was happier for having seen her. Many pleasant thoughts were scattered in many minds by her performance of Maid Marian, and no one who saw it will ever part with the remembrance of it.

XIX.

IT was perhaps an auspicious portent, it certainly is an interesting fact, that the first play that was ever acted in America at a regular theatre and by a regular theatrical company was Shakespeare's comedy of *The Merchant of Venice*. Such at least is the record made by William Dunlap, the first historian of the American theatre, who names Williamsburg, Virginia, as the place and September 5, 1752 as the date of that production. It ought to be noted, however (so difficult is it to settle upon any fact in this uncertain world), that the learned antiquarian Judge C. P. Daly, fortified likewise by the scrupulously accurate Ireland, dissents from Dunlap's statement and declares that Cibber's alteration of Shakespeare's *Richard the Third* was acted by a regular company in a large room in Nassau Street, New York, at an earlier date, namely, on March 5, 1750. All the same,

it appears to have been Shakespeare's mind
that started the dramatic movement in
America.   The American stage has under-
gone great changes since that time, but
both *The Merchant of Venice* and *Richard
the Third* are still acted, and in the *Merchant*, if not in *Richard*, the public interest
is still vital.   In New York, under Edwin
Booth's management, at the Winter Garden theatre, January 28, 1867, and subsequently at Booth's theatre, and in London,
under Henry Irving's management, at the
Lyceum theatre, November 1, 1879, sumptuous productions of the *Merchant* have
brilliantly marked the dramatic chronicle
of our times.   Discussion of the great character of Shylock steadily proceeds and
seems never to weary either the disputants
or the audience.   The sentiment, the fancy,
and the ingenuity of artists are often ex-
pended not only upon the austere, picturesque, and terrible figure of the vindictive
Jew, but upon the chief related characters
in the comedy — upon Bassanio and Portia,
Gratiano and Nerissa, Lorenzo and Jessica,
the princely and pensive Antonio,   the
august Duke and his stately senators, and
the shrewd and humorous Gobbo.   More
than one painting has depicted the ardent

Lorenzo and his fugitive infidel as they
might have looked on that delicious summer night at Belmont when they saw
"how the floor of heaven is thick inlaid
with patines of bright gold," and when the
blissful lover, radiant with happiness and
exalted by the sublime, illimitable, unfath-
omable spectacle of the star-strewn firma-
ment, murmured, in such heaven-like ca-
dence, of the authentic music of heaven.

It is not to be denied that lovely words
are spoken to Jessica, and that almost
equally lovely words are spoken by her.
Essayists upon the *Merchant* havè generally accepted her without a protest — so
much do youth and beauty in a woman
count in the scale when weighed against
duty and integrity. There is no indication
that Shylock was ever unjust or unkind to
Jessica. Whatever he may have been to
others he seems always to have been good
to her ; and she was the child of that lost
Leah of his youthful devotion whom he
passionately loved and whom he mourned
to the last. Yet Jessica not only abandoned
her father and his religion, but robbed him
of money and jewels (including the betrothal ring, the turquoise, that her mother
had given to him), when she fled with the

young Christian who had won her heart.
It was a basely cruel act; but probably
some of the vilest and cruelest actions that
are done in this world are done by persons
who are infatuated by the passion of love.
Mrs. Jameson, who in her beautiful essay
on Portia extenuates the conduct of Jessica,
would have us believe that Shylock valued
his daughter far beneath his wealth, and
therefore deserved to be deserted and plun-
dered by her; and she is so illogical as to
derive his sentiments on this subject from
his delirious outcries of lamentation after
he learned of her predatory and ignomini-
ous flight. The argument is not a good
one. Fine phrases do not make wrong deeds
right. It were wiser to take Jessica for
the handsome and voluptuous girl that certainly she is, and to leave her rectitude out
of the question. Shakespeare in his draw-
ing of her was true to nature, as he always
is; but the student who wants to know
where Shakespeare's heart was placed when
he drew women must look upon creatures
very different from Jessica. The women
that Shakespeare seems peculiarly to have
loved are Imogen, Cordelia, Isabella, Rosalind, and Portia — Rosalind, perhaps, most
of all; for although Portia is finer than

T

Rosalind, it is extremely probable that
Shakespeare resembled his fellow-men suffi-
ciently to have felt the preference that Tom
Moore long afterward expressed:

> "Be an angel, my love, in the morning,
>   But, oh! be a woman to-night."

When Ellen Terry embodied Portia — in
Henry Irving's magnificent revival of *The
Merchant of Venice* — the essential womanhood of that character was for the first time
in the modern theatre adequately interpreted and conveyed. Upon many play-
going observers indeed the wonderful wealth
of beauty that is in the part — its winsome
grace, its incessant sparkle, its alluring because piquant as well as luscious sweetness,
its impetuous ardour, its enchantment of
physical equally with emotional condition, its
august morality, its perfect candour, and its
noble passion — came like a surprise. Did
the great actress find those attributes in
the part (they asked themselves), or did
she infuse them into it? Previous representatives of Portia had placed the emphasis
chiefly, if not exclusively, upon morals and
mind. The stage Portia of the past has
usually been a didactic lady, self-contained,
formal, conventional, and oratorical. Ellen

Terry came, and Portia was figured exactly as she lives in the pages of Shakespeare — an imperial and yet an enchanting woman, dazzling in her beauty, royal in her dignity, as ardent in temperament as she is fine in brain and various and splendid in personal peculiarities and feminine charm. After seeing that matchless impersonation it seemed strange that Portia should ever have been represented in any other light, and it was furthermore felt that the inferior, mechanical, utilitarian semblance of her could not again be endured. Ellen Terry's achievement was a complete vindication of the high view that Shakespearean study has almost always taken of that character, and it finally discredited the old stage notion that Portia is a type of decorum and declamation.

Aside from Hazlitt, who thought that Portia is affected and pedantic, and who did not like her because he did not happen to appreciate her, the best analytical thinkers about Shakespeare's works have taken the high view of that character. Shakespeare himself certainly took it ; for aside from her own charming behaviour and delightful words it is to be observed that everybody in the play who speaks of her at all speaks her praise. It is only upon the stage that she has been made artificial, prim, and preachy. That misrepresentation of her has, perhaps, been caused, in part, by the practice long prevalent in our theatre of cutting and compressing the play so as to make Shylock the chief figure in it. In that way Portia is shorn of much of her splendour and her meaning. The old theatrical records dwell almost exclusively upon Shylock, and say little if anything about Portia. In Shakespeare's time, no doubt, *The Merchant of Venice* was acted as it is written, the female persons in it being played by boys, or by men who could " speak small." Alexander Cooke (1588–1614) played the light heroines of Shakespeare while the poet was alive. All students of the subject are aware that Burbage was the first Shylock, and that when he played the part he wore a red wig, a red beard, and a long false nose. No record exists as to the first Portia. The men who were acting female characters upon the London stage when that institution was revived immediately after the Restoration were Kynaston, James Nokes, Angel, William Betterton, Mosely, and Floid. Kynaston, it is said, could act a woman so well that when at length women themselves began to appear as actors it was for some time doubted whether any one of them could equal him. The account of his life, however, does not mention Portia as one of his characters.

Indeed the play of *The Merchant of Venice*, after it languished out of sight in that decadence of the stage which ensued upon the growth of the Puritan movement in England, did not again come into use until it was revived in Lord Landsdowne's alteration of it produced at the theatre in Lincoln's Inn Fields in 1701, and even then it was grossly perverted. Forty years later, however, on St. Valentine's Day 1741, at Drury Lane, when Macklin regenerated the character of Shylock, the original piece was restored to the theatre. Women in the meantime had come upon the stage. The garrulous and delightful Pepys, who had seen Kynaston play a female part, records in his marvellous Diary that he first saw women as actors on January 3, 1661. Those were members of Killigrew's company, which preceded that of Davenant by several months, if not by a year; and therefore the common statement in theatrical books that the first woman that ever appeared on the English stage was Mrs. Sanderson, of Dave-

nant's company, at Lincoln's Inn Fields, is
erroneous : and indeed the name of the first
English actress is as much unknown as the
name of the first Portia. When Macklin
restored Shakespeare's *Merchant of Venice*
to the stage it is not likely that the character
of Portia was dwarfed, for its representative
then was Kitty Clive, and that actress was
a person of strong will. With Clive the
long list begins of the Portias of the stage.
She was thirty years old when she played
the part with Macklin, and it is probable
that she played it with dignity and certain
that she played it with sparkling animation
and piquant grace. The German Ulrici,
whose descriptive epithets for Portia are
" roguish and intellectual," would doubtless
have found his ideal of the part fulfilled in
Clive. The Nerissa that night was Mrs.
Pritchard, then also thirty years old, but
not so famous as she afterward became.

The greatest actress on the British stage
in the eighteenth century undoubtedly was
Margaret Woffington (1719–1760). Sarah
Siddons, to whom the sceptre passed, was
only five years old when Woffington died.
Both those brilliant names are associated
with Portia. Augustin Daly's *Life of Woffington* — the best life of her that has been

written, and one of the most sumptuous
books that have been made — contains this
reference to her performance of that part:
" All her critics agree that her declamation
was accurate and her gesture grace and
nature combined ; but in tragic or even dramatic speeches her voice probably had its
limits, and in such scenes, being overtaxed,
told against her. As Portia she appeared
to great advantage ; but when Lorenzo says,
' This is the voice, or I am much deceived,
of Portia,' and Portia replies, ' He knows
me, as the blind man knows the cuckoo, by
the bad voice,' the audience laughed out-
right, and Woffington, conscious of her
deficiency, with great good-humour joined
with them in their merriment." The incident is mentioned in the *Table Talk* (1825)
of Richard Ryan, to which book Daly
refers. Mrs. Siddons made her first appearance on the London stage as Portia December 29, 1775, and conspicuously failed in
the part on that occasion, but she became
distinguished in it afterward ; yet it is
probable that Mrs. Siddons expressed its
nobility more than its tenderness, and much
more than its buoyant and glittering glee,
which was so entirely and beautifully given
by Ellen Terry. After Peg Woffington and

before Mrs. Siddons the most conspicuous
Portia was Mrs. Dancer, whom Hugh Kel-
ley, in his satirical composition of *Thespis*,
calls a "moon-eyed idiot," — from which
barbarous bludgeon phrase the reader derives a hint as to her aspect. Some of the
tones of Mrs. Dancer's voice were so tender
that no one could resist them. Spranger
Barry could not, for he married her, and
after his death she became Mrs. Crawford.
Miss Maria Macklin, daughter of the first
true Shylock of the stage, acted Portia,
April 13, 1776, with her father. She is
recorded as an accomplished woman but
destitute of genius — in which predicament
she probably was not lonesome. On June
11, 1777 Portia was acted at the Haymarket by Miss Barsanti, afterward Mrs. Lister,
an actress who, since she excelled in such
parts as were customarily taken by Fanny
Abington (the distinct opposite of Portia-
like characters), must have been unsuited
for it. The names of Miss Younge, Miss
Farren, Miss E. Kemble, Miss Ryder, Mrs.
Pope, Miss De Camp, and Miss Murray
are in the record of the stage Portias that
comes down to 1800. Probably the best of
all those Portias was Mrs. Pope.

The beautiful Mrs. Glover played Portia

in 1809 at the Haymarket theatre.   Mrs.
Ogilvie played it, with Macready as Shylock (his first appearance in that part), on
May 13, 1823.   Those figures passed and
left no shadow.   Two English actresses of
great fame are especially associated with
Portia — Ellen Tree, afterward Mrs. Charles
Kean, and Helen Faucit, now Lady Martin;
and no doubt their assumptions of the part
should be marked as exceptions from the
hard, didactic, declamatory, perfunctory
method that has customarily characterised
the Portia of the stage.   Lady Martin's
written analysis of Portia is noble in
thought and subtle and tender in penetra-
tion and sympathy.   Charlotte Cushman
read the text superbly, but she was much
too formidable ever to venture on assuming
the character.   Portia is a woman who
deeply loves and deeply rejoices and exults
in her love, and she is never ashamed of
her passion or of her exultation in it; and
she says the finest things about love that
are said by any of Shakespeare's women;
the finest because, while supremely passionate, the feeling in them is perfectly sane.
It is as a lover that Ellen Terry embodied
her, and while she made her a perfect woman, in all the attributes that fascinate,

she failed not, in the wonderful trial scene, to invest her with that fine light of celestial anger — that momentary thrill of moral austerity — which properly appertains to the character at the climax of a solemn and almost tragical situation.

On the American stage there have been many notable representatives of the chief characters in *The Merchant of Venice*. In New York, when the comedy was done at the old John Street theatre in 1773, Hallam was Shylock and Mrs. Morris Portia. Twenty years afterward, at the same house, Shylock was played by John Henry, and Portia by Mrs. Henry, while the brilliant Hodgkinson appeared as Gratiano. Cooper, whose life has been so well written by that ripe theatrical scholar Joseph N. Ireland, in one of the books of the Dunlap Society, assumed Shylock in 1797 at the theatre just then opened in Greenwich Street. The famous Miss Brunton (then Mrs. Merry), was the Portia, and the cast included Moreton as Bassanio, Warren as Antonio, Bernard as Gratiano, and Blissett as Tubal. How far away and how completely lost and forgotten those once distinguished and admired persons are ! Yet Cooper in his day was idolised : he had a fame as high, if not as widely spread, as that of Henry Irving or Edwin Booth at present. William Creswick — lately dead at an advanced age in London — was seen upon the New York stage as Shylock in 1840; Macready in 1841; Charles Kean in 1845. With the latter, Ellen Tree played Portia. Charles W. Couldock enacted Shylock on September 6, 1852, at the Castle Garden theatre, in a performance given to commemorate the alleged centenary of the introduction of the drama into America. The elder Wallack, the elder Booth, Edwin Forrest, G. V. Brooke, George Vandenhoff, Wyzeman Marshall, and E. L. Davenport are among the old local representatives of the Jew. Madam Ponisi used to play Portia, and so did Mrs. Hoey.

In December 1858, when *The Merchant of Venice* was finely revived at Wallack's theatre, with the elder Wallack as Shylock, the cast included Lester Wallack as Bassanio, John Brougham as Gratiano, A. W. Young — a quaintly comic actor, too soon cut off — as Launcelot Gobbo, Mary Gannon — the fascinating, the irresistible — as Nerissa, and handsome Mrs. Sloan as Jessica. The eminent German actor Davison played Shylock, in New York, in his

own language; and many German actors,
no one of them comparable with him, have
been seen in it since. Lawrence Barrett
often played it, and with remarkable force
and feeling. The triumphs won in it by
Edwin Booth are within the remembrance
of many playgoers of this generation.
When he last acted the Jew Helena
Modjeska was associated with him as
Portia. Booth customarily ended the piece
with the trial scene, omitting the last
act; and indeed that was long the stage
custom; but with the true Portia of Ellen
Terry and a good cast in general the last
act went blithely and with superb effect.
The comedy was not written for Shylock
alone. He is a tremendous identity, but
he is not the chief subject. The central
theme is Portia and her love. That theme
takes up a large part of the play, — which
is like a broad summer landscape strewn
with many-coloured flowers that flash and
glitter in the sun, while slowly a muttering
thunder-storm gathers and lowers, and
presently sweeps overhead, casting one
black shadow as it passes, and leaving the
fragrant and glistening plain all the brighter
and sweeter for the contrast with its defeated menace and vanishing gloom.

XX.

RICHARD MANSFIELD AS RICHARD THE THIRD.

THE ideal of Richard that was expressed by this actor did not materially differ from that which has been manifested by great tragic actors from Garrick to Booth. He embodied a demoniac scoffer who, nevertheless, is a human being. The infernal wickedness of Richard was shown to be impelled by tremendous intellect but slowly enervated and ultimately thwarted and ruined by the cumulative operation of remorse — corroding at the heart and finally blasting the man with desolation and frenzy. That, undoubtedly, was Shakespeare's design.   But Richard Mansfield's expression of that ideal differed from the expression to which the stage has generally been accustomed, and in this respect his impersonation was distinctive and original.

The old custom of playing Richard was to take the exaggerated statements of the

opening soliloquy in a literal sense, to pro-
vide him with a big hump, a lame leg, and
a fell of straight black hair, and to make
him walk in, scowling, with his lower lip
protruded, and declare with snarling vehemence and guttural vociferation his amiable
purpose of specious duplicity and miscel-
laneous slaughter.   The opening speech,
which is in Shakespeare's juvenile manner —
an orotund, verbose manner, which perhaps
he had caught from Marlowe, and which
he outgrew and abandoned — was thus
utilised for displaying the character in a
massed aspect, as that of a loathsome hypocrite and sanguinary villain ; and, that being
done, he was made to advance through about
two-thirds of the tragedy, airily yet fero-
ciously slaying everybody who came in his
way, until at some convenient point, defin-
able at the option of the actor, he was suddenly smitten with a sufficient remorse to
account for his trepidation before and during the tent-scene ; and thereafter he was
launched into combat like a meteoric butcher,
all frenzy and all gore, and killed, amid general acclamation, when he had fenced himself out of breath.

That treatment of the character was,
doubtless, in part a necessary consequence

of Shakespeare's perfunctory adoption of
the Tudor doctrine that Richard was a
blood-boltered monster; but in a larger
degree it was the result of Cibber's vulgar distortion of the original piece.   The
actual character of the king, — who seems
to have been one of the ablest and wisest
monarchs that ever reigned in England —
has never recovered, and it never will re-
cover, from the odium that was heaped
upon it by the Tudor historians and accepted and ratified by the great genius of
Shakespeare.   The stage character of the
king has been almost as effectually damned
by the ingenious theatrical claptrap with
which Cibber misrepresented and vulgar-
ised Shakespeare's conception, assisted by
the efforts of a long line of blood-and-thun-
der tragedians, only too well pleased to depict a gory, blathering, mugging miscreant,
such as their limited intelligence enabled
them to comprehend.   The stage Richard,
however, may possibly be redeemed.   In
Cibber he is everything that Queen Margaret calls him, and worse than a brute.
In Shakespeare, although a miscreant, he
is a man.   The return to Shakespeare,
accordingly, is a step in the right direction.   That step was taken some time ago,

although not maintained, first by Macready,
then by Samuel Phelps, then by Edwin
Booth, and then by Henry Irving. Their
good example was followed by Richard
Mansfield. He used a version of the tragedy, made by himself, — a piece indicative of
thoughtful study of the subject as well as a
keen intuitive grasp of it. He did not stop
short at being a commentator. Aiming to
impersonate a character he treated Shakespeare's prolix play in such a manner
as to make it a practicable living picture
of a past age. The version was in five
acts, preserving the text of the original,
much condensed, and introducing a few
lines from Cibber. It began with a bright
processional scene before the Tower of London, in which Elizabeth, Queen of Edward
IV., was conspicuous, and against that
background of " glorious summer " it placed
the dangerous figure of the Duke of Gloster.
It comprised the murder of Henry VI., the
wooing of Lady Anne, — not in a London
street, but in a rural place, on the road to
Chertsey ; the lamentation for King Edward
IV. ; the episode of the boy princes ; the
condemnation of Hastings, — a scene that
brilliantly denotes the mingled artifice and
savagery of Shakespeare's Gloster ; the
Buckingham plot ; the priest and mayor

scene ; the temptation of Tyrrel ; the fall of
Buckingham ; the march to battle ; the episode of the spectres ; and the fatal catastrophe on Bosworth Field. Enough of the story
was thus related to satisfy the Shakespeare
scholar.

The notable peculiarity was the assumption that there are considerable lapses of
time at intervals during the continuance of
the story. The effort to reconcile poetry
with history produced little if any appreciable practical result upon the stage, — seeing that an audience would not think of
lapses of time unless those lapses were
mentioned in the play-bill. An incessant
continuity of action, a ceaseless rush and
whirl of events, is the essential life of the
play. No auditor can feel that Richard
has waited twelve years before making any
movement or striking any blow, after his
aspiration that heaven will take King Edward and leave the world for him "to bustle in."   That word "bustle" is a favourite
word with Richard. And furthermore there
is no development of his character in Shakespeare's play : there is simply the presentation of it, complete and rounded at the
outset, and remaining invariably and in-
flexibly the same to the close.

Mansfield, however, deduced this effect from his consideration of the flight of time: a contrast between Richard at nineteen and Richard at thirty-three, a contrast strongly expressive of the reactionary influence that an experience of evil deeds has produced upon a man who at first was only a man of evil thoughts and evil will. This imported into the performance a diversity of delineation without, however, affecting the formidable weight of the figure of Richard, or its brilliancy, or its final significance. The embodiment was splendid with it, and would be just as splendid without it. The presence of heart and conscience in that demoniac human creature is denoted by Shakespeare and must be shown by the actor. Precisely at what point his heaven-defying will should begin to waver is not defined. Mansfield chose to indicate the operation of remorse and terror in Richard's soul as early as the throne scene and before yet the king has heard that the royal boys have been murdered. The effect of his action, equally with the method of it, was magnificent. You presently saw him possessed of the throne for which he had so terribly toiled and sinned, and alone upon it, bathed in

blood-red light, the pitiable personification
of gorgeous but haunted evil, marked off
from among mankind and henceforth desolate.   Throughout that fine scene Mansfield's portrayal of the fearful struggle
between wicked will and human weakness
was in a noble vein of imagination, profound in its sincerity, affecting in its pathos,
and pictorial in its treatment.   In the
earlier scenes his mood and his demeanour
had been suffused with a cool, gay, mockery of elegant cynicism.   He killed King
Henry with a smile, in a scene of gloomy
mystery that might have come from the
pencil of Gustave Dore.   He looked upon
the mourning Lady Anne with cheerful
irony and he wooed her with all the fervour
that passion and pathos can engender in the
behaviour of a hypocrite.   His dissimulation with the princes and with the mayor
and the nobles was to the last degree specious.   One of his finest points was the
temptation of Buckingham to murder the
princes.   There, and indeed at all points,
was observed the absence of even the faint-
est reminiscence of the ranting, mouthing,
flannel-jawed king of clubs who has so
generally strutted and bellowed as Shakespeare's Gloster.   All was bold and telling

in the manner, and yet the manner was reticent with nature and fine with well-bred continence.

With the throne scene began the spiritual conflict. At least it then began to be disclosed; and from that moment onward the state of Richard was seen to be that of Orestes pursued by the furies. But Mansfield was right, and was consistent, in making the monarch faithful in his devotion to evil. Richard's presentiments, pangs, and tremors are intermittent. In the great, empty, darkening throne-room, with its shadowy nooks and dim corners, shapeless and nameless spectres may momentarily come upon him and shake his strong spirit with the sinister menace of hell. Along the dark plains, on the fateful night before the battle, the sad ghosts may drift and wander, moaning and wailing in the ghastly gloom; and in that hour of haunted desolation the doomed king may feel that, after all, he is but mortal man, and that his pre-ordered destruction is close at hand and not to be averted; but Richard never deceives himself; never palters with the goodness that he has scorned. He dies as he has lived, defiant and terrible.

Mansfield's treatment of the ghost scenes

at Bosworth was novel, original, and poetic, and his death scene was not only a
display of personal prowess but a repro-
duction of historical fact. With a detail
like this the truth of history becomes useful, but in general the actor cannot safe-
ly go back of the Shakespearean scheme.
To present Richard as he probably was
would be to present a man of some virtue
as well as great ability. Mansfield's acting revealed an amiable desire to infuse
as much goodness as possible into the
Shakespearean conception, but he obtained
his chief success by acting the part substantially according to Shakespeare and by
setting and dressing the play with exceptional if not altogether exact fidelity to
the time, the places, and the persons that
are implicated in the story.

Shakespeare's Richard is a type of colossal will and of restless, inordinate, terrific
activity. The objects of his desire and his
effort are those objects which are incident
to supreme power; but his chief object is
that assertion of himself which is irresistibly
incited and steadfastly compelled by the
overwhelming, seething, acrid energy of his
feverish soul, burning and raging in his
fiery body. He can no more help pro-

jecting himself upon the affairs of the
world than the malignant cobra can help
darting upon its prey. He is a vital, elemental force, grisly, hectic, terrible, impelled by volcanic heat and electrified and
made lurid and deadly by the infernal
purpose of restless wickedness. No actor
can impersonate Richard in an adequate
manner who does not possess transcendent
force of will, combined with ambitious,
incessant, and restless mental activity.
Mansfield in those respects is qualified for
the character, and out of his professional
resources he was able to supply the other
elements that are requisite to its constitution and fulfilment. He presented as
Richard a sardonic, scoffing demon, who
nevertheless, somewhere in his complex
nature, retains an element of humanity.
He embodied a character that is tragic in
its ultimate effect, but his method was
that of the comedian. His portrayal of
Richard, except at those moments when
it is veiled with craft and dissimulation, or
at those other and grander moments, infrequent but awful and agonising, when it
is convulsed with terror or with the anguish
of remorse, stood forth boldly in the sunshine, a crystallised and deadly sarcasm,

equally trenchant upon itself and all the
world, equally scornful of things human
and things divine. That deadly assumption
of keen and mordant mockery, that cool,
glittering, malignant lightness of manner,
was consistently sustained throughout the
performance, while the texture of it was
made continuously entertaining by diversity of colour and inflection, sequent on
changing moods; so that Richard was
shown as a creature of the possible world
of mankind and not as a fiction of the
stage.

The part was acted by him : it was not de-
claimed. He made, indeed, a skilful use of
his uncommon voice—keeping its tones light,
sweet, and superficial during the earlier
scenes (while yet, in accordance with his
theory of development, Gloster is the personification of evil purpose only beginning
to ripen into evil deed), and then permitting them to become deeper and more significant and thrilling as the man grows old
in crime and haggard and convulsed in
self-conflict and misery. But it was less
with vocal excellence that the auditor was
impressed than with the actor's identification with the part and his revelation of the
soul of it. When first presented Gloster

was a mocking devil. The murder of King
Henry was done with malice, but the malice was enwrapped with glee. In the wooing of Lady Anne there was both heart and
passion, but the mood was that of light-
some duplicity. It is not until years of
scheming and of evil acts, engendering, pro-
moting, and sustaining a condition of mental horror and torture, have ravaged his
person and set their seal upon him, in
sunken cheek and hollow eye, in shattered
nerves and deep and thrilling voice, sur-
charged at once with inveterate purpose
and with incessant agony, that this light
manner vanishes, and the demeanour and
action of the wicked monarch becomes ruthless, direct, and terrible. Whether, upon
the basis of a play so discursive, so episod-
ical, so irresolutely defined as Shakespeare's
Richard the Third, that theory of the development of its central character is logically
tenable is a dubious question. In Shakespeare the character is presented full-grown
at the start, and then, through a confused
tangle of historical events, is launched into
action. Nevertheless in his practical application of it Mansfield made his theory
effective by a novel, powerful, interesting
performance. You could not help perceiv-

ing in Mansfield's embodiment that Gloster was passing through phases of experience — that the man changed, as men do change in life, the integral character remaining the same in its original fibre, but the condition varying, in accordance with the reaction of conduct upon temperament and conscience.

Mansfield deeply moved his audience in the repulse of Buckingham, in the moody menace of the absent Stanley, in the denunciation of Hastings, and in the awakening from the dream on the night before the battle. Playgoers have seldom seen a dramatic climax so thrilling as his hysterical recognition of Catesby, after the moment of doubt whether this be not also a phantom of his terrific dream. It was not so much by startling theatrical effects, however, as by subtle denotements, now of the tempest and now of the brooding horror in the king's heart, that the actor gained his victory. The embodiment lacked incessant fiery expedition — the explosive, meteoric quality that astounds and dazzles. Chief among the beauties was imagination. The attitude of the monarch toward his throne — the infernal triumph, and yet the remorseful agony and withering fear — in the moment of ghastly loneliness when he knows that the innocent princes have been murdered and that his imperial pathway is clear, made up one of the finest spectacles of dramatic illumination that the stage has afforded. You saw the murderer's hideous exultation, and then, in an instant, as the single ray of red light from the setting sun streamed through the Gothic window and fell upon his evil head, you saw him shrink in abject fear, cowering in the shadow of his throne; and the dusky room was seemingly peopled with gliding spectres. That treatment was theatrical, but in no derogatory sense theatrical — for it comports with the great speech on conscience; not the fustian of Cibber, about mutton and short-lived pleasure, but the speech that Shakespeare has put into Richard's mouth; the speech that inspired Mansfield's impersonation — the brilliant embodiment of an intellectual man, predisposed to evil, who yields to that inherent impulse, and thereafter, although intermittently convulsed with remorse, fights with tremendous energy against the goodness that he scorns and defies, till at last he dashes himself to pieces against the adamant of eternal law.

XXI.

GENEVIEVE WARD : FORGET ME NOT.

IN the season of 1880–81 Genevieve Ward
made a remarkably brilliant hit with
her embodiment of Stephanie De Mohrivart,
in the play of *Forget Me Not*, by Herman
Merivale, and since then she has acted that
part literally all round the world. It was
an extraordinary performance — potent
with intellectual character, beautiful with
refinement, nervous and steel-like with in-
domitable purpose and icy glitter, intense
with passion, painfully true to an afflicting
ideal of reality, and at last splendidly tragic :
and it was a shining example of ductile and
various art. Such a work ought surely to
be recorded as one of the great achievements
of the stage. Genevieve Ward showed herself to possess in copious abundance peculiar qualities of power and beauty upon
which mainly the part of Stephanie is
reared. The points of assimilation between
the actress and the part were seen to consist

in an imperial force of character, intellectual
brilliancy, audacity of mind, iron will, perfect elegance of manners, a profound self-
knowledge, and unerring intuitions as to
the relation of motive and conduct in that
vast network of circumstance which is the
social fabric. Stephanie possesses all those
attributes ; and all those attributes Genevieve Ward supplied, with the luxuriant
adequacy and grace of nature. But Stephanie superadds to those attributes a bitter,
mocking cynicism, thinly veiled by artificial
suavity and logically irradiant from natural
hardness of heart, coupled with an insensi-
bility that has been engendered by cruel
experience of human selfishness. This,
together with a certain mystical touch of
the animal freedom, whether in joy or
wrath, that goes with a being having neither
soul nor conscience, the actress had to supply — and did supply — by her art. As interpreted by Genevieve Ward the character
was reared, not upon a basis of unchastity
but upon a basis of intellectual perversion.
Stephanie has followed — at first with self-
contempt, afterward with sullen indifference, finally with the bold and brilliant
hardihood of reckless defiance — a life of
crime. She is audacious, unscrupulous,

cruel; a consummate tactician; almost sex-less, yet a siren in knowledge and capacity to use the arts of her sex; capable of any wickedness to accomplish an end, yet trivial enough to have no higher end in view than the reinvestiture of herself with social recognition; cold as snow; implacable as the grave; remorseless; wicked; but, beneath all this depravity, capable of self-pity, capable of momentary regret, capable of a little human tenderness, aware of the glory of the innocence she has lost, and thus not altogether beyond the pale of compassion. And she is, in externals, — in everything visible and audible, — the ideal of grace and melody.

In the presence of an admirable work of art the observer wishes that it were entirely worthy of being performed and that it were entirely clear and sound as to its applicability — in a moral sense, or even in an intellectual sense — to human life. Art does not go far when it stops short at the revelation of the felicitous powers of the artist; and it is not altogether right when it tends to beguile sympathy with an unworthy object and perplex a spectator's perceptions as to good and evil. Genevieve Ward's performance of Stephanie, brilliant though it was, did not redeem the character from its bleak exile from human sympathy. The actress managed, by a scheme of treatment exclusively her own, to make Stephanie, for two or three moments, piteous and forlorn; and her expression of that evanescent anguish — occurring in the appeal to Sir Horace Welby, her friendly foe, in the strong scene of the second act — was wonderfully subtle. That appeal, as Genevieve Ward made it, began in artifice, became profoundly sincere, and then was stunned and startled into a recoil of resentment by a harsh rebuff, whereupon it subsided through hysterical levity into frigid and brittle sarcasm and gay defiance. For a while, accordingly, the feelings of the observer were deeply moved. Yet this did not make the character of Stephanie less detestable. The blight remains upon it — and always must remain — that it repels the interest of the heart. The added blight likewise rests upon it (though this is of less consequence to a spectator), that it is burdened with moral sophistry. Vicious conduct in a woman, according to Stephanie's logic, is not more culpable or disastrous than vicious conduct in a man : the woman, equally with the man, should have a social license to sow

the juvenile wild oats and effect the middle-
aged reformation ; and it is only because
there are gay young men who indulge in
profligacy that women sometimes become
adventurers and moral monsters. All this
is launched forth in speeches of singular
terseness, eloquence, and vigour; but all
this is specious and mischievous perversion
of the truth — however admirably in character from Stephanie's lips. Every observer
who has looked carefully upon the world is
aware that the consequences of wrongdoing
by a woman are vastly more pernicious than
those of wrongdoing by a man ; that society
could not exist in decency, if to its already
inconvenient coterie of reformed rakes it
were to add a legion of reformed wantons ;
and that it is innate wickedness and evil
propensity that makes such women as
Stephanie, and not the mere existence of
the wild young men who are willing to
become their comrades — and who generally
end by being their dupes and victims. It
is natural, however, that this adventurer —
who has kept a gambling-hell and ruined
many a man, soul and body, and who now
wishes to reinstate herself in a virtuous
social position — should thus strive to pal-
liate her past proceedings. Self-justifica-

tion is one of the first laws of life. Even
Iago, who never deceives himself, yet an-
nounces one adequate motive for his fearful crimes. Even Bulwer's Margrave —
that prodigy of evil, that cardinal type of
infernal, joyous, animal depravity — can yet
paint himself in the light of harmless loveliness and innocent gayety.

Forget Me Not tells a thin story, but its
story has been made to yield excellent
dramatic pictures, splendid moments of intellectual combat, and affecting contrasts of
character. The dialogue, particularly in
the second act, is as strong and as brilliant
as polished steel. In that combat of words
Genevieve Ward's acting was delicious with
trenchant skill and fascinating variety.
The easy, good-natured, bantering air with
which the strife began, the liquid purity of
the tones, the delicate glow of the arch
satire, the icy glitter of the thought and
purpose beneath the words, the transition
into pathos and back again into gay indifference and deadly hostility, the sudden and
terrible mood of menace, when at length
the crisis had passed and the evil genius
had won its temporary victory — all those
were in perfect taste and consummate harmony. Seeing that brilliant, supple, relent-
less, formidable figure, and hearing that

incisive, bell-like voice, the spectator was
repelled and attracted at the same instant,
and thoroughly bewildered with the sense
of a power and beauty as hateful as they
were puissant. Not since Ristori acted
Lucretia Borgia has the stage exhibited
such an image of imperial will, made radiant with beauty and electric with flashes of
passion. The leopard and the serpent are
fatal, terrible, and loathsome; yet they
scarcely have a peer among nature's supreme symbols of power and grace. Into
the last scene of *Forget Me Not*, — when
at length Stephanie is crushed by physical
fear, through beholding, unseen by him,
the man who would kill her as a malignant
and dangerous reptile, — Genevieve Ward
introduced such illustrative " business," not
provided by the piece, as greatly enhanced
the final effect. The backward rush from
the door, on seeing the Corsican avenger
on the staircase, and therewithal the inci-
dental, involuntary cry of terror, was the
invention of the actress: and from that moment to the final exit she was the incarnation of abject fear. The situation is one
of the strongest that dramatic ingenuity
has invented: the actress invested it with a
colouring of pathetic and awful truth.

v

XXII.

EDWARD S. WILLARD IN THE MIDDLEMAN AND JUDAH.

E. S. WILLARD accomplished his first appearance upon the American stage (at Palmer's theatre, November 10, 1890), in the powerful play of *The Middleman*, by Henry Arthur Jones. A representative audience welcomed the modest and gentle stranger and the greeting that hailed him was that of earnest respect. Willard had long been known and esteemed in New York by the dramatic profession and by those persons who habitually observe the changeful aspects of the contemporary stage on both sides of the ocean; but to the American public his name had been comparatively strange. The sentiment of kindness with which he was received deepened into admiration as the night wore on, and before the last curtain fell upon his performance of Cyrus Blenkarn he had gained an unequivocal and auspicious victory. In

no case has the first appearance of a new
actor been accompanied with a more brilliant exemplification of simple worth; and
in no case has its conquest of the public enthusiasm been more decisive. Not the least
impressive feature of the night was the steadily increasing surprise of the audience as the
performance proceeded. It was the actor's
way to build slowly, and at the opening of
the piece the poor inventor's blind ignorance of the calamity that is impending is
chiefly trusted to create essential sympathy.
Through those moments of approaching sorrow the sweet unconsciousness of the loving father was expressed by Willard with
touching truth. In this he astonished even
as much as he pleased his auditors; for
they were not expecting it.

One of the most exquisite enjoyments
provided by the stage is the advent of a
new actor who is not only new but good.
It is the pleasure of discovery. It is the
pleasure of contact with a rich mind hitherto unexplored. The personal appearance,
the power of the eye, the variety of the
facial expression, the tones of the voice,
the carriage of the person, the salient attributes of the individual character, the altitude of the intellectual development, the

quality of the spirit, the extent and the nature of those artistic faculties and resources that constitute the professional equipment, — all those things become the subject first of interested inquiry and next of pleased recognition. Willard is neither of the stately, the weird, the mysterious, nor the ferocious order of actor. There is nothing in him of either Werner, Manfred, or Sir Giles Overreach. He belongs not to either the tradition of John Kemble or of Edmund Kean. His personality, nevertheless, is of a distinctive and interesting kind. He has the self-poise and the exalted calm of immense reserve power and of tender and tremulous sensibility perfectly controlled. His acting is conspicuously marked by two of the loveliest attributes of art — simplicity and sincerity. He conceals neither the face nor the heart. His figure is fine and his demeanour is that of vigorous mental authority informed by moral purity and by the self-respect of a manly spirit. Goodness, although a quality seldom taken into the critical estimate, nevertheless has its part in spiritual constitution and in consequent effect. It was, for instance, an element of artistic potentiality in the late John McCullough. It operated spontaneously; and just

so it does in the acting of Willard, who,
first of all, gives the satisfying impression
of being genuine.   A direct and thorough
method of expression naturally accompanies that order of mind and that quality
of temperament.   Every movement that
Willard makes upon the stage is clear, free,
open, firm, and of an obvious significance.
Every tone of his rich and resonant voice is
distinctly intended and is distinctly heard.
There are no "flaws and starts."   He has
formed a precise ideal.   He knows exactly
how to embody and to utter it, and he makes
the manifestation of it sharp, defined, positive, and cogent.   His meaning cannot be
missed.   He has an unerring sense of proportion and symmetry.   The character that
he represents is shown, indeed, all at once,
as a unique identity; but it is not all at
once developed, the manifestation of it being
made gradually to proceed under the stress
of experience and of emotion.   He rises
with the occasion.   His feelings are deep,
and he is possessed of extraordinary power
for the utterance of them — not simply vocal
power, although that, in his case, is exceptional, but the rare faculty of becoming
convulsed, inspired, transfigured, by passion,
and of being swept along by it, and of

sweeping along his hearers. His manner covers, without concealing, great intensity. This is such a combination of traits as must have existed — if the old records are read aright — in that fine and famous actor, John Henderson, and which certainly existed in the late Benjamin Webster. It has, however, always been rare upon the stage, and, like all rare jewels, it is precious. The actor who, from an habitual mood of sweet gravity and patient gentleness, can rise to the height of delirious passion, and there sustain himself at a poise of tempestuous concentration which is the fulfilment of nature, and never once seem either ludicrous or extravagant, is an actor of splendid power and extraordinary self-discipline. Such an actor is Willard. The blue eyes, the slightly olive complexion, the compact person, the picturesque appearance, the melodious voice, the flexibility of natural action, and the gradual and easy ascent from the calm level of domestic peace to the stormy summit of passionate ecstasy recall personal peculiarities and artistic methods long passed away. The best days of Edwin L. Davenport and the younger James Wallack are brought to mind by them.

In the drama of *The Middleman* Wil-

lard had to impersonate an inventor, of
the absorbed, enthusiastic, self-regardless,
fanatical kind. Cyrus Blenkarn is a potter. His genius and his toil have enriched
two persons named Chandler, father and
son, who own and conduct a porcelain
factory in an English town of the present
day. Blenkarn has two daughters, and
one of them is taken from him by the
younger Chandler. The circumstances of
that deprivation point at disgrace, and the
inventor conceives himself to have suffered
an odious ignominy and irreparable wrong.
Young Chandler has departed and so has
Mary Blenkarn, and they are eventually to
return as husband and wife; but Cyrus
Blenkarn has been aroused from his rev-
eries over the crucible and furnace, —
wherein he is striving to discover a lost
secret in the potter's art that will make
him both rich and famous, — and he utters
a prayer for vengeance upon these Chand-
lers, and he parts from them. A time of
destitution and of pitiful struggle with dire
necessity, sleepless grief, and the maddening impulse of vengeance now comes upon
him, so that he is wasted almost to death.
He will not, however, abandon his quest
for the secret of his art. He may die of

hunger and wretchedness ; he will not yield.
At the last moment of his trial and his misery — alone — at night — in the alternate
lurid blaze and murky gloom of his firing-
house — success is conquered : the secret is
found.   This climax, to which the prelimi-
naries gradually and artfully lead, affords
a great opportunity to an actor ; and Willard greatly filled it.   The old inventor
has been bowed down almost to despair.
Grief and destitution, the sight of his remaining daughter's poverty, and the conflict of many feelings have made him a
wreck.   But his will remains firm.   It is
not, however, until his last hope has been
abandoned that his success suddenly comes
— and the result of this is a delirium.   That
situation, one of the best in modern drama,
has been treated by the author in such a
manner as to sustain for a long time the
feeling of suspense and to put an enor-
mous strain upon the emotion and the resources of an actor.   Willard's presentment
of the gaunt, attenuated figure of Cyrus
Blenkarn — hollow-eyed, half-frantic, hysterical with grief and joy — was the complete incarnation of a dramatic frensy ;
and this, being sympathetic, and moving
to goodness and not to evil, captured the

heart. It was a magnificent exhibition, not alone of the physical force that sometimes is so essential in acting but of that fervour of the soul without which acting is a mockery.

The skill with which Willard reserved his power, so that the impersonation might gradually increase in strength, was one of the best merits of his art. Blenkarn's prayer might readily be converted into the climax of the piece, and it might readily be spoken in such a way that no effect would be left for the culmination in the furnace-room. Those errors were avoided, and during three out of the four acts the movement of the piece was fluent, continuous, and cumulative. In this respect both the drama and the performance were instructive. Henry Arthur Jones has diversified his serious scenes with passages of sportive humour and he has freighted the piece with conventional didacticism as to the well-worn question of capital and labour. The humour is good: the political economy need not detain attention. The value of the play does not reside in its teaching but in its dramatic presentation of strong character, individual experience, and significant story. The effect produced by *The Middleman* is that of moral elevation. Its auditor is touched and ennobled by a spectacle of stern trial, pitiable suffering, and stoical endurance. In the purpose that presides over human destiny — if one may accept the testimony equally of history and of fiction — it appears to be necessary first to create strong characters and then to break them ; and the manner in which they are broken usually involves the elements alike of dramatic effect and of pathos. That singular fact in mortal experience may have been noticed by this author. His drama is a forcible exposition of it. *The Middleman* was set upon Palmer's stage in such a way as to strengthen the dramatic illusion by the fidelity of scenery. The firing-house, with its furnaces in operation, was a copy of what may be seen at Worcester. The picture of English life was excellent.

When Willard played the part of Judah Llewellyn for the first time in America (December 29, 1890), he gained from a sympathetic and judicious audience a verdict of emphatic admiration. Judah Llewellyn is a good part in one of the most striking plays of the period — a play that tells an interesting and significant story by expressive, felicitous, and incessant action ;

affects the feelings by situations that are
vital with dramatic power ; inspires useful
thought upon a theme of psychological importance ; cheers the mind with a fresh
breeze of satirical humour ; and delights the
instinct of taste by its crisp and pungent
style.   Alike by his choice of a comparatively original subject and his deft method
in the treatment of it Henry Arthur Jones
has shown a fine dramatic instinct ; and
equally in the evolution of character and
the expression of experience and emotion he
has wrought with feeling and vigour.   Most
of the plays that are written, in any given
period, pass away with the period to which
they appertain.   *Judah* is one of the exceptions ; for its brilliantly treated theme is
one of perennial interest, and there seems
reason to believe, of a work so vital, that
long after the present generation has vanished it still will keep its place in the
theatre, and sometimes be acted, not as a
quaint relic but as a living lesson.

That theme is the psychic force in human
organism.   The author does not obtrude
it ; does not play the pedant with it ; does
not lecture upon it ; and above all does
not bore with it.   He only uses it ; and he
has been so true to his province as a drama-

tist and not an advocate that he never once
assumes to decide upon any question of
doctrine that may be involved in the assertion of it.   His heroine is a young woman
who thinks herself to be possessed of a certain inherent restorative power of curing
the sick.   This power is of psychic origin
and it operates through the medium of
personal influence.   This girl, Vashti Dethick, has exerted her power with some
success.   Other persons, having felt its
good effect, have admitted its existence.
The father of Vashti, an enterprising scamp,
has thereupon compelled the girl to trade
upon her peculiar faculty ; little by little to
assume miraculous powers ; and finally to
pretend that her celestial talent is refreshed
and strengthened by abstinence from food,
and that her cures are wrought only after
she has fasted for many days.   He has
thus converted her into an impostor ; yet,
as her heart is pure and her moral principle naturally sound, she is ill at ease in
this false position, and her mental distress
has suddenly become aggravated, almost to
the pitch of desperation, by the arrival of
love.   She has lost her heart to a young
clergyman, Judah Llewellyn, the purity of
whose spirit and the beauty of whose life

are a bitter and burning rebuke to her enforced deceitfulness of conduct. Here is a
woman innocently guilty, suddenly aroused
by love, made sensitive and noble (as that
passion commonly makes those persons who
really feel it), and projected into a condition of aggrieved excitement. In this
posture of romantic and pathetic circumstances the crisis of two lives is suddenly
precipitated in action.

Judah Llewellyn also is possessed of spiritual sensibility and psychic force. In boyhood a shepherd, he has dwelt among the
mountains of his native Wales, and his imagination has heard the voices that are in
rocks and trees, in the silence of lonely
places, in the desolation of the bleak hills,
and in the cold light of distant stars. He is
now a preacher, infatuated with his mis-
sion, inspired in his eloquence, invincible
in his tremendous sincerity. He sees Vashti
and he loves her. It is the first thrill of
mortal passion that ever has mingled with
his devotion to his Master's work. The
attraction between these creatures is human ; and yet it is more of heaven than of
earth. It is a tie of spiritual kindred that
binds them. They are beings of a different
order from the common order — and, as

happens in such cases, they will be tried by
exceptional troubles and passed through a
fire of mortal anguish.   For what reason
experience should take the direction of misery with fine natures in human life no philosopher has yet been able to ascertain ;
but that it does take that direction all competent observation proves.   To Vashti and
Judah the time speedily comes when their
love is acknowledged, upon both sides —
the preacher speaking plainly ; the girl,
conscious of turpitude, shrinking from a
spoken avowal which yet her whole personality proclaims.   Yielding to her father's
malign will she has consented to make one
more manifestation of curative power, to go
through once more, — and for the last time,
— the mockery of a pretended fast.   The
scene is Lord Asgarby's house ; the patient
is Lord Asgarby's daughter — an only child,
cursed with constitutional debility, the fore-
doomed victim of premature decline.   This
frail creature has heard of Vashti and believes in her, and desires and obtains her
society.   To Professor Dethick this is, in
every sense, a golden opportunity, and he
insists that the starvation test shall be thoroughly made.   Lord Asgarby, willing to do
anything for his idolised daughter, assents

to the plan, and his scientific friend, cynical Professor Jopp, agrees, with the assistance of his erudite daughter, to supervise the experiment. Vashti will fast for several days, and the heir of Asgarby will then be healed by her purified and exalted influence.

The principal scene of the play shows the exterior of an ancient, unused tower of Asgarby House, in which Vashti is detained during the fast. The girl is supposed to be starving. Her scampish father will endeavour to relieve her. Miss Jopp is vigilant to prevent fraud. The patient is confident. Judah, wishful to be near to the object of his adoration, has climbed the outer wall and is watching, beneath the window, unseen, in the warder's seat. The time is summer, the hour midnight, and the irrevocable vow of love has been spoken. At that supreme instant, and under conditions so natural that the picture seems one of actual life, the sin of Vashti is revealed and the man who had adored her as an angel knows her for a cheat. With a difference of circumstances that situation — in the fibre of it — is not new. Many a lover, male and female, has learned that every idol has its flaw. But the situation is new in its dramatic structure. For Judah the

discovery is a terrible one, and the resultant agony is convulsive and lamentable.
He takes, however, the only course he could
be expected to take : he must vindicate the
integrity of the woman whom he loves, and
he commits the crime of perjury in order to
shield her reputation from disgrace.

What will a man do for the woman whom
he loves ? The attributes of individual character are always to be considered as forces
likely to modify passion and to affect conduct.   But in general the answer to that
question may be given in three words —
anything and everything ! The history of
nations, as of individuals, is never rightly
read until it is read in the light of knowledge of the influence that has been exerted
over them by women. Cleopatra, in ancient
Egypt, changed the history of Rome by the
ruin of Marc Antony. Another heroine re-
cently toppled Ireland down the fire-escape
into the back-yard. So goes the world.   In
Judah, however, the crime that is done for
love is pursued to its consequence of ever-
accumulative suffering, until at length, when
it has been expiated by remorse and repent-
ance, it is rectified by confession and oblit-
erated by pardon.   No play ever taught a
lesson of truth with more cogent dramatic

force. The cynical, humorous scenes are
delightful.

Willard's representation of Cyrus Blenkarn stamped him as one of the best actors
of the age. His representation of Judah
Llewellyn deepened that impression and
reinforced it with a conviction of marked
versatility. In his utterance of passion
Willard showed that he has advanced far
beyond the Romeo stage. The love that he
expressed was that of a man — intellectual,
spiritual, noble, a moral being and one essentially true. Man's love, when it is real,
adores its object ; hallows it ; invests it with
celestial attributes ; and beholds it as a part
of heaven. That quality of reverence was
distinctly conveyed by the actor, and therefore to observers who conceive passion to
be delirious abandonment (of which any
animal is capable), his ardour may have
seemed dry and cold. It was nevertheless
true. He made the tempestuous torrent of
Judah's avowal the more overwhelming
by his preliminary self-repression and his
thoughtful gentleness of reserve ; for thus
the hunger of desire was beautiful with
devotion and tenderness ; and while the
actor's feelings seemed borne away upon
a whirling tide of irresistible impulse his

w

exquisite art kept a perfect control of face, voice, person, demeanour, and delivery, and not once permitted a lapse into extravagance. The character thus embodied will long be remembered as an image of dignity, sweetness, moral enthusiasm, passionate fervour, and intellectual power; but, also, viewed as an effort in the art of acting, it will be remembered as a type of consummate grace in the embodiment of a beautiful ideal clearly conceived. The effect of spiritual suffering, as conveyed in the pallid countenance and ravaged figure, in the last act, was that of noble pathos. The delivery of all the speeches of the broken, humiliated, haunted minister was deeply touching, not alone in music of voice but in denotement of knowledge of human nature and human suffering and endurance. The actor who can play such a part in such a manner is not an experimental artist. Rather let him be called — in the expressive words of one of his country's poets —

> " Sacred historian of the heart
> And moral nature's lord."

XXIII.

SALVINI AS KING SAUL AND KING LEAR.

SALVINI was grander and finer in King
Saul than in any other embodiment that
he presented. He seized the idea wholly,
and he executed it with affluent power.
He brought to the part every attribute necessary to its grandeur of form and its afflicting sympathy of spirit. His towering
physique presented, with impressive accuracy, the Hebrew monarch, chosen of God,
who was " lifted a head and shoulders above
the people." His tremulous sensibility, his
knowledge of suffering, his skill in depicting it, his great resources of voice, his vigour
and fineness of action, his exceptional commingling of largeness and gentleness — all
these attributes combined in that performance, to give magnificent reality to one
of the most sublime conceptions in literature. By his personation of Saul Salvini
added a new and an immortal figure to the
stage pantheon of kings and heroes.

Alfieri's tragedy of *Saul* was written in
1782–83, when the haughty, impetuous, and
passionate poet was thirty-four years old,
and at the suggestion of the Countess of
Albany, whom he loved. He had suffered a
bereavement at the time, and he was in
deep grief. The Countess tried to con-
sole him by reading the Bible, and when
they came upon the narrative of Saul
the idea of the tragedy was struck out between them. The work was written with
vigorous impulse and the author has
left, in his autobiography, the remark
that none of his tragedies cost him so little
labour. *Saul* is in five acts and it contains
1567 lines — of that Italian *versi sciolti*
which inadequately corresponds to the
blank verse of the English language. The
scene is laid in the camp of Saul's army.
Six persons are introduced, namely, Saul,
Jonathan, David, Michel, Abner, and
Achimelech. The time supposed to be
occupied by the action — or rather, by the
suffering — of the piece is a single day,
the last in the king's life. Act first is devoted to explanation, conveyed in warn-
ings to David, by Jonathan, his friend,
and Michel, his wife. Act second presents
the distracted monarch, who knows that

God has forsaken him and that death is
at hand.   In a speech of terrible intensity he relates to Abner the story of the
apparition of Samuel and the doom that
the ghost has spoken.   His children humour and soothe the broken old man,
and finally succeed in softening his mind
toward David — whom he at once loves,
dreads, and hates, as the appointed instru-
ment of his destruction and the successor
to his crown.   Act third shows David playing upon the harp before Saul, and chanting
Saul's deeds in the service and defence of Is-
rael — so that he calms the agonised delirium
of the haunted king and wins his blessing;
but at last a boastful word makes discord
in the music's charm, and Saul is suddenly
roused into a ghastly fury.   Acts fourth
and fifth deal with the wild caprices and
maddening agonies of the frenzied father;
the ever-varying phenomena of his mental
disease; the onslaught of the Philistines;
the killing of his sons; the frequent recur-
rence, before his mind's eye, of the shade
of the dead prophet; and finally his sui-
cidal death.   It is, in form, a classical
tragedy, massive, grand, and majestically
simple; and it blazes from end to end with
the fire of a sublime imagination.

Ardent lovers of Italian literature are fond of ranking *Saul* with *Lear*. The claim is natural but it is not valid. In *Lear* — not to speak of its profound revelations of universal human nature and its vast philosophy of human life — there is a tremendous scope of action, through which mental condition and experience are dramatically revealed ; and there is the deepest deep of pathos, because the highest height of afflicted goodness. In *Saul* there is simply — upon a limited canvas, without adjuncts, without the suggestion of resources, without the relief of even mournful humour, and with a narrative rather than a dramatic background — the portraiture of a condition ; and, because the man displayed is neither so noble nor so human, the pathos surcharging the work is neither so harrowing nor so tender. Yet the two works are akin in majesty of ideal, in the terrible topic of mental disease that shatters a king, and in the atmosphere of desolation that trails after them like a funeral pall ; and it is not a wonder that Alfieri's *Saul* should be deemed the greatest tragedy ever originated in the Italian language. It attains a superb height, for it keeps an equal pace with the severe simplicity of the

Bible narrative on which it is founded.   It
depicts the condition of an imaginative
mind, a stately and robust character, an
arrogant, fiery spirit, a kind heart, and
a royal and regally poised nature, that
have first been undermined by sin and the
consciousness of sin, and then crazed by
contact with the spirit world and by a
nameless dread of the impending anger of
an offended God.   It would be difficult to
conceive of a more distracting and piteous
state.   Awe and terror surround that august sufferer, and make him both holy and
dreadful.   In his person and his condition, as those are visible to the imaginative
mind, he combines elements that irresistibly
impress and thrill.   He is of vast physical
stature, that time has not bent, and of
great beauty of face, that griefs have ravaged but not destroyed.   He is a valiant
and sanguinary warrior, and danger seems
to radiate from his presence.   He is a magnanimous king and a loving father, and he
softens by generosity and wins by gentleness.   He is a maniac, haunted by spectres
and scourged with a whip of scorpions, and
his red-eyed fury makes all space a hell
and shatters silence with the shrieks of the
damned.   He is a human soul, burdened

with the frightful consciousness of Divine
wrath and poised in torment on the preci-
pice that overhangs the dark, storm-beaten
ocean of eternity. His human weakness is
frighted by ghastly visions and indefinite
horrors, against which his vain struggle
only makes his forlorn feebleness more
piteous and drear. The gleams of calm
that fall upon his tortured heart only light
up an abyss of misery — a vault of darkness peopled by demons. He is already cut
off from among the living, by the doom
of inevitable fate, and while we pity him
we fear him. His coming seems attended
with monstrous shapes; he diffuses disso-
nance; his voice is a cry of anguish or a
wail of desolation; his existence is a tempest; there can be no relief for him save
death, and the death that ends him comes
like the blessing of tears to the scorched
eyelids of consuming misery. That is the
Saul of the Bible and of Alfieri's tragedy;
and that is the Saul whom Salvini embodied.
It was a colossal monument of human suffering that the actor presented, and no one
could look upon it without being awed and
chastened.

Salvini's embodiment of King Lear was a
remarkable manifestation of physical re-

sources and of professional skill.   The
lofty stature, the ample and resonant voice,
the copious animal excitement, the fluent
elocution and the vigorous, picturesque,
and often melodramatic movements, ges-
tures, and poses of Salvini united to ani-
mate and embellish a personality such as
would naturally absorb attention and diffuse excitement.   Every artist, however,
moves within certain specific and positive
limitations — spiritual, mental, and physical.   No actor has proved equal to every
kind of character.   Salvini, when he acted
Hamlet, was unspiritual — giving no effect
to the haunted tone of that part or to its
weird surroundings ; and when he acted
Macbeth he was unimaginative, obscure,
common, and therefore inadequate.   The
only Shakespearean character that he excelled in is Othello, and even in that
his ideal displayed neither the magnanimity nor the tenderness that are in
Shakespeare's conception.   The chief attributes of the Moor that he interpreted
were physical ; the loftiest heights that
he reached were terror and distracted
grief ; but he worked with a pictorial
method and a magnetic vigour that en-
thralled the feelings even when they did not
command the judgment.

His performance of King Lear gave new
evidence of his limitations. During the
first two acts he made the king a merely
restless, choleric, disagreeable old man,
deficient in dignity, destitute of grandeur,
and especially destitute of inherent personal fascination — of the suggestiveness
of ever having been a great man. Lear
is a ruin — but he has been a Titan ; the
delight of all hearts no less than the monarch of all minds. The actor who does not
invest him with that inherent, overwhelming personal fascination does not attain to
his altitude. The cruel afflictions that occur in the tragedy do not of themselves
signify : the pity is only that they should
occur to him. That is the spring of all the
pathos. In Salvini's Lear there were beautiful moments and magnificent bits of action. "I gave you all" and "I'm cold
myself" were exquisite points. He missed
altogether, however, the more subtle significance of the reminiscent reference to Cordelia — as in "No more of that, I have
noted it well" — and he gave, at the beginning, no intimation of impending madness.
In fact he introduced no element of lunacy
till he reached the lines about "red-hot
spits" in Edgar's first mad scene.

Much of Salvini's mechanism in Lear was crude. He put the king behind a table, in the first scene — which had the effect of preparation for a lecture; and it pleased him to speak the storm speech away back at the upper entrance, with his body almost wholly concealed behind painted crags. With all its moments of power and of tenderness the embodiment was neither royal, lovable, nor great. It might be a good Italian Lear: it was not the Lear of Shakespeare. Salvini was particularly out of the character in the curse scene and in the frantic parting from the two daughters, because there the quality of the man, behind the action, seemed especially common. The action, though, was theatrical and had its due effect.

XXIV.

HENRY IRVING AS EUGENE ARAM.

HENRY IRVING'S impersonation of Eugene Aram — given in a vein that is distinctly unique — was one of strange and melancholy grace and also of weird poetical and pathetic power.

More than fifty years ago, just after Bulwer's novel on the subject of Eugene Aram was published, that character first came upon the stage, and its first introduction to the American theatre occurred at the Bowery, where it was represented by John R. Scott. Aram languished, however, as a dramatic person, and soon disappeared. He did not thrive in England, neither, till, in 1873, Henry Irving, who had achieved great success in *The Bells*, prompted W. G. Wills to effect his resuscitation in a new play, and acted him in a new manner. The part then found an actor who could play it, — investing psychological subtlety with tender human feeling and romantic grace, and making an imaginary experience of suffering vital and heartrending in its awful reality. The performance ranks with the best that Henry Irving has given — with *Mathias, Lesurques, Dubosc, Louis XI.,* and *Hamlet;* those studies of the night-side of human nature in which his imagination and intellect and his sombre feeling have been revealed and best exemplified.

Eugene Aram was born at Ramsgill, in Nidderdale, Yorkshire, in 1704. His father, Peter Aram, was a man of good family but becoming reduced in circumstances he took service as a gardener on the estate of Sir Edward Blackett, of Newby Hall. In 1710 Peter Aram and his family were living at Bondgate, near Ripon, and there Eugene went to school and learned to read the New Testament. At a considerably later period he was instructed, during one month, by the Rev. Mr. Alcock, of Burndall. This was the extent of the tuition that he ever received from others. For the rest he was self-taught. He had a natural passion for knowledge and he displayed wonderful industry in its acquisition. When sixteen years old he knew something of Latin, Greek, and Hebrew, and later he made himself acquainted with Chaldaic and Arabic.

His occupation, up to this time, was that of assistant to his father, the gardener ; but about 1720 he was employed in London as a clerk to a merchant, Mr. Christopher Blackett, a relative to his father's patron, Sir Edward.   He did not remain there long. A serious illness prostrated him, and on recovering he returned to Nidderdale, with which romantic region his fate was to be forever associated.   He now became a tutor, and not long after he was employed as such at a manor-house, near Ramsgill, called Gowthwaite Hall, a residence built early in the seventeenth century by Sir John Yorke, and long inhabited by his descendants.   While living there he met and courted Anna Spance, the daughter of a farmer, at the lonely village of Lofthouse, and in 1731 he married her.   The Middlesmoor registry contains the record of this marriage, and of the baptism and death of their first child.   In 1734 Eugene Aram removed to Knaresborough, where he kept a school.   He had, all this while, sedulously pursued his studies, and he now was a scholar of extraordinary acquirements, not only in the languages but in botany, heraldry, and many other branches of learning.   His life seemed fair and his future

bright : but a change was at hand. He had
not resided long at Knaresborough before
he became acquainted with three persons
most unlike himself in every way. These
men were Henry Terry, Richard Houseman, and Daniel Clarke. Houseman was
a flax-dresser. Clarke was a travelling
jeweller. All of them were intemperate ;
and it is supposed that the beginning of
Eugene Aram's downfall was the appetite
for drink. The confederacy that he formed
with these men is not easily explicable, and
probably it never has been rightly explained.
The accepted statement is that it was a confederacy for fraud and theft. Clarke was
reported to be the heir presumptive to a
large fortune. He purchased goods, was
punctual in his payments, and established
his credit. He was supposed to be making
purchases for a merchant in London. He
dealt largely in gold and silver plate and in
watches, and soon he made a liberal use of
his credit to accumulate valuable objects.
In 1744 he disappeared, and he never was
seen or heard of again.· His frauds became
known, and the houses of Aram and Houseman, suspected as his associates, were
searched, but nothing was found to impli-
cate either of them.

Soon after this event Aram left Knaresborough — deserting his wife — and proceeded to London, where for two years he
had employment as a teacher of Latin.
He was subsequently an usher at the
boarding school of the Rev. Anthony Hin-
ton, at Hayes, in Middlesex, and there it
was observed that he displayed an extraordinary and scrupulous tenderness and solicitude as to the life and safety of even worms
and insects — which he would remove from
the garden walks and put into places of
security. At a later period he found employment as a transcriber of acts of Parliament, for registration in chancery. Still
later he became an usher at the Free
School of Lynn, in Norfolk, where, among
other labours, he undertook to make a comparative lexicon, and with this purpose col-
lated over 3000 words in English, Latin,
Greek, Hebrew, and Celtic. He had ample
opportunity to leave England but he never
did so. At length, in 1759, a labourer who
was digging for limestone, at a place known
as St. Robert's Cave, Thistle Hill, near
Knaresborough, came upon a human skeleton, bent double and buried in the earth.
Suspicion was aroused. These bones, it
was surmised, might be those of Daniel

Clarke. His mysterious disappearance and his associates were remembered. The authorities sent forth and arrested Terry, Houseman, and Eugene Aram, and those persons were brought to their trial at York. A bold front would have saved them, for the evidence against them was weak. Aram stood firm, but Houseman quailed, and presently he turned "state's evidence" and denounced Aram as the murderer of Clarke. The accused scholar spoke in his own defence, and with astonishing skill, but he failed to defeat the direct and decisive evidence of his accomplice. Houseman declared that on the day of the murder Clarke, Aram, and himself were in company, and were occupied in disposing of the property which they had obtained; that Aram proposed to walk in the fields, and that they proceeded, thereupon, at nightfall, to the vicinity of St. Robert's Cave. Clarke and Aram, he said, went over the hedge and advanced toward the cave, and Aram struck Clarke several times upon the breast and head, and so killed him. It was a dark night, and in the middle of winter, but the moon was shining through drifting clouds, and Houseman said he could see the movement of Aram's hand but not the weapon that it held. He was about twelve yards from the spot of the murder. He testified that the body of Clarke was buried in the cave. The presiding justice charged against the prisoner and Eugene Aram was convicted and condemned. He subsequently, it is said, confessed the crime, alleging to the clergyman by whom he was attended that his wife had been led into an intrigue by Clarke, and that this was the cause of the murder. Here, doubtless, is the indication of the true nature of this tragedy. Aram, prior to his execution, was confined in York Castle, where he wrote a poem of considerable length and some merit, and also several shorter pieces of verse. On the morning of his execution it was found that he had opened a vein in his arm, with the intent to bleed to death, but the wound was staunched, and he was taken to Knaresborough and there hanged, and afterward his body was hung in chains in Knaresborough Forest. His death occurred on August 13, 1759, in the fifty-fifth year of his age. On the night before his execution he wrote a rhythmical apostrophe to death : —

"Come, pleasing rest! eternal slumber fall!
  Seal mine, that once must seal the eyes of
    all!
  Calm and composed my soul her journey
    takes;
  No guilt that troubles and no heart that
    aches."

Such is the story of Eugene Aram — a
story that has furnished the basis of various fictions, notably of Bulwer's famous
novel, and which inspired one of the best
of the beautiful poems of Thomas Hood.
Wills gathered hints from it, here and
there, in the making of his play; but he
boldly departed from its more hideous and
repulsive incidents and from the theory of
the main character that might perhaps be
justified by its drift. In the construction of
the piece Henry Irving made many material
suggestions. The treatment of the character of Aram was devised by him, and the
management of the close of the second act
denotes his felicity of invention.

The play opens in the rose-garden of a
rural rectory in the sweet, green valley of
the shining Nidd. The time is twilight;
the season summer; and here, in a haven
of peace and love, the repentant murderer
has found a refuge. Many years have

passed since the commission of his crime,
and all those years he has lived a good life,
devoted to study, instruction, and works of
benevolence. He has been a teacher of the
young, a helper of the poor, and he has
gained respect, affection, and honourable
repute. He is safe in the security of
silence and in the calm self-poise of his
adamantine will. His awful secret sleeps
in his bosom and is at rest forever. He
has suffered much and he still suffers ;
yet, lulled into a false security by the un-
eventful lapse of years and by that drifting, desolate, apathetic recklessness which
is sequent on the subsiding storm of passionate sorrow, he has allowed himself to
accept a woman's love and to love her in
return, and half to believe that his long
misery has expiated his sin and that even
for him there may be a little happiness yet
possible on earth. Eugene Aram, the village school-master, and Ruth Meadows, the
vicar's daughter, are betrothed lovers ; and
now, on the eve of their wedding morning,
they stand together among the roses, while
the sun is going down and the sweet summer wind plays softly in the leaves, and
from the little gray church close by a solemn
strain of music — the vesper hymn — floats

out upon the stillness of the darkening day.
The woman is all happiness, confidence,
and hope ; the man, seared and blighted by
conscious sin and subdued by long years of
patient submission to the sense of his own
unworthiness, is all gentleness, solicitude,
reverence, and sorrow. At this supreme
moment, when now it seems that everything
is surely well, the one man in the world
who knows Eugene Aram's secret has become, by seeming chance, a guest in the
vicarage ; and even while Ruth places her
hand upon her lover's heart and softly
whispers, " If guilt were there, it still should
be my pillow," the shadow of the gathering
night that darkens around them is deepened by the blacker shadow of impending
doom. The first act of the play is simply
a picture. It involves no action. It only
introduces the several persons who are
implicated in the experience to be displayed, denotes their relationship to one
another, and reveals a condition of feeling and circumstance which is alike romantic, pathetic, and perilous, and which is soon
to be shattered by the disclosure of a fatal
secret. The act is a preparation for a
catastrophe.

In the second act the opposed characters clash: the movement begins, and the catastrophe is precipitated. The story opens at nightfall, proceeds the same evening, and ends at the dawn of the ensuing day. The scene of act second is a room in the vicarage. Aram and Parson Meadows are playing chess, and Ruth is hovering about them and roguishly impeding their play. The purpose accomplished here is the exhibition of domestic comfort and content, and this is further emphasised by Ruth's recital of a written tribute that Aram's pupils have sent to him, on the eve of his marriage. Wounded by this praise the conscience-stricken wretch breaks off abruptly from his pastime and rushes from the room — an act of desperate grief which is attributed to his modesty. The parson soon follows, and Ruth is left alone. Houseman, their casual guest, having accepted the vicar's hospitable offer of a shelter for the night, has now a talk with Ruth, and he is startled to hear the name of Eugene Aram, and thus to know that he has found the man whose fatal secret he possesses, and upon whose assumed dread of exposure his cupidity now purposes to feed. In a coarsely jocular way this brutish creature provokes the indignant resentment

of Ruth, by insinuations as to her betrothed
lover's past life; and when, a little later,
Ruth and Aram again meet, she wooingly
begs him to tell her of any secret trouble
that may be weighing upon his mind. At
this moment Houseman comes upon them,
and utters Aram's name. From that point
to the end of the act there is a sustained
and sinewy exposition, strong in spirit and
thrilling in suspense, — of keen intellect
and resolute will standing at bay and
making their last battle for life, against the
overwhelming odds of heaven's appointed
doom. Aram defies Houseman and is denounced by him; but the ready adroitness
and iron composure of the suffering wretch
still give him supremacy over his foe — till,
suddenly, the discovery is announced of
the bones of Daniel Clarke in St. Robert's
Cave, and the vicar commands Aram and
Houseman to join him in their inspection.
Here the murderer suffers a collapse. There
has been a greater strain than even he can
bear; and, left alone upon the scene, he
stands petrified with horror, seeming, in an
ecstasy of nameless fear, to look upon the
spectre of his victim. Henry Irving's management of the apparition effect was such
as is possible only to a man of genius, and

such as words may record but never can describe.

The third act passes in the churchyard. Aram has fled from the sight of the skeleton, and has fallen among the graves. It is almost morning. The ghastly place is silent and dark. The spirit of the murderer is broken, and his enfeebled body, long since undermined by the grief of remorse and now chilled by the night dews, is in the throes of death. The incidents of the closing scene are simple, but they are heartbreaking in their pathos and awful in their desolation. The fugitive Houseman finds Aram here, and spurns him as a whimpering lunatic. Then, in this midnight hour and this appalling place, alone in the presence of God, the murderer lifts his hands toward heaven, confesses his crime, and falls at the foot of the cross. Here Ruth finds him, and to her, with dying lips, he tells the story of the murder and of all that he has since endured. And just as his voice falters into silence and his heart ceases to beat, the diamond light of morning gleams in the eastern sky and the glad music of an anthem floats softly from the neighbouring church. Upon that beautifully significant picture the final curtain fell.

Wills's literary framework for the display of character and experience is scarcely to be considered a perfect play. It begins by assuming on the part of its auditor a knowledge of the mystery upon which it is based. Such a knowledge the auditor ought certainly to have, but in presence of an exact drama he derives it from what he sees and not from remembrance of what he has read. The piece is, perhaps, somewhat irrational in making Aram a resident, under his own name, of the actual neighbourhood of his crime. It lowers the assumed nobility of his character, furthermore, by making this remorseful and constantly apprehensive murderer willing to yoke a sweet, innocent, and idolised woman to misery and shame by making her his wife. And it mars its most pathetic scene — the awful scene of the midnight confession in the churchyard — by making Eugene Aram declare, to the woman of his love, the one human being who comforts and sustains him on the brink of eternity, that he has loved another woman for whose sake he did the murder. Since the whole story was to be treated in a fanciful manner, a still wider license in the play of fancy would, perhaps, have had a more

entirely gracious and satisfying effect. The
language is partly blank verse and partly
prose ; and, while its tissue is rightly and
skilfully diversified by judicious allowance
for the effect of each character upon the
garment of individual diction, and while
its strain, here and there, rises to eloquence
of feeling and beauty of imagery, there is
a certain lack of firmness in its verbal fibre.
The confession speech that has to be spoken
by Aram comprises upward of ninety lines
— and that is a severe and perilous strain
upon an actor's power of holding the
public interest. The beauties of the play,
however, are many and strong. Its crowning excellence is that it gives dramatic
permanence to a strangely interesting character.

The knowledge of human nature that
Henry Irving revealed in this part and
the manner in which he revealed it were
nothing less than wonderful. The moment he walked upon the scene you
saw the blighted figure of a man who
has endured, and is enduring, spiritual
torment. The whole personality was suffused with a mournful strangeness. The
man was isolated and alone. It was a
purely ideal view of the character that

the actor denoted; for he made Eugene
Aram a noble, tender, gentle person,
whom ungovernable passion, under circumstances of overwhelming provocation, had
once impelled to an act of half-justifiable
homicide, and who had for years been
slowly dying with remorse. He touched
no chord of terror, but only the chord of
pity. Like his portrayal of Mathias, the
picture showed the reactionary effect of
hidden sin in the human soul; but the
personality of the sufferer was entirely different. Each of those men has had experience of crime and of resultant misery, but
no two embodiments could possibly be more
dissimilar, alike in spiritual quality and
in circumstances. Mathias is dominated
by paternal love and characterised by a
half-defiant, ever-vigilant, and often self-
approbative pride of intellect, in being able
to guard and keep a terrible and dangerous
secret. Eugene Aram is dominated by a
saint-like tenderness toward a sweet woman
who loves him, and characterised by a profound, fitful melancholy, now humble and
submissive, now actively apprehensive and
almost frenzied. Only once does he stand
at bay and front his destiny with a defiance
of desperate will; and even then it is for

the woman's sake rather than for his own.
Henry Irving's acting made clear and beautiful that condition of temperament. A
noble and affectionate nature, shipwrecked,
going to pieces, doomed, but making one
last tremendous though futile effort to avert
the final and inevitable ruin — this ideal
was made actual in his performance.
The intellectual or spiritual value of such
a presentment must depend upon the
auditor's capacity to absorb from a tragedy its lessons of insight into the relations of the human soul to the moral
government of the world. Many spectators
would find it merely morbid and gloomy ;
others would find it superlatively illuminative and eloquent. Its artistic value the
actor himself made evident to every comprehension. There is a moment of the
performance when the originally massive
and passionate character of Eugene Aram
is suddenly asserted above his meek-
ness, contrition, and sorrow ; when, at the
sound of his enemy's voice, he first becomes petrified with the sense of peril, and
then calmly gathers all his powers to meet
and conquer the danger. The splendid
concentration, the perfect poise, the sustained intensity, the copious and amazing

variety and force of emotion, and the positive, unerring, and brilliant art with which
Henry Irving met that emergency and displayed that frightful and piteous aspect of
assailed humanity, desperate and fighting
for life, made up such an image of genius
as seldom is seen and never will be forgotten. Rapid transition has ever been one
of the commonest and most effective expedients used in histrionic art. This, on the
contrary, was an example of sustained,
prolonged, cumulative, artistic expression
of the most harrowing and awful emotions
with which the human soul can be convulsed; and it was a wonder of consummate acting. The same thoroughness of
identification and the same astonishing
adequacy of feeling pervaded the scene in
the churchyard. At first, in the dusky
starlight, only a shapeless figure, covered
with a black cloak, was seen among the
gravestones, crouched upon a tomb; but
the man that rose, as if out of the grave,
pallid, emaciated, ghastly, the spectre of
himself, was the authentic image of majestic despair, not less sublime than pitiable,
and fraught with a power that happiness
could never attain. Not in our time upon
the stage has such a lesson been taught,

with such overwhelming pathos, of the utter helplessness of even the strongest human will, when once the soul has· been vitiated by sin and the eternal law of right defied by mortal passion. In the supplication to his astonished accomplice the actor seemed like one transfigured, and there the haunted effect was extremely awful.

XXV.

CHARLES FISHER.

IN old times Charles Fisher often figured in the old comedies, and he was one of the last of the thin and rapidly lessening group of actors capable of presenting those pieces — wherein, although the substance be human nature, the manner is that of elaborate and diversified artifice. When he played Lieutenant Worthington, in *The Poor Gentleman*, he was a gentleman indeed — refined, delicate, sensitive, simply courageous, sustained by native integrity, and impressive with a dignity of manner that reflected the essential nobility of his mind; so that when he mistook Sir Robert Bramble for a bailiff, and roused that benevolent baronet's astonishment and rage, he brought forth all the comic humour of a delightful situation with the greatest ease and nature. He played Littleton Coke, Sir Harcourt Courtly, old Laroque — in which he gave a wonderful picture of the working

of remorse in the frail and failing brain of
age — and Nicholas Rue, in *Secrets worth
Knowing*, a sinister and thrilling embodiment of avarice and dotage. He played
Dr. Bland, the elegant medical cynic of
Nos Intimes; De la Tour, the formidable,
jealous husband of Henriette, in *Le Patte
de Mouche;* Horace, in *The Country Squire;*
Goldfinch, in which he was airy, sagacious,
dashing, and superb, in *The Road to Ruin;*
and Captain Cozzens, the nonchalant rascal
of *The Knights of the Round Table*, which
he embodied in a style of easy magnificence, gay, gallant, courageous, alert, im-
perturbable, and immensely comic. He
was the original Matthew Leigh in Lester Wallack's romantic play of *Rosedale*
(1863). He acted Joseph Surface in the
days when Lester Wallack used to play
Charles, and he always held his own in
that superior part. He was equally fine in
Sir Peter and Sir Oliver. When the good
old play of *The Wife's Secret* was revived
in New York, in 1864, he gave a dignified
and impetuous performance of Sir Walter
Amyott. I remember him in those parts,
with equal wonder at his comprehensive
variety of talent and admiration for his
always adequate skill. I saw him as the

volatile Ferment, in *The School of Reform*,
and nothing could be more comic than his
unwitting abuse of General Tarragon, in
that blustering officer's presence, or his
equally ludicrous scene of cross purposes
with Bob Tyke. He was a perfect type, as
Don Manuel Velasco, in *The Compact*, of
the gallant, stately Spanish aristocrat. He
excelled competition when, in a company
that included George Holland, W. Holston,
A. W. Young, Mark Smith, Frederick C.
P. Robinson, and John Gilbert, he enacted
the convict in *Never Too Late to Mend.*
He was equally at home whether as the
King in *Don Cæsar de Bazan* or as Tom
Stylus the literary hack, in *Society.* He
passed easily from the correct and sentimental Sir Thomas Clifford, of *The Hunch-
back*, to the frivolous Mr. Willowear, of
To Marry or Not to Marry. No one could
better express than he did, when playing
Wellborn, both pride of birth and pride of
character. One of his most characteristic
works was Hyssop, in *The Rent Day.* His
scope and the rich resources of his experience are denoted in those citations. It is
no common artist who can create and sustain a perfect illusion, and please an audience equally well, whether in such a part

Y

as Gilbert Featherstone, the villain, in *Lost in London*, or old Baptista, in *The Taming of the Shrew*. The playgoer who never saw Charles Fisher as Triplet can scarcely claim that he ever saw the part at all. The quaint figure, the well-saved but threadbare dress, the forlorn air of poverty and suffering commingled with a certain jauntiness and pluck, the profound feeling, the unconscious sweetness and humour, the spirit of mind, gentility, and refinement struggling through the confirmed wretchedness of the almost heart-broken hack — who that ever laughed and wept at sight of him in the garret scene, sitting down, "all joy and hilarity," to write his comedy, can ever forget those details of a true and touching embodiment? His fine skill in playing the violin was touchingly displayed in that part, and gave it an additional tone of reality. I once saw him acting Mercutio, and very admirable he was in the guise of that noble, brave, frolicsome, impetuous young gentleman. The intense vitality, the glancing glee, the intrepid spirit — all were preserved; and the brilliant text was spoken with faultless fluency. It is difficult to realise that the same actor who set before us that perfect image of comic

perplexity, the bland and benevolent Dean,
in *Dandy Dick*, could ever have been
the bantering companion of Romeo and
truculent adversary of fiery Tybalt. Yet
this contrast but faintly indicates the versatile character of his mind. Fisher was
upon the American stage for thirty-eight
years, from August 30, 1852, when he came
forth at Burton's theatre as Ferment.
Later he went to Wallack's, and in 1872
he joined Daly's company, in which he
remained till 1890. It may be conjectured
that in some respects he resembled that
fine comedian Thomas Dogget, to whom
Sir Godfrey Kneller, the painter, said, "I
can only copy Nature from the originals
before me, while you vary them at pleasure and yet preserve the likeness." Like
Dogget he played, in a vein of rich, hearty,
jocose humour, and with great breadth of
effect and excellent colour, the sailor Ben,
in *Love for Love*. The resemblance was
in mental characteristics, not physique —
for Dogget was a slight and sprightly
man, whereas Fisher could represent majesty as well as frolic. After he went to
Daly's theatre he manifested a surprising range of faculty. He first appeared
there on October 28, 1872, as Mr. Dorn-

ton, in *The Road to Ruin*, and on November 19, following, he acted Falstaff for
the first time.   He presented there the
other Shakespearean parts of Leonatus, Ar-
mado, and Malvolio — the last of these
being a model of fidelity to the poet, and
now a classic in reputation.   He also assumed Adam and Jaques.   He presented
the living image of Shakespeare himself, in
Yorick, and his large, broad, stately style
gave weight to Don Manuel, in *She Would
and She Wouldn't;* to that apt type of
the refined British aristocrat, Sir Geoffrey
Champneys, in *Our Boys;* and to many a
noble father or benevolent uncle of the
adapted French society drama.   Just as
Dogget was supreme in such parts as Fon-
dlewife, so was Fisher superb in the uxori-
ous husband whom the demure child-wife
bamboozles, in the comedies of Molière.
No man has ever better depicted than he
did a sweet nature shocked by calamity
and bowed down with grief, or, as in Joe
Chirrup, in *Elfie*, manliness chastened by
affliction and ennobled by true love : yet
his impersonation of Fagin was only second
to that of J. W. Wallack, Jr. ; his Moody,
in *The Country Girl*, was almost tragic in
its grim and grizzled wretchedness and

snarling wrath ; and I have seen him assume to perfection the gaunt figure and crazy mood of Noah Learoyd, in *The Long Strike,* and make that personality a terrible embodiment of menace. From the time he first acted the comic Major Vavasour, in *Henry Dunbar,* no actor of equal quaintness has trod our stage. He died on June 11, 1891, and was buried at Woodlawn.

XXVI.

STUDENTS of the English stage find in books on that subject abundant information about the tragedy queens of the early drama, and much likewise, though naturally somewhat less (because comedy is more difficult to discuss than tragedy), about the comedy queens. Mrs. Cibber still discomfits the melting Mrs. Porter by a tenderness even greater than the best of Belvideras could dispense. Mrs. Bracegirdle and Mrs. Oldfield still stand confronted on the historic page, and still their battle continues year after year. All readers know the sleepy voice and horrid sigh of Mrs. Pritchard in Lady Macbeth's awful scene of haunted somnambulism ; the unexampled and unexcelled grandeur of Mrs. Yates in Medea ; the infinite pathos of Mrs. Dancer (she that became in succession Mrs. Spranger Barry and Mrs. Crawford) and her memorable scream, as Lady Ran-

dolph, at " Was he alive ? " ; the comparative discomfiture of both those ladies by
Mrs. Siddons, with her wonderful, wailing
cry, as Isabella, " O, my Biron, my Biron,"
her overwhelming Lady Macbeth and her
imperial Queen Katharine. The brilliant
story of Peg Woffington and the sad fate
of Mrs. Robinson, the triumphant career
of Mrs. Abington and the melancholy
collapse of Mrs. Jordan — all those things,
and many more, are duly set down in the
chronicles. But the books are comparatively silent about the Old Women of the
stage — an artistic line no less delightful
than useful, of which Mrs. G. H. Gilbert
is a sterling and brilliant representative.
Mrs. Jefferson, the great-grandmother of
the comedian Joseph Jefferson, who died
of laughter, on the stage (1766–68), might
fitly be mentioned as the dramatic ancestor
of such actresses as Mrs. Gilbert. She was
a woman of great loveliness of character
and of great talent for the portrayal of " old
women," and likewise of certain " old men "
in comedy. " She had," says Tate Wilkin-
son, " one of the best dispositions that ever
harboured in a human breast " ; and he
adds that " she was one of the most elegant women ever beheld."   Mrs. Gilbert

has always suggested that image of grace,
goodness, and piquant ability. Mrs. Vernon was the best in this line until Mrs.
Gilbert came; and the period which has
seen Mrs. Judah, Mrs. Vincent, Mrs. Ger-
mon, Mary Carr, Mrs. Chippendale, Mrs.
Stirling, Mrs. Billington, Mrs. Drew, Mrs.
Phillips, and Madam Ponisi, has seen no
superior to Mrs. Gilbert in her special walk.
She was in youth a beautiful dancer, and
all her motions have spontaneous ease and
grace. She can assume the fine lady, without for an instant suggesting the parvenu.
She is equally good, whether as the formal
and severe matron of starched domestic
life, or the genial dame of the pantry. She
could play Temperance in *The Country
Squire*, and equally she could play Mrs.
Jellaby. All varieties of the eccentricity of
elderly women, whether serious or comic,
are easily within her grasp. Betsy Trot-
wood, embodied by her, becomes a living
reality; while on the other hand she suffused with a sinister horror her stealthy,
gliding, uncanny personation of the dumb,
half-insane Hester Dethridge. That was the
first great success that Mrs. Gilbert gained,
under Augustin Daly's management. She
has been associated with Daly's company

since his opening night as a manager,
August 16, 1869, when, at the Fifth Avenue
theatre, then in Twenty-fourth Street, she
took part in Robertson's comedy of *Play*.
The first time I ever saw her she was acting
the Marquise de St. Maur, in *Caste*, on
the night of its first production in America,
August 5, 1867, at the Broadway theatre,
the house near the southwest corner of
Broadway and Broome Street, that had
been Wallack's but now was managed by
Barney Williams. The assumption of that
character, perfect in every particular, was
instinct with pure aristocracy ; but while
brilliant with serious ability it gave not
the least hint of those rich resources of
humour that since have diffused so much
innocent pleasure. Most of her successes
have been gained as the formidable lady
who typifies in comedy the domestic pro-
prieties and the Nemesis of respectability.
It was her refined and severely correct demeanour that gave soul and wings to the
wild fun of *A Night Off.* From Miss Garth
to Mrs. Laburnum is a far stretch of imi-
tative talent for the interpretation of the
woman nature that everybody, from Shakespeare down, has found it so difficult to
treat. This actress has never failed to

impress the spectator by her clear-cut, brilliant identification with every type of character that she has assumed; and, back of this, she has denoted a kind heart and a sweet and gentle yet never insipid temperament — the condition of goodness, sympathy, graciousness, and cheer that is the flower of a fine nature and a good life. Scenes in which Mrs. Gilbert and Charles Fisher or James Lewis have participated, as old married people, on Daly's stage, will long be remembered for their intrinsic beauty — suggestive of the touching lines :

" And when with envy Time, transported,
    Shall think to rob us of our joys,
  You'll in your girls again be courted,
    And I'll go wooing with my boys."

XXVII.

JAMES LEWIS.

A PROMINENT representative type of character is "the humorous man," and that is Shakespeare's phrase to describe him. Wit is a faculty; humour an attribute. Joseph Addison, Laurence Sterne, Washington Irving — whatever else they might have been they were humourists. Sir Roger de Coverley, Tristram Shandy, Uncle Toby, Diedrich Knickerbocker, Ichabod Crane — these and other creations of their genius stand forth upon their pages to exemplify that aspect of their minds. But the humourist of the pen may, personally, be no humourist at all. Addison's character was austere. Irving, though sometimes gently playful, was essentially grave and decorous.

Comical quality in the humorous man whom nature destines for the stage must be personal. His coming brings with it a sense of comfort. His presence warms the

heart and cheers the mind. The sound of
his voice, "speaking off," before he emerges
upon the scene, will set the theatre in a
roar. This was notably true of Burton and
of William Warren. The glance, motion,
carriage, manner, and the pause and stillness of such a man, instil merriment. Cibber says that Robert Nokes had a palpable
simplicity of nature which was often as
unaccountably diverting in his common
speech as on the stage. John E. Owens,
describing the conduct of a big bee in an
empty molasses barrel, once threw a circle
of his hearers, of whom I was one, almost
into convulsions of laughter. Artemas
Ward made people laugh the moment
they beheld him, by his wooden composure
and indescribable sapience of demeanour.
The lamented Daniel E. Setchell, a comedian who would have been as famous as he
was funny had he but lived longer, presented a delightful example of spontaneous
humour. It is ludicrous to recall the simple gravity, not demure but perfectly solemn, with which, on the deck of a Hudson
River steamboat, as we were passing West
Point, he indicated to me the Kosciuszko
monument, saying briefly, "That's the
place where Freedom shrieked." It was

the quality of his temperament that made his playfulness delicious. Setchell was the mental descendant of Burton, as Burton was of Reeve and as Reeve was of Liston. Actors illustrate a kind of heredity. Each species is distinct and discernible. Lester Wallack maintained the lineage of Charles Kemble, William Lewis, Elliston, and Mountfort — a line in which John Drew has gained auspicious distinction. John Gilbert's artistic ancestry could be traced back through Farren and Munden to King and Quin, and perhaps still further, to Lowin and Kempe.

The comedian intrinsically comical, while in his characteristic quality eccentric and dry, has been exemplified by Fawcett, Blisset, Finn, and Barnes, and is conspicuously presented by James Lewis. No one ever saw him without laughter — and it is kindly laughter, with a warm heart behind it. The moment he comes upon the stage an eager gladness diffuses itself throughout the house. His refined quaintness and unconscious drollery capture all hearts. His whimsical individuality never varies; yet every character of the many that he has portrayed stands clearly forth among its companions, a distinct, unique embodiment. The graceful urbanity, the elaborate yet natural

manner, the brisk vitality, the humorous
sapience of Sir Patrick Lundy — how completely and admirably he expressed them!
How distinct that fine old figure is in the
remembrance of all who saw it! But he
has never played a part that he did not
make equally distinct. A painter might
fill a gallery with odd, characteristic creations by merely copying his compositions
of "make-up." The amiable professor in
A Night Off, the senile Gunnion in *The
Squire*, Lissardo in *The Wonder*, Grumio
in *The Shrew* — those and many more he
has made his own; while in the actor's
province of making comic characters really
comical to others there is no artist who
better fulfils the sagacious, comprehensive
injunction of Munden (imparted to a youthful actor who spoke of being "natural"
in order to amuse), "Nature be d——d!
Make the people laugh!" That, aside
from all subtleties, is not a bad test of the
comic faculty, and that test has been met
and borne by the acting of James Lewis.

XXVIII.

A LEAF FROM MY JOURNAL.

[November 23, 1867.]

THIRTY years hereafter many who are now active and honoured in dramatic life will be at rest — their work concluded, their achievements a fading tradition. But they will not be wholly forgotten. The same talisman of memory that has preserved to our time the names and the deeds of the actors of old will preserve to future times the names and the deeds that are distinguished now in the mimic world of the stage. Legend, speaking in the voice of the veteran devotee of the drama, will say, for example, that of all the actors of this period there was no light comedian comparable with Lester Wallack; that he could thoroughly identify himself with character, — though it did not always please him to do so; that his acting was so imaginative and so earnest as to make reality of the most gossamer fiction; and that his vivacity — the essential element and the crown of comedy-acting — was like the dew on the opening rose. And therewithal the veteran may quaff his glass to the memory of another member of the Wallack family, and speak of James Wallack as Cassius, and Fagin, and the Man-in-the-Iron-Mask, and the King of the Commons, and may say, with truth, that a more winning embodiment of bluff manliness and humour was never known to our stage than the versatile actor who made himself foremost in those characters. It will be impossible to remember him without recalling his intimate professional associate, Edwin L. Davenport. He was the only Brutus of his time, our old friend will say, and in his prime the best Macbeth on the American stage ; and he could play almost any part in the drama, from the loftiest tragedy to mere trash ; and he was an admirable artist in all that he did. There will be plenty of evidence to fortify that statement ; and if the veteran shall also say that Wallack's company contained, at the same time, the best "old men" in the profession, no dissentient voice, surely, will challenge the names of George Holland, John Gilbert, James H. Stoddart, and Mark Smith.

Cibber could play Lord Foppington at seventy-three; but George Holland played Tony Lumpkin at seventy-seven. A young part, — but the old man was as joyous as a boy and filled it with a boisterous, mischievous humour at once delightful and indescribable. You saw him to the best advantage, though, in Mr. Sulky, Humphrey Dobbin, and kindred parts, wherein the fineness of his temperament was veiled under a crabbed exterior and some scope was allowed for his superb skill in painting character. So the discourse will run; and, when it touches upon John Gilbert, what else than this will be its burden? — that he was perfection as the old fop; that his Lord Ogleby had no peer; that he was the oddest conceivable compound of dry humour, quaint manners, frolicsome love of mischief, honest, hearty mirth, manly dignity, and tender pathos. To Mark Smith it will render a kindred tribute. Squire Broadlands, Old Rapid, Sir Oliver Surface — they cannot be forgotten. Extraordinary truthfulness to nature, extraordinary precision of method, large humanity, strong intellect, and refined and delicate humour that always charmed and never offended — those were the qualities that enrolled him among the best actors of his time. And it will not be strange if Old Mortality passes then into the warmest mood of eulogium, as he strives to recall the admirable, the incomparable "old woman" Mrs. Vernon. She was a worthy mate of those worthies, he will exclaim. She could be the sweet and loving mother, gentle and affectionate ; the stately lady, representative of rank and proud of it and true to it ; and the most eccentric of ludicrous old fools. She was the ideal Mrs. Malaprop, and she surpassed all competitors in the character of Mrs. Hardcastle. Mary Gannon was her stage-companion and her foil, he will add — the merriest, most mischievous, most bewitching player of her time, in her peculiar line of art. As Hester, in *To Marry or Not to Marry*, and as Sophia, in *The Road to Ruin*, she was the incarnation of girlish grace and delicious ingenuousness, and also of crisp, well-flavoured mirth. No taint of tameness marred her acting in those kindred characters, and no air of effort made it artificial. Nor was Fanny Morant less remarkable for the glitter of comedy and for an almost matchless precision of method. So will our friend of the future prose on, in a vein that will be tedious enough to mat-

ter-of-fact people; but not tedious to
gentle spirits who love the stage, and sympathise with its votaries, and keep alive
its traditions — knowing that this mimic
world is as real and earnest as the strife
that roars and surges around it; that there
as everywhere else humanity plays out
its drama, whereof the moral is always the
same — that whether on the stage or in
the mart, on the monarch's throne or in
the peasant's cot,

> "We are such stuff
> As dreams are made on, and our little life
> Is rounded with a sleep."

THE END.

THE WORKS OF

WILLIAM WINTER.

SHAKESPEARE'S ENGLAND. 18MO, CLOTH, 75 CENTS.

GRAY DAYS AND GOLD. 18MO, CLOTH, 75 CENTS.

SHADOWS OF THE STAGE. 18MO, CLOTH, 75 CENTS.

SHADOWS OF THE STAGE. Second Series. 18MO, CLOTH, 75 CENTS.

OLD SHRINES AND IVY. 18MO, CLOTH, 75 CENTS.

Also a Small Limited LARGE PAPER EDITION. 4 Vols. Uniform. $8.00.

WANDERERS: A Collection of Poems. NEW EDITION. WITH A PORTRAIT. 18MO, CLOTH, 75 CENTS.

" The supreme need of this age in America is a practical conviction that progress does not consist in material prosperity, but in spiritual advancement. Utility has long been exclusively worshipped. The welfare of the future lies in the worship of beauty. To that worship these pages are devoted, with all that implies of sympathy with the higher instincts, and faith in the divine destiny of the human race." — *From the Preface to Gray Days and Gold.*

MACMILLAN & CO.,

66 FIFTH AVENUE,   NEW YORK

SHADOWS OF THE STAGE.

18MO, CLOTH, 75 CENTS.

"The fame of the actor more than that of any other artist is an evanescent one — a 'bubble reputation' — indeed, and necessarily so from the conditions under which his genius is exercised. While the impression it makes is often more vivid and inspiring for the moment than that of the poet and the painter, it vanishes almost with the occasion which gave it birth, and lives only as a tradition in the memory of those to whom it had immediately appealed. 'Shadows they are, and shadows they pursue.'

"The writer, therefore, who, gifted with insight and a poetic enthusiasm which enables him to discern on the one hand the beauties in a dramatic work not perceived by the many, and on the other the qualities in the actor which have made him a true interpreter of the poet's thought, at the same time possessing the faculty of revealing to us felicitously the one, and the other is certainly entitled to our grateful recognition.

"Such a writer is Mr. William Winter, easily the first, — for we know of none other living in this country, or in the England he loves so much, in whose nature the critic's vision is united with that of the poet so harmoniously. . . .

"Over and above all this, there is in these writings the same charm of style, poetic glamour and flavor of personality which distinguish whatever comes to us from Mr. Winter's pen, and which make them unique in our literature." — *Home Journal*, New York.

MACMILLAN & CO.,

66 FIFTH AVENUE,   NEW YORK.

OLD SHRINES AND IVY.

18MO, CLOTH, 75 CENTS.

CONTENTS.

SHRINES OF HISTORY.

SHRINES OF LITERATURE.

"Whatever William Winter writes is marked by felicity of diction and by refinement of style, as well as by the evidence of culture and wide reading. 'Old Shrines and Ivy' is an excellent example of the charm of his work."— *Boston Courier*.

MACMILLAN & CO.,

66 FIFTH AVENUE,   NEW YORK.

SHAKESPEARE'S ENGLAND.

18MO, CLOTH, 75 CENTS.

"... It was the author's wish, in dwelling thus upon the rural loveliness, and the literary and historical associations of that delightful realm, to afford sympathetic guidance and useful suggestion to other American travellers who, like himself, might be attracted to roam among the shrines of the mother-land. Temperament is the explanation of style; and he has written thus of England because she has filled his mind with beauty and his heart with mingled joy and sadness; and surely some memory of her venerable ruins, her ancient shrines, her rustic glens, her gleaming rivers, and her flower-spangled meadows will mingle with the last thoughts that glimmer through his brain when the shadows of the eternal night are falling and the ramble of life is done." — *From the Preface.*

"He offers something more than guidance to the American traveller. He is a convincing and eloquent interpreter of the august memories and venerable sanctities of the old country." — *Saturday Review.*

"The book is delightful reading." — *Scribner's Monthly.*

"Enthusiastic and yet keenly critical notes and comments on English life and scenery." — *Scotsman.*

MACMILLAN & CO.,

66 FIFTH AVENUE,   NEW YORK.

(5)

GRAY DAYS
AND GOLD.

18MO, CLOTH, 75 CENTS.

CONTENTS.

Classic Shrines.
        Haunted Glens and Houses.
The Haunts of Moore.   Old York.
      Beautiful Bath.
           The Lakes and Fells of Wordsworth.
Shakespeare Relics at Worcester.
      Byron and Hucknall Torkard.
          Historic Nooks and Corners.
Up and Down the Avon.   Shakespeare's Town.
    Rambles in Arden.
         The Stratford Fountain.
           Bosworth Field.
              The Home of Dr. Johnson.
From London to Edinburgh.
     Into the Highlands.
         Highland Beauties.
           The Heart of Scotland.
Elegiac Memorials.   Sir Walter Scott.
    Scottish Pictures.
        Imperial Ruins.
          The Land of Marmion.
             At Vesper Time.

   This book, which is intended as a companion to *Shakespeare's England*, relates to the gray days of an American wanderer in the British Isles, and to the gold of thought and fancy that can be found there.

MACMILLAN & CO.,

66 FIFTH AVENUE,   **NEW YORK.**

GRAY DAYS
AND GOLD.

18MO, CLOTH, 75 CENTS.

PRESS NOTICES.

"Mr. Winter's graceful and meditative style in his English sketches has recommended his earlier volume upon (Shakespeare's) England to many readers, who will not need urging to make the acquaintance of this companion book, in which the traveller guides us through the quiet and romantic scenery of the mother-country with a mingled affection and sentiment of which we have had no example since Irving's day." — *The Nation.*

"As friendly and good-humoured a book on English scenes as any American has written since Washington Irving." — *Daily News, London.*

"Much that is bright and best in our literature is brought once more to our dulled memories. Indeed, we know of but few volumes containing so much of observation, kindly comment, philosophy, and artistic weight as this unpretentious little book." — *Chicago Herald.*

"They who have never visited the scenes which Mr. Winter so charmingly describes will be eager to do so in order to realize his fine descriptions of them, and they who have already visited them will be incited by his eloquent recital of their attractions to repeat their former pleasant experiences." — *Public Ledger, Philadelphia.*

MACMILLAN & CO.,

66 FIFTH AVENUE, NEW YORK.

(7)